IN SEARCH OF FOOD

Traditional Eating & Drinking in Britain

DEDICATION

FOR
JULIE

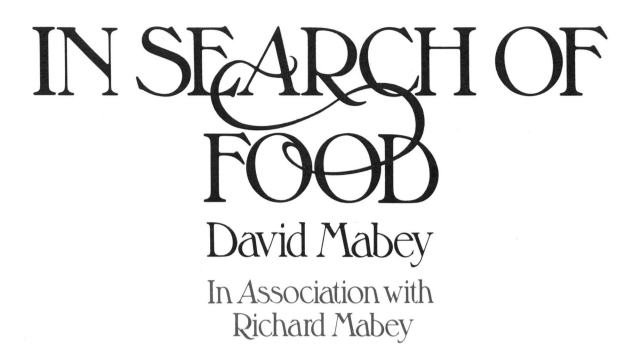

IN SEARCH OF FOOD

David Mabey

In Association with
Richard Mabey

Traditional Eating & Drinking
in Britain

MACDONALD & JANE'S LONDON

Published 1978 by
Macdonald and Jane's Publishers Limited
Paulton House, 8 Shepherdess Walk, London N1 7LW

Designed by David Fordham

ISBN 0 354 04190 8

Printed and bound in Great Britain by
Waterlow and Sons Limited, London and Dunstable

CONTENTS

ACKNOWLEDGEMENTS

Much of the work for this book was done 'in the field', and we have talked to hundreds of people throughout Britain about food and drink. Often we gleaned information from chance encounters in pubs and markets with people whose names we never knew. So it is not possible to list everyone who helped us. We thank them all for their enthusiasm and co-operation, particularly as we were inquisitive strangers to most of them.

Food producers and breweries, both large and small, have helped by allowing us to visit their premises and by providing answers to questions and illustrative material as well. We would like to thank all the breweries mentioned in the book, from Adnams to Youngs, and also Colmans Foods, C. & T. Harris (Calne), Lea and Perrins, Wiltshire Tracklements, Dickinson and Morris, Tuxford and Tebbutt, Suttons of Great Yarmouth, Bowyers of Trowbridge, Bulmers Cider Company, The Taunton Cider Company, The Merrydown Wine Company, The Colchester Oyster Fishery, The Whitstable Oyster Fishery, and Wipers, Wilsons, Quiggins and Romneys, all manufacturers of Kendal Mint Cake.

Many other people have allowed us to take photographs of their work and products: Martin Griffiths at Penrhos Court; Michael Waterfield at Marriage Farm, Wye; Bronwen Nixon at Rothay Manor, Ambleside; the proprietors of Sarah Nelson's Grasmere Gingerbread Shop; Richard Pinney at the Butley Oysterage; John Chevallier-Guild at the Aspall Cyder House; Bartlett and Son (Butchers) of Bath; F. Cooke and Sons (Eel and Pie Shop) in East London; Robinson's butcher's shop in Penrith, and the owners of the black pudding stalls on Bury market in Lancashire. Many other shopkeepers, stall holders and publicans helped in this way, and we would like to thank them all.

Colleges of agriculture, museums and libraries have been very kind and we would like to thank The Campaign for Real Ale, The Fish Friers' Association, The National Federation of Women's Institutes, The British Bacon Curers Federation, The Ministry of Agriculture, Fisheries and Food, The Torry Research Station, The English Vineyards Association, Wye College of Agriculture, Lackham College of Agriculture, Banbury Museum, Gloucester Folk Museum, Kendal Museum of Lakeland Life, The Welsh Folk Museum, Rutland County Museum, The Museum of English Rural Life at the University of Reading, The Highland Folk Museum at Kingussie, Beamish Museum and the Bridewell Museum in Norwich. Among the libraries, Norwich City Library has been particularly efficient and patient.

Many individuals have been helpful and generous with their knowledge, in particular Joan Poulson, Judith Guise and Jennifer Dunn. Scores of friends have kept their eyes and ears open during our research and have provided valuable leads and ideas. We would especially like to thank Nick and Chris Heipher for looking after us in Kent, and Maz and Ian Sherratt for doing the same in Hereford, as well as allowing us the use of their kitchen and living room for photography. Thanks also to Trishi, Debbie and Julie for working unsociable hours as typists.

Finally we would like to thank all those people who worked with us on the book: Trevor Wood, David Cleveland and Sheila Nightingale who took many of the original photographs; Mr A. Spark who made the maps; Geoffrey Dickinson who provided the cartoons; Edward Arnor and Carol Fowke who drew the line illustrations. Last of all, thanks to our designer, David Fordham, and editor, Susan Egerton-Jones, who not only showed patience, tolerance, unflagging enthusiasm and imagination, but also added their own knowledge of regional food to the book.

We would like to thank the editors of the many newspapers and magazines who provided us with photographs which are acknowledged in the text. We would also like to thank Faber and Faber for permission to use an extract from *The Days That We Have Seen* by George Ewart Evans; Mrs Sonia Brownell Orwell and the publishers Secker and Warburg for permission to quote extracts from *The Collected Essays, Journalism, and Letters of George Orwell Vol. 1*; and J. E. Brownlow and the Leicestershire Archaeological and Historical Society for permission to quote from *The Melton Mowbray Pork Pie Industry*.

PREFACE
THE ART OF
FOOD HUNTING

David Mabey

The idea of a book about regional food and of going out in search of it sprang from my deep curiosity about what we eat in Britain, and how much of the food – and drink as well – that we associate with various parts of the land actually still exists. My brother Richard shares much of my enthusiasm in this, so it was natural that we should embark on the book as a joint venture. We wanted to get to the truth about regional food, to explode myths where necessary, to inform people, and, above all, to point out the links between food and its locality. We wanted it to be a personal view as well, suggestive and encouraging, rather than completely comprehensive.

The first time I visited Melton Mowbray, in Leicestershire, I went in search of a pie. Not just any pie, but the famous Melton Mowbray Pork Pie. I wanted to see them, to find out how they were made and to eat them on their own home ground. On arrival I felt that I needed to absorb the atmosphere of the place, so I went to a pub. As it was market day, the pub, in customary fashion, had an afternoon extension. I drank, listened and observed. A while later I set off to explore the streets. Taking my time, I gazed into shop windows and noted how food was being displayed and what was on sale. The next morning I tracked down one of the shops where the pies were made. Slightly cautious about introducing myself and my interest to complete strangers, I was nevertheless made welcome and shown round the whole premises. I watched the raising of the pastry crust and the baking as well. I had found the real thing.

The notion of food hunting has something in common with the study of natural history. More often than not it is outdoor work, and the most exciting finds are the unexpected ones. You can search out a rare pie with as much enthusiasm and spirit as you can travel to watch avocets. And the pie had the added advantage of being edible. Taking the natural history analogy a little further, there's an element of conservation as well. The food hunter is an agent; by discovering and popularizing local food he can help it to survive.

The hunting grounds for travellers in search of food are shops, markets, pubs, improvised stalls by the roadside, quayside or beach. Food that is made and eaten in the family kitchen is not so accessible to the food hunter; it has a different character; it is more individual and dishes belonging to one family rarely migrate and turn up in other places. But publicly available food has a strong sense of locality; it will belong to a particular area for particular reasons. Sometimes that area may be one town, sometimes a county or even a whole region, but there will always be an identifiable link between the food and the place where it is made and eaten. It may be the geography of the place, the landscape, the soil, the influence of one crop which does better than others, an important industry or a quirkish local predilection for a particular food. Or it may be a combination of several factors, natural and man-made.

To *explain* the survival and, in some cases, the exploitation of local and regional food, one has to put it into context – both historically and contemporarily. These foods are not museum pieces, quaint relics from the past which nobody needs now; they are still made, still eaten, still to be found and tasted by anyone with the curiosity to go and look. They have a sturdy resilience to withstand or adapt to economic pressure from the food industry and the supermarket. But, they do survive, and there is tremendous local pride and enthusiasm for them.

Richard Mabey

In this book we have used the word 'food' rather more frequently than 'dish' because most authentic foods are simple. They *can* be turned into fine dishes with a little culinary expertise, but usually they are available complete in themselves: bread, cheese, pies, cooked meat, smoked fish, beer, cider and so on. And it is often because of their simplicity or 'plainness', in the best sense of the word, that they continue to be valued and enjoyed.

The farmer who makes cider, the fisherman who smokes herrings in a shed, the lady who knows cheese, the men who catch salmon in specially designed nets, or scoop elvers – the marvellous tiny fry of the eel – from the waters of the Severn, and the bakers and butchers who prepare and sell everything from pork pies to black puddings and brawn are all remarkable for the traditions and skills that have become their specialities. Once you have talked to these people, listened to their tales and the private language of their trade, and watched them at work, their food takes on a new value and intimacy.

As I stood watching the chief 'raiser' at work with the pastry for the pies in Melton Mowbray, moulding and turning the dough as a potter might handle clay, I knew I was watching tradition at work – food being made in the right place by the right people.

Both Richard and I are aware that we could not possibly do justice to all the fascinating regional foods that are there for the finding in the whole of the British Isles. Many readers may be disappointed not to find their own local speciality mentioned at all; for us the writing of this book was an expedition and it would have taken us a lifetime to have searched for and found all there is to be found. But if we have encouraged you to take to the road with a new purpose, we will have achieved something. And if you feel able to let us know of your own discoveries, then a 'Further Search for Food' will be well on the way to existence.

David Mabey, 1978

INTRODUCTION:
THE SOURCES OF FOOD, BASIC FOODS

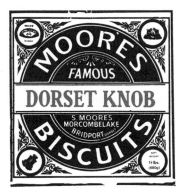

Much of our local and regional food dates back to the time when it was common for families and whole communities to be centred around a small market town. Transport was slow, and travel usually inconvenient and often unnecessary. Consequently people in one area seldom knew about the local dishes made and eaten by their fellow countrymen in neighbouring districts. The food, like the people, stayed where it was. Today the situation is very different. All of us have become travellers: we can move easily around the country, and, as a result, local and regional foods have become more accessible. Going in search of food either as sideline or as a planned expedition is now a practical proposition, with enough rewards and surprises to justify embarking on such a journey.

To provide a few general hints to successful food hunting, I have set out in this introduction an indication of where to look, what to take with you in the way of equipment, and essential information, sources and guide books, plus some important rules about gathering wild foods; and, finally, a brief look at three basic foods which we take for granted, but which form a fundamental part of our traditions and eating habits.

SOURCES OF FOOD

Food hunters begin their search in shops, pubs, markets and restaurants, as well as roadside stalls and beach huts. Not surprisingly, shops are the richest source of local and regional food, and as a general rule shops in market towns and in the outskirts of big cities are the most rewarding. Small village shops may supply the odd interesting item, but they tend to be less productive than one might expect. And the modern stores which now stand in large shopping precincts are seldom geared to the specialist foods of their area, although it is worth keeping your eyes open for good delicatessens. Selective window shopping is a useful way of scanning the produce of a town; you soon learn what to look for and what to avoid, and whether the place is going to yield anything in the way of local food.

Pubs are primarily for drinking, so it is worth sampling any locally-brewed beers, cider, or wine when in a new pub. Be curious. Don't be embarrassed about buying bottles to take away. Bottle collecting has become fashionable recently, and there's nothing wrong with it, provided, of course, that the contents are eventually drunk. A number of pubs feature local and regional foods, and, as a rule, if the food is simple the better it will be. After tasting a large number of pub lunches during the writing of this book I am now very suspicious of hostelries that advertise obscure local dishes cooked by the landlord's wife.

Markets are often more fun to investigate than shops. They have the advantage that you can be much more openly curious about all the produce on display. Market stallholders tend to be more knowledgeable and willing to talk than shop assistants, and the larger markets also provide a range of goods close together on different stalls, which makes comparison worthwhile. Markets, however, normally close quite early in the afternoon and are only held once or twice a week in most towns, so check days and times before setting out.

Restaurants can be fruitful, although they are tremendously varied in their approach, often missing the really important local foods and featuring a grandiose menu of vaguely English dishes quite out of keeping with their region or their culinary capabilities. Some, however, do succeed, and should be encouraged and supported. Be enthusiastic, but go carefully.

Roadside stalls are special because they are usually rather makeshift affairs and always unexpected. They vary in number and in the goods displayed, on their locality and the season – late summer cobnuts in Kent, crabs in East Anglia and so on. Never pass one without checking its wares. Also look out for signs and advertisements for 'picking your own', and, if you are on the coast, make enquiries about fish; huts and stalls on the beach often sell part of the day's catch, fresh from the boats, at much lower than shop prices.

THE FOOD HUNTER'S KIT

There are a number of pieces of equipment that every food hunter should keep with him. Food is bought either to be taken away or to be eaten on the spot. So you must be prepared.

One of the first principles of food hunting is that foods *belong* in particular areas, and to get real pleasure from them you need to be greedy, impatient and curious. Whether you have found lardy cake in Wiltshire, or Melton Mowbray pies in Leicestershire, or a bottle of Broadside strong ale in Suffolk, you need to be able to deal with it efficiently.

I always carry a bottle opener, a corkscrew, a couple of good knives – one for cutting, one for spreading – a fork and a spoon. A penknife is useful when you have to improvize with crabs and other resilient foods, and there are times when you will need some nutcrackers as well. There's no real need to have plates or mugs – use wrapping and paper bags, and drink straight from the bottle. At this level, the enjoyment of food has a rough informal edge to it, and extra refinements are cumbersome and unnecessary.

If you are taking food back home you will need some containers. Unless you want to build a fridge into your car, perishables such as sausages, fresh meat and fish products are not worth collecting. But cakes, cheeses, cured meat and cured fish, pies, sweets, bread and many other foods can be easily transported, and it is only sensible to ensure that the food doesn't go dry or stale during its journey, and that it doesn't smell, stain, or contaminate anything else. Kitchen foil is invaluable, as are different-sized freezer bags and a few miscellaneous containers with lids will come in handy. (Tinfoil containers, like those used by Chinese takeaways, are particularly good, and easy to buy.)

Don't, however, become too obsessed with the idea of collecting. Make full use of what you find. Eat it straight away if possible, but if there are left-overs put them by for another day.

GATHERING WILD FOODS

The rules to follow when gathering food from the wild are precisely the same as those which should govern ordinary purchases: be quite sure that you know what you are picking and are confident of its quality. Ignore generalizations which purport to separate poisonous plants from edible ones. They are not foolproof. If you have any doubts about the identity of a food, leave it alone!

coarse grain mustard with white wine

Gathering, preparing and eating wild food is perfectly safe if you follow the simple guidelines below:

FLOWERING AND FRUITING PLANTS:

1) Use a good field guide for identification, such as *The Wild Flowers of Britain and Northern Europe*, (Fitter and Blamey, Collins).

2) Check that the leaves or berries that you pick are young and fresh and are not obviously affected by infection.

3) Avoid picking too close to major roads or near farmland where chemical sprays may have been used.

4) Pick into an open basket whenever possible to avoid squashing and to conserve the freshness and bloom of your crop.

5) Consider the plant's health as well as your own: pick only very small quantities from each individual specimen, so that its appearance and survival are not threatened.

6) Remember that it is now an offence to pull up any wild plant by the roots, unless it is growing on your own land or you have the landowner's permission.

MUSHROOMS AND TOADSTOOLS:

1) Absolutely correct identification is doubly important here, as there are a few deadly poisonous species (mostly uncommon) which resemble edible species. (A good field guide is *The New Field Guide to Fungi*, Soothill and Fairhurst, Michael Joseph.) One way of simplifying the identification process is to learn half-a-dozen easily recognized and excellent tasting species (eg: giant puffball, shaggy ink-cap, chanterelle, cep, blewit, field mushroom) and stick to these.

2) Discard any specimens which are old, decaying, sodden with water or infested with maggots. You can usually detect the latter by the entry holes they have bored through the stalk. Avoid also any specimens which are too small to have developed their identifying characteristics.

3) Don't cut the fungi with a knife, but twist them gently free of the ground. You will need the whole stalk and any attendant 'sheaths' for identification; removing them in this way also stimulates the growth of a new 'flush'. (The toadstools we see above the ground are just the 'fruits' of the whole fungus plant.)

4) Gather the crop into an open basket, and keep in cool, dry, well-ventilated surroundings. Fungi can absorb great quantities of water, which spoils their taste and encourages decay. Most cases of fungal food-poisoning result not from poisonous species but from edible varieties that have been kept too long and in the wrong conditions.

5) Clean your fungi before cooking and slice open the caps to double-check for decayed maggoty portions. There is, however, no need to wash them.

6) If you are trying a new species for the first time begin with a small portion, to cover the remote possibility that you may have a personal allergy to it.

SHELLFISH:

Correct identification here is less important than quality control. There are no poisonous species among British shellfish, but a good proportion of dubious individuals. Molluscs feed by pumping water through their shells and filtering out plankton, and if this should happen to include micro-organisms derived from sewage, say, these may be concentrated by the molluscs and cause a bad digestive upset to anyone who eats them.

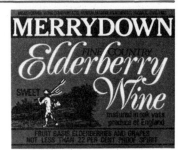

1) Never gather shellfish from shorelines near large towns or industrial complexes.

2) Avoid gathering during the hot summer months. All shellfish are slightly out of condition during the breeding season, which coincides with the period when populations of potentially dangerous micro-organisms in the sea are most virulent.

3) Avoid East Coast mussels altogether during spring and summer. Outbreaks of the protozoan *Gonyaulax tamarensis*, which produces paralytic shellfish poisoning (PSP) in humans, now occur every summer in the North Sea. All sea creatures are susceptible to 'red tides' which signal a bloom of this species, but mussels, straining up to ten gallons of water a day, can concentrate especially large quantities of the toxins.

4) Never gather 'spats', the small, young generation of shellfish. Leave them to grow into adult specimens.

5) Before cooking, wash your shellfish well, and allow them to stand in fresh water for at least six hours to clean out the mud and sand.

6) Immediately *before* cooking discard any shellfish that are *open* or smell offensive. Check any doubtful specimens by gently forcing the shell open a fraction of an inch. It should shut again quickly as soon as you remove the pressure. If it opens with ease, or fails to shut again, it is best to assume the fish is dead so throw it away.

7) *After* cooking discard any that remain *shut*.

SOURCES OF INFORMATION

Reference books:
It's not practical to take a whole library (see p. 256) with you when you are travelling. However, a couple of guides are useful in the field: *The Good Beer Guide*, issued each year by the Campaign for Real Ale (CAMRA), is essential for anyone interested in the beers of Britain. And *The Good Food Guide*, although not an entirely reliable guide to eating houses serving regional food, does pinpoint a number of restaurants that really have achieved a balance between local and national food.

Libraries:
If there are any important local foods in an area, it is likely that the library will have some historical and factual information about them. Melton Mowbray library, for instance, is full of useful material about the local pork pie industry. Library staff are helpful provided you explain what you are looking for and give them time to find it. Even if they cannot help directly they may be able to suggest other lines of enquiry.

Newspapers:
Local newspapers help to complete the picture of any area. They will give details of fruit-picking, markets, food festivals and general tit-bits, anecdotes and news about local food. The advertisements and 'for sale' columns will also tell you something about the character and life of the area.

Museums:
There are no museums devoted to food, but throughout the country there are many that include details and exhibits which reflect the local food of the past. Folk museums and those specializing in agriculture or domestic life are the most useful. There's hardly a town which does not have a museum of some sort, and they are worth a visit. A copy of *Museums and Galleries in Great Britain and Ireland*, published by ABC Historic Publications, is easily available and gives a complete list with details of opening times and the main features of each museum.

BASIC FOODS

Most of the foods described in this book are strictly regional specialities; they are associated with and belong to one particular area and have resisted standardization. But three of our basic foods – bread, cheese and beer – have had to struggle to survive in the face of intense commercial pressure to rob them of their different and quite specific local and regional characters. The aim of the food industry has been to make all our bread look and taste the same, with similar levelling affecting cheese and beer.

These three foods still collectively make up our 'staff of life', and they have to be produced in very large quantities. So it is economically convenient to try and eliminate those local variations which might be valued by people living in one small area but are no more than a persistent thorn in the side of the large brewers, bakers and creameries.

Food hunters can help to preserve the produce of local bakers, brewers and cheese-makers by buying what they make and by positive support and encouragement. The Campaign for Real Ale won a magnificent victory by turning the tide of the big brewers who, in the early 1970s, were threatening to replace traditionally-brewed beer with a predictable, mediocre liquid called 'keg'. CAMRA proved that there was still tremendous interest in draught beer and the difference in taste, strength, aroma and intoxicating effect between brews. They showed that we *can* make a successful stand in the face of so-called progress. We do not have to accept what companies think is good for us.

To help food hunters understand a little more about bread, cheese and beer when they encounter them during their travels, I have included here something about their history, their regional origins, how they are actually produced and some details about the regional and local variations still available.

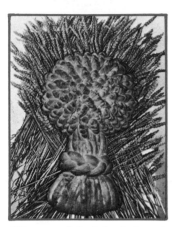

(Photograph by John L. Jones)

BREAD

We have relied on bread as our staple food for thousands of years, and it has undergone many changes since the primitive cereal mixed with water was heated and dried. Bread was made from anything that was available from acorns, peas and beans to barley, oats, rye and wheat. White, wheat bread was a luxury reserved for the rich, while the poor survived on brown or black bread made from barley and rye.

Today's bread is still broadly divided into brown and white. But it's no longer simply a matter of class or income. It is too easy to say white bread is bad, and brown bread is good. White bread can be tasty and nutritious, and it is not unknown for brown to be almost inedible, or even white bread coloured brown. The real division is now between the bread produced by the two remaining big bakery firms, Allied Bakeries and Rank Hovis MacDougall, and that produced by the 50 smaller companies and the 5,000 or so local bakers in the country.

Sliced bread in its usual indigestible, tasteless form is little short of a national disgrace but it is still baked and bought in vast quantities. That anyone can prefer it, when there are such good alternatives available in small bakeries in almost every town in the country, is extraordinary. Bread is such a fundamental part of our diet, and it is surprising how little most of us care about what we buy. Only when the big bakers go on strike do people make their own, or patronize the small bakers at the expense of the supermarket.

There's a distinct similarity between the baking and brewing industries, and, recently, The Campaign for Real Bread (CAMREB) was launched by The Vegetarian Society as a younger brother to The Campaign for Real Ale (CAMRA). There's the same imbalance between a few very large firms and a great many small ones, and a similar levelling of what is produced so that it all tastes and looks alike, and there is the same intense promotion of the big firms' products.

Holborn Bakeries Ltd.

ESTD. – 1740

But it is encouraging that more people are beginning to take an interest in bread made from wholemeal flour and in the different types of bread produced by the small bakers. In response to this demand big firms have had to start producing wholemeal loaves. While much of our regional bread is a thing of the past – the tradition was lost before anyone was prepared to do anything about it – there is still a great deal of distinctly regional bread and yeast cookery. The oatcakes of Derbyshire, Lancashire, Yorkshire and Scotland are good examples, as are the home-made crumpets and muffins in the north-west, and the whole range of rolls like baps and barm cakes. Then there are the fruit breads, like Wiltshire lardy cake and *bara brith* from Wales, and buns from all parts of the country. In all, a rich baking tradition that will not disappear easily.

CHEESE

Cheese, which was being made in Britain at least 2,000 years ago, has always been one of our staple foods: nutritious, easy to store and transport, a neat, compact way of concentrating food. Cheese-making was an essential feature of farmhouse and country life right up to the 19th century, and almost every region of the country had its own specialities, huge rounds of cheese which were sold at fairs and on market stalls throughout the land. A cheese weighing 200lbs was not an uncommon sight in those days either in a farmhouse cheese store or on a market stall.

But in 1860 disease killed off many thousands of cattle in Britain and the amount of milk, and therefore cheese, produced dropped drastically. American cheese might have swamped the market had not British cheese-makers decided to work together as co-operatives and to open factories, or creameries. These factories could produce much more cheese more efficiently and more quickly than the farmhouse dairy. More cheese was needed because it was an essential food for people in the fast-expanding cities which grew up with the Industrial Revolution. In 1870 the first cheese factory opened in Derby and by 1875 it had expanded to six factories. The change to factory production meant that farm cheese-makers gradually stopped making cheese. In 1900, for instance, there were 2,000 farmers producing cheese in Cheshire. Today there are less than 30.

A few cheese-makers continued to produce farmhouse cheese until 1914, when wartime restrictions and the need for quantity rather than quality put an end to their activities. Although most of Britain's cheese has been produced in creameries since then, there are signs of a renewed interest in farm-produced cheese and local variations.

In 1955 the English Country Cheese Council was set up to promote English cheese and there is no doubt that it has helped to encourage interest in different types of English cheese made in the traditional way. They recognize nine main cheeses: Cheddar, Cheshire, Double Gloucester, Caerphilly, Wensleydale, Derby, Lancashire, Leicester and Stilton. But there are plenty of others. There is Sage Derby (flavoured with sage leaves and juice), a rare Blue Cheshire, white unveined Stilton and a Cotswold cheese which is sold in some places. Some cheeses, like Lancashire, are still made in farmhouses, and Double Gloucester is once again being made from the milk of Old Gloucester cows – the breed originally associated with the cheese. So there is still plenty of good cheese in Britain, although many of the lesser types have disappeared altogether. You won't find Bath cheese, or Banbury cheese, or Daventry cheese, and there is no cheese now associated with Wiltshire or Cambridgeshire.

Most of the cheese bought in supermarkets today is in pieces cut from large blocks and wrapped in hygienic transparent plastic, which makes it sweat and does little for its flavour or texture. And cheese that is sold without packaging often isn't matured for long enough, because it is uneconomical to have whole

(Reproduced by kind permission of J. Sainsbury Ltd)

cheeses on the shelves of the creamery for too long. A good piece of properly matured cheese is now almost a luxury, although it wasn't originally made for that reason.

The most active campaigner for the preservation of farmhouse cheese is Major Patrick Rance, who runs an excellent cheese shop in Streatley-on-Thames in Berkshire.

BEER

In the 1950s, Britain's beer was suddenly threatened to a degree that had not been known before. Big business moved in, and for the next decade there were endless mergers and takeovers and many local breweries were either closed or absorbed by a handful of brewing giants. Almost everyone has fond memories of a brewery that once sold fine beer, but was forced to close its doors because of pressure applied by the big brewers. Remember Bullards, Morgans or Steward and Pattersons from Norwich, or Flowers from Stratford, or Harmans from Uxbridge and scores of others?

The small breweries weren't the only casualties; the beer itself suffered. The big brewers decided to package and standardize, aiming for a type of beer that could be distributed nationally and would taste the same whether it was consumed in Yorkshire or Sussex. They started to filter and pasteurize the beer before it left the brewery, storing it in pressurized canisters with carbon dioxide. The resulting bland, fizzy brew was called 'keg'. Another beer called 'top-pressure' has also come into being. In this case it is the dispensing that is important. The beer is stored in barrels and forced through the cellar pipes to the bar by an injection of gas.

In comparison traditional beer seemed difficult to keep, difficult to serve and too variable in quality. In the eyes of the big brewers it had to be replaced. It almost was, completely. But the situation changed in 1971 when The Campaign for Real Ale (CAMRA) was formed. Its members have fought strongly not only for the survival of traditional beer, but for the drinkers who were being deprived of choice.

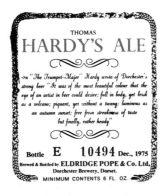

The number of breweries operating in Britain has declined steadily since the turn of the century from 6,447 in 1900 to 162 in 1973. Even so, beer drinkers now have a chance to sample a great many different brews which might now be extinct had not CAMRA alerted those who cared about what went into their glass. But, to put the situation in perspective, about three-quarters of the Britain's beer is produced by the big brewers, and most of it is pressurized in some way. And some of the beer produced in the traditional way by the independent breweries can be truly awful if it is not looked after and served properly.

Some areas of the country are still beer wildernesses, like parts of East Anglia and the West Country, but in most places there is good beer to be found and drunk, and its availability is increasing all the time. Some new breweries are also starting up to add to the list of local and regional brews available. There are strong and weak bitters, some hoppy, some sweet and fruity; there are dark and light milds, barley wines, old ales and a whole range of bottled beers from the Thomas Hardy Ale brewed by Eldridge Pope in Dorset – the strongest beer of its kind in Britain – to the Broadside, which is Adnams contribution to the list of strong bottled beers.

Throughout this book, I have mentioned quite a number of the independent breweries in the different regions, but I have concentrated on those which are indigenous to any particular area. Traditional beer moves about much more than it used to. You can drink Sam Smith's beer from Yorkshire in Hertfordshire, and Hook Norton from Oxfordshire in Hereford for example, and the situation is changing all the time. Look out for the breweries I have listed, but expect to find others as well, and try as many types as you can.

LONDON
STREET SELLERS, MARKETS AND EATING HOUSES

Unlike the other areas dealt with in this book, London is not strictly a region. It is a single city, albeit a vast and sprawling one with suburbs and swallowed up villages, and for a long time it has existed as a cosmopolitan metropolis with a whole range of different communities – Welsh, Irish, Jewish, German, Chinese, Indian and so on. As a result the food of London is as varied as the people who live and work in the city. It's much harder to characterize, it's more difficult to find a common underlying theme for the food that has evolved in London than in other areas.

London's traditional food is openly for sale in pubs, markets, restaurants and on street stalls. Home-cooking, such an important factor in other regions, has had little effect on the foods that have become associated with London. For centuries, chefs in the city's hotels and restaurants have been creating many of the dishes like steak and kidney pudding which have become intimately linked with England's capital.

It wasn't just the grand eating houses either which shaped the food of London. Out on the streets pie-sellers, muffin men, men selling roasted

The Chinese restaurants in Lisle Street and Gerrard Street are as much a part of London life these days as the jellied eel and whelk stalls in the East End.

Street-walkers clustered around a London seller. From 'The Book of Shops' by F. D. Bedford. (Reproduced by kind permission of The Mary Evans Picture Library)

A glance through 'The Good Food Guide' will direct you to quite a number of new restaurants in London claiming to specialize in traditional English food in general, and food associated with the city in particular.

chestnuts, and hot baked potatoes, as well as jellied eel and shellfish stalls all made their contribution. This was the type of food, along with fish and chips, which the ordinary working people of London depended on, so, in a sense, it is a more direct reflection of the life and traditions of the city.

Some of the grand dishes along with the eating houses that created them have disappeared, just as some of the street sellers have gone, but there is still plenty to find and enjoy as you make your way around the city.

FISH IN THE CITY

Billingsgate is the largest fish market in the country – a vast clearing house for all kinds of fish from different parts of the world. So you would expect plenty of good fish to be had in London. The River Thames may yet become a fish river as it was years ago, if the cleaning programme continues with as much success as it has recently. It may, once again, be tolerable for salmon and anchovies, two fish that once lived in its waters.

In the last two hundred year three fish have become closely associated with London: whitebait, eels and oysters.

WHITEBAIT

Whitebait isn't actually a species of fish, but the collective term for the fry of the herring and sprat. They were once caught in vast shoals by vessels moored in the Thames tideway just of Blackwall. Because the fish was so delicate and fragile and quickly lost its freshness, it was eaten on the spot as soon as the catch was taken from the water. Every July, Londoners converged on Blackwall and Greenwich where they knew the taverns would be selling the fish quickly fried in flour.

The Ship Tavern, Greenwich in the 1890s. Members of the Opposition would eat their whitebait dinners here. (Reproduced by kind permission of The Mary Evans Picture Library)

Whitebait dinners did not originate at Greenwich. Dagenham was their birthplace, when such a dinner celebrated the completion of the land drainage scheme in Essex. The story goes that Prime Minister Pitt was invited to a dinner on one occasion and brought several ministers with him. They enjoyed it so much that they decided to make it a regular occasion, and it wasn't long before Greenwich became the regular meeting place.

The taste for whitebait also extended to the Houses of Parliament, and it was the custom for members of the government to enjoy a whitebait dinner at the end of the parliamentary session. The ministers dined at the *Trafalgar Tavern*, while the opposition went to the nearby *Old Ship Tavern* to ensure that no debating spoiled their eating.

"Three Cheers for Salisbury"

'Three Cheers for Salisbury'. Government Ministers at the whitebait dinner of 1878. (From The Graphic Magazine. Reproduced by kind permission of The Mary Evans Picture Library)

As a prelude to their whitebait, the ministers would be served 'water-souchy', a kind of fish soup that had been popular since the 17th century. It was a tasty way of using up any stray fish that had been caught in the whitebait nets, although sometimes specific fish, like the Windermere char, were requested by the diners.

No whitebait are caught in the Thames today, and the old taverns in Greenwich like *Swigg's Hotel* in King William Walk no longer serve whitebait dinners. Frozen packets of whitebait are the nearest we can get to this tradition.

EELS

Londoners have always enjoyed eels which were once caught in the Thames, and traditionally they have been prepared in three ways.

Eel pies:

In *The Cook's Oracle* (1843) there is a recipe for 'Eel Pie worthy of Eel-pie Island'. This island is situated in the Thames near Richmond, and was a popular place for fairs and picnics. Eel pies were so popular that the island was named after them. The pies consisted of eels, parsley, sherry, shallots, butter and lemon, all covered with puff pastry. Dr Kitchener, author of *The Cook's Oracle*, adds a note to his recipe that: '*It is a great question debated for ages on Richmond Hill whether the pie is best hot or cold. It is perfect either way.*'

Pleasure seekers of more modern times used to frequent Eel-Pie Island because of its pub and jazz club and because of its appealing remoteness. The arm of the law, however, eventually clamped down and it is more respectable these days.

Jellied eels:

People either love or loath jellied eels. Certainly if you have been brought up in the East End of London you will know how excellent they can be. The eels are

'When I go to dress an Eel thus, I wish he were as long and as big as that which was caught in Peterborough river, in the year 1667; which was a yard and three quarters long. If you will not believe me, then go and see at one of the coffee-houses in King Street in Westminster' – Izaac Walton.

BILLINGSGATE

Billingsgate fish market is the major wholesale distribution centre of every kind of fish from all parts of Britain and further afield as well.

Billingsgate fish market. (Photographs by Sheila Nightingale)

In the entrance at Cooke's Eel Shop in Dalston there is a mosaic 'door-mat', depicting an eel entwined in the letters of the firm's name. (Photograph by Trevor Wood)

One Robert Cooke, who was known as the Jellied Eel King, made a great deal of money from his trade. He died leaving £42,000.

simply chopped into pieces, cooked in stock and left to get cold, when the liquor sets to a clear, slightly lemon-coloured jelly. Traditionally the eels are cooked in large white basins and dispensed from large enamel bowls; these days a portion of jellied eels usually comes in a carton of some kind, but the product inside is the same as it was years ago.

The jellied eel stalls in the East End and other parts of London usually sell shellfish as well, such as cockles, mussels and whelks, served on tiny china saucers. You help yourself to a saucer, pay your money and season the shellfish with vinegar and pepper.

The gory details of eel-killing are visible to everyone who passes the window of Cooke's shop. (Photograph by Trevor Wood)

A busy weekday lunchtime at Cooke's. (Photograph by Trevor Wood)

Eels and mash:

This dish has always been associated with the eel and pie shops that at one time were as popular as fish and chip shops in London. Now, sadly, only a few are left, but those that have survived have done so in grand style. One of the finest

A monastic stained-glass window built into one of the doors in Cooke's shop. (Photograph by Trevor Wood)

is Cooke's shop in Kingsland High Street. It is not only a good place to buy eels or pies, but it is also a marvellously preserved building, with its interior unchanged for something like fifty years: the tables are marble-topped, the rows of seats are simple wooden benches, there is sawdust on the floor and huge mirrors on the walls, and everywhere there are pale green, blue and white tiles.

You can buy jellied eels at the shop, but most customers go for 'pie and mash' or 'eel and mash' both served with 'liquor' – a thin green parsley sauce. The steak pies are made in the kitchens at the back of the shop, and pie connoisseurs always turn them upside down before they eat them. The eels come from Billingsgate by the ton each week and are kept alive in tanks until they are ready for the chopping block, which is displayed for all to see in the front window of the shop. Once the pieces of eel have been cooked in a bowl of stock they are served with a generous lump of roughly mashed potato and the green liquor.

The food, whether it is pie or eel, is eaten with a spoon and fork: you will have to search hard to find a knife in the shop. This custom goes back to the time when eel and pie shops were much more rowdy places attracting a lot of dubious characters, especially at night. So many knives were stolen, no doubt for weapons or for pawning, that the only course left to the shop owners was to take them away from the boxes of cutlery.

The beautifully-preserved frontage of Cooke's Eel shop. (Photograph by Trevor Wood)

OYSTERS

In the 19th century, oysters were common, cheap food in London, and appeared on stalls alongside other shellfish. This account from a stallholder of the time gives some idea of the trade:

'Oysters, whelks and liquor go together invariable; consequence where there's fewest stalls and most publics is the choicest spot for a pitch. . . . Hoysters wants no cooking, but whelks, eels, and herrings should be kept in stock cooked to a turn . . . It don't pay more than a poor living, although me and the missus are at this corner with the barrow in all weathers, specially the missus, as I take odd jobs beating carpets etc . . . So the old gal has the most of the weather to herself. I have to start every morning about five for Billingsgate . . . the oysters on the barrow, with pepper, salt and vinegar fetch from a penny to three halfpence.'[1]

It is claimed that oysters are powerful aphrodisiacs, but I suspect it is more the act of eating them than the oysters themselves which can induce thoughts of pleasure. (Imagine what ecstasy the people of Dickens' time must have experienced, eating oysters in vast quantities almost every day!)

There is more about oysters on p. 32

[1] *Street Life in London* by J. Thompson and Adolphe Smith, 1876.

The Supper Rooms at the Haymarket. Oysters were very popular here – fried, stewed and 'scolloped'. From 'Twice Round the London Clock', 1858. (Reproduced by kind permission of the Mary Evans Picture Library)

BREWERIES

FULLER, SMITH AND TURNER LTD
The Griffin Brewery, Chiswick, London W4

Fuller's produce two outstanding bitters; the extra special bitter (ESB) is the strongest draught bitter in the country, while the London Pride is less potent but perhaps more popular. They also produce a dark mild called Hock.

Most Fuller's pubs are in the west and south of London. *The Star Tavern* in Belgravia is probably the most central, but you can try *The Red Lion* in Acton, *The Warwick Arms* in Kensington or *The Hole in the Wall* in Waterloo.

(Reproduced by permission of Fuller, Smith and Turner Ltd)

YOUNG AND CO'S BREWERY LTD
Ram Brewery, Wandsworth, London, SW18

Young's is one of a handful of breweries in the vanguard of the draught beer revolution. They have never wavered in the belief that they could survive by producing traditional beer. Their Special Bitter and Ordinary Bitter are both excellent, although their mild, Best Malt Ale, is not so highly thought of. They also produce Winter Warmer, a strong old ale, usually available in the winter months.

Most of Young's London pubs are in the south-west. Recommended ones include *The Coach and Horses* in Barnes, *The Duke of Cambridge* in Battersea, *The Olde Windmill* in Clapham and *The Brittania Tap* in Kensington.

(Reproduced by permission of Young and Co's Brewery)

MARKETS

London's street markets are very extensive and food is only one of many types of goods for sale, so I have only listed those which are particularly good sources of food. Because of the cosmopolitan nature of the city the markets are not always devoted to regional English produce, but they are fascinating nevertheless. Don't be surprised to find yams and green bananas on stalls next to potatoes and apples.

Berwick Street Market, W1.   *Monday – Saturday*
Brixton Market, SW9.   *Monday – Saturday (early closing Wednesday)*
Chapel Street Market, N1.   *Tuesday – Sunday*
Deptford Market, Douglas Way, SE8.   *Friday and Saturday*
East Street Market, Walworth Road, SE17.   *Monday – Saturday*
Hessel Street Market, E1.   *Monday – Friday*
Kingsland Road Market, E8.   *Monday – Saturday*
North End Road Market, SW6.   *Monday – Saturday*
Portobello Road Market, W10.   *Monday – Saturday*
(early closing Wednesday)
Wentworth Street Market, E1.   *Monday – Friday*
Whitecross Street Market, EC1.   *Monday – Saturday*

Chapel Street market in the 1890s. At that time Sainsbury's had a general shop at No 43, a small dairy in a terrace at No 44½ (!) and a poultry and game shop at No 51. In 1965 these were amalgamated into a single supermarket at No 54. (Reproduced by kind permission of J. Sainsbury Ltd)

COVENT GARDEN AND VEGETABLES

An enigmatic moment in the old Covent Garden market. (Photograph by Max Green)

A scene such as this suggests that the market should have been named Convent, not Covent, Garden! (Reproduced by kind permission of The Museum of English Rural Life, University of Reading)

Vegetable stalls on London's street markets. (Photographs by Sheila Nightingale)

An artist's impressions of Covent Garden in the 19th century. (From 'Sketches of London', reproduced by kind permission of The Museum of English Rural Life, University of Reading)

STREET SELLERS

The shellfish sellers weren't the only ones to be found in London in the 19th century. Some of the oldest, according to Henry Mayhew, writing in 1851, were the muffin and crumpet sellers, who walked the streets with a bell and a tray of wares on their heads. You could still see and hear them in London until the 1930s but they have disappeared altogether now. Muffins and crumpets were only eaten during the winter months, so it must have been an uncomfortable trade, having to continue whatever the weather. (Muffins are still made and eaten in the north-west of England see p. 189.)

The Muffin Man. (From London Street Cries. A postcard dated 1909)

Although the muffin men have gone, there are still traders on street corners selling hot roasted chestnuts and baked potatoes. It is worth stopping on a winter's day to warm your hands by the red hot braziers and buy a bag of chestnuts or a potato to eat as you walk along the streets. And you will still see costermongers on many street corners with their barrows of apples and other fruit. The food they sell may not be strictly local, but their presence in the city is part of its history.

'The Pig Pye Man'. Pie men selling all kinds of pies were much in demand on the streets of London.

Roasted chestnuts were also very popular, and you can still find chestnut sellers in many parts of London today. (Reproduced by kind permission of The Mary Evans Picture Library)

Make use of these street sellers. You will often come across them quite unexpectedly so stop if you can and have a look at what they are selling, and buy anything that looks like a bargain.

SOME DISHES FROM LONDON'S EATING HOUSES

London was well-known for its taverns and chop houses in the 18th century. Taverns and ale-houses sold food such as toasted cheese, oysters or soup, while the chop houses specialized in grilled meat, such as steaks and thick mutton chops eaten with pickles and potatoes. Often there would be more substantial dishes for those who needed them: stews and hot-pots which were wholesome, simple and served in large quantities. They were neither the food of the rich, who frequented the more exclusive hotels and clubs, nor of the very poor who relied on the wares of the street sellers and on basic food cooked at home. This food formed a kind of middle ground and many of the dishes have become some of our most famous *national* specialities.

It is sad that so much pub food in London nowadays is a drastically diluted version of the fare sold in the old chop houses and eating houses.

BOILED BEEF AND CARROTS

A piece of salted brisket or silverside is cooked with onions and carrots and served with boiled potatoes, dumplings, and often pease pudding as well. The whole dish is moistened with some of the meat liquor and served with parsley sauce. The only other essential ingredient is strong English mustard.

This was a favourite in the pubs and eating houses of London and it is still one of the city's best dishes. Londoners hold it in great affection and it has been celebrated in the music hall song *Boiled Beef and Carrots*. Not many dishes can claim that kind of immortality!

STEAK AND KIDNEY PUDDING

Cockneys call this 'Kate and Sydney Pud' and it is surprising how the dish has been alternately frowned or smiled upon through the years. In Dr Johnson's day it was an opulent affair. He described it *'entombed there-in beefsteaks, kidneys, oysters, larks, mushrooms and wondrous spices and gravies, the secret of which is only known to the compounder'*. In later years it was thought rather vulgar – popular with working-class men who appreciated its bulk. Then, by 1900, it had been absorbed into country house cooking on an elaborate scale. Today the best steak and kidney puddings are made at home, but quite a few of the more dedicated English restaurants in London, like *The Cheshire Cheese* (Dr Johnson's haunt), *Rule's* and *Simpson's-in-the-Strand* produce it regularly, although they don't attempt the monster fifty-pounders that were once their speciality.

Rule's was originally an oyster house when it opened in 1798. It was run by Thomas Rule and his three sons. There is a verse which says:
'And the three young Rules rush wildly about;
With dozens of oysters and pewters of stout.'

TOAD-IN-THE-HOLE

This is another dish which has been simplified over the years. In its original form it included pieces of rumpsteak, oysters, mushrooms, kidneys, chops or even a whole boned and stuffed chicken. Today's toad-in-the-hole still has the Yorkshire pudding batter, but it usually contains nothing more elaborate than a few sausages. I have eaten it with chops and kidneys and the flavour is delicious because the juices from the meat are absorbed into the batter, giving a clue to the kind of flavour people in the 18th and 19th century expected from their food.

The important point about bubble and squeak is to ensure that the outside is really browned – almost burnt – and the inside is soft and moist. At the last minute some people whisk the two together.

BUBBLE AND SQUEAK

Judging from the recipe given by Queen Victoria's chef, Francatelli, in his book *The Modern Cook*, 19th-century bubble and squeak bore only a passing resemblance to the dish we make today. It originally consisted of slices of cold

SMITHFIELD

Smithfield meat market. (Photographs by Sheila Nightingale)

Smithfield market as it appeared in the latter half of the 19th century. (Reproduced by kind permission of The Museum of English Rural Life, University of Reading)

salt beef with freshly cooked cabbage, fried in dripping and served with a little thin brown sauce poured over it. The dish we know that sizzles when it cooks in the pan is made from cold green vegetables, cold potato and onion, all fried until the mixture is browned on both sides. While Francatelli was making his version, poor housewifes in other parts of London were no doubt using up left-over vegetables by frying them together, and it is their bubble and squeak that has survived.

TRIPE

Although we tend to think of tripe as a northern food it was in fact very popular in London about 100 years ago when it was stewed, curried and even stuffed and roasted on a spit. Imagine Mr Codlin waiting in *The Jolly Sandboys* for his supper of stewed tripe:

The only unfamiliar items in this amazing stew are cow-heel, which the is the bovine equivalent to a pig's trotter, and sparrow-grass, which is merely an old name for asparagus.

'*Mr. Codlin drew his sleeve across his lips, and said in a murmuring voice, "What is it?" "It's a stew of tripe," said the landlord smacking his lips, "and cow-heel" smacking them again, "and bacon" smacking them once more "and steak" smacking them for the fourth time "and peas, cauliflowers, new potatoes and sparrow grass, all working up together in one delicious gravy." Having come to the climax, he smacked his lips a great many times, and taking a long hearty sniff of the fragrance that was hovering about, put on the cover again with the air of one whose toils on earth were over.*'[1]

Tripe is still sold in London and a few places will serve you with a dish of tripe and onions. But, reflecting on the atmosphere in *The Jolly Sandboys*, I wonder if perhaps we have lost some of that enthusiasm and excitement about simple food. Tripe, to many of us, seems pallid only because we do nothing interesting with it. A pity.

CHELSEA BUNS

The Original Old Chelsea Bun House situated in Pimlico Road was destroyed in 1839. Crowds would come from all parts of London on a Sunday afternoon to eat the buns (as many as a quarter of a million are said to have been sold in one day), to look at the freaks' museum in the Bun House, and perhaps to

The exterior of The Chelsea Bun House. From 'The Mirror', 6th April 1839. (Reproduced by kind permission of The Mary Evans Picture Library)

1 *The Old Curiosity Shop* by Charles Dickens, 1840.

The interior of The Chelsea Bun House. From 'The Mirror', 6th April 1839. (Reproduced by kind permission of The Mary Evans Picture Library)

glimpse the king, George III, munching a bun in the company of Queen Charlotte. And they would look for 'Captain Bun', the owner Mr Richard Hand, as he strolled around in a long dressing gown with a fez on his head. The outing would have provided some jolly entertainment and sustenance as well.

The buns are made from a sheet of bun dough, which is brushed with butter and sprinkled evenly with sugar, currants and candied peel. Then the dough is rolled up and divided into a number of coiled pieces which are placed side by side in baking tins and brushed with egg before being put in the oven. As the buns cook they rise and swell, and consequently the sides join together. The almost square buns have to be separated, and the doughy, rough, white inner surfaces contrast neatly with the sticky brown top.

OYSTERS

'... poverty and oysters always seem to go together ... the poorer a place is, the greater call there seems to be for oysters ... here's a oyster stall to every half-dozen houses[in Whitechapel]. The street's lined with 'em. Blessed if I don't think that ven a man's wery poop, he rushes out of his lodgings, and eats oysters in reg'lar desperation.' Those words spoken by Sam Weller in *The Pickwick Papers*, applied to London in the 1830s, and the tradition had existed for something like 300 years. Oysters were cheap food (at the end of the 15th century they were 4d a bushel when beef was 3½d a lb); they weren't only eaten by the poor, but by more well-heeled folk as well. Judging by the frequent references to 'barrels of oysters' in his diary, Pepys must

'The first day of oysters in London'.　(Reproduced by kind permission of the Mary Evans Picture Library)

have had a great craving for them. Out in the streets of London in the 17th and 18th centuries you could buy oysters from barrows which also supplied gilt ginger-bread.

But by the 1850s oysters had become a rare luxury. The main reason for this was the over-fishing and plundering of stocks to satisfy the demands of England's new industrial towns. Fortunately the first artificial oyster beds were already being prepared, otherwise the shellfish would have disappeared altogether from English waters. One of the first was a project started in 1865 by the South-East England Oyster Company using a site near Hayling Island.

Oysters 'stored' under water in baskets. (Photograph by Trevor Wood)

Today, the main supplies of oysters still come from areas around the south-east corner of England, especially Whitstable and Colchester, as well as the Helford River in Cornwall. (Wivenhoe in Essex was the old centre of the industry. Here there were big storage pits where the oysters were kept before being shipped to London and the eastern counties.)

The common oyster (*Ostrea edulis*) lives off-shore in shallow water. After it has spawned, the fertilized larvae or 'spats' sink to the sea bed and must attach themselves very rapidly to rocks or pebbles. If they fail and finish up on mud or sand they cannot survive. Although oysters are farmed they are still vulnerable and have suffered in recent years from bad winter conditions, attack by creatures like the sting winkle and by being outnumbered by marauding sting limpets,

Mr Pinney's oysters grow in beds which occupy a stretch of river near his home. (Photograph by Trevor Wood)

who use the same food supplies as the oyster. Consequently a lot of oysters are imported, particularly from Portugal, to meet the large demand in this country.

But if you are searching for locally grown oysters today go to Colchester, or further south round the Thames estuary to Kent. The season, the months with an 'r' in them, begins in October and continues until April, and in Colchester they hold a prodigious Oyster Feast to mark the beginning of the season. However, this is a formal, rather un-festive occasion, no more than a gathering of civil dignitaries and invited guests. It is much more fun to catch one of the informal celebrations that some Essex pubs now hold around the time of the Feast.

My favourite haunt for oyster eating (and for fine smoked fish as well) is further north, in Suffolk. The Butley Oysterage, in the village of Orford, is famous for its 'native' (home-grown) oysters and its smoked salmon. The Pinney family, who run the Oysterage, grow tiny Japanese *gigasc* oysters, feeding the seeds on home-made plankton produced in glass jars like bubbling, thick green wine. An eight acre stretch of river is all they need for their hatchery. It's an ingenious and very successful local enterprise.

Oysters are, first of all, raw food. They need to be freshly opened with their liquor still in the shell, kept cool on a bed of ice and flavoured with lemon juice and perhaps a little cayenne pepper. You will need brown bread and butter as well, and a bottle of Guinness to drink. But they are eaten cooked as well: they were once put into Lancashire hot-pot, and steak and oyster pie – a traditional London speciality.

The Butley Orford Oysterage in Orford, Suffolk sells fine native oysters grown locally by Richard Pinney. (Photograph by Trevor Wood)

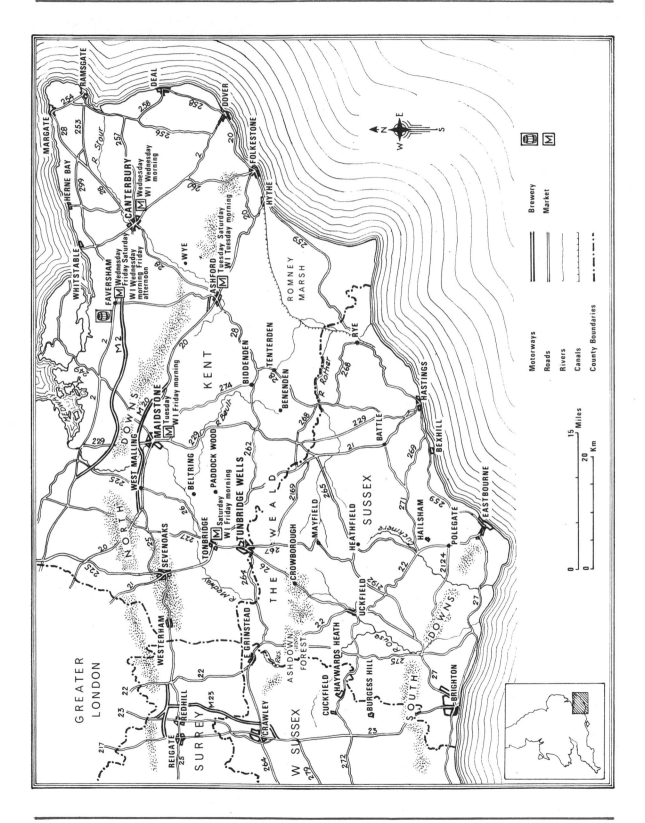

THE WEALD OF KENT
FARMS, GARDENS AND FRUIT PICKING

The Weald is a mainly wooded region lying between the North and South Downs, and stretching through Kent and Sussex. It is an area that was colonized and turned into pasture as early as the 7th century. The village names of the Weald have an ancient ring to them: Tenterden, Benenden, Biddenden (the suffix *den* is from the Old English word meaning valley). Sheep were the first animals to be farmed on the downlands and on reclaimed marsh to the south of the Weald, but the region had a warm climate and the rich soil was ideal for market gardens and organized plantations.

The Weald was once an important iron-mining area, and during the 16th and 17th centuries, when wood was the basic fuel needed for much of this work, large areas of woodland were cut down causing irrevocable changes in the landscape.

Many of the fruit and vegetables that we know today were being grown in the gardens of large manor houses in the Middle Ages, but not until the 16th century was there a general upsurge of interest in the subject of fruit growing. Many estates developed large orchards, new varieties were introduced from abroad, and the idea of market gardening was established – principally by immigrant French gardeners. By the middle of the 17th century there were plantations of apples, pears, cherries and plums, with plenty of space given to strawberries, gooseberries and other soft fruit. The Weald was perfectly positioned to become the 'garden of England'.

A flock of Romney Marsh sheep grazing on flat meadows in the south of the Weald. (Reproduced by kind permission of The Museum of English Rural Life, University of Reading)

One of the first farm-shops to be opened in south-east England, at Uckfield in Sussex. (Reproduced by kind permission of The Museum of English Rural Life, University of Reading)

The reputation of the Weald, and indeed the whole south-east corner of England, has never been challenged since those days. But, along with the growth of commercial market gardening and trading on a national scale, a healthy local market aimed directly at people living in or travelling through the area has developed over the years. The idea of 'farm shops' started in this part of the country, farmers and smallholders make full use of roadside stalls as an extra outlet for selling their produce, and they encourage people to 'pick their own' – a notion which helps the farmer to get a crop off the land, and gives the customer a chance to select really fresh produce at a reasonable price as well as a taste of the pleasures (or hardships) of picking.

'The manifold vertues in Hops do manifestly argue the holsomnesse of Beere above Ale; for the Hops rather make it a Physicall drinke to keep the body in health, than an ordinary drinke for the quenching of our thirst'. Gerard's Herbal, 1597.

HOPS

These days, we associate hops with brewing, and, of course, they are one of the essential ingredients of beer. But it was not always so. The Romans brought hops to Britain, but used them as a vegetable, eating the young shoots in salads. When they left, hops appear to have left with them, for they aren't mentioned again until the 15th century, and it wasn't until a century later that they began to be cultivated in Kent by Flemish settlers. Up till that time people in Britain had drunk an unhopped brew called ale, which was made from malt, and was fermented and flavoured with honey and herbs.

Humulus lupulus, the hop, was regarded by many people in the 16th century as an unwelcome intruder, tainting the drink they had preserved for centuries. But it had advantages and eventually even the most conservative ale-drinker had to concede. Then brewers found that hops helped to preserve and clarify their beer, and drinkers discovered that their drink had a new bitter flavour and aroma. Hops were accepted and have been used in brewing ever since.

Botanically the hop is a perennial vine, with a square stem bristly with rough hairs. At the end of each growing season it dies down to near ground level, producing new shoots in the spring. These shoots grow rapidly, and are trained up a framework of poles, wires and strings. The strings are actually made of tough yarn, and hop-stringing is still a skilled art. The hop shoots or 'bines' grow to something like 25 feet, so originally the stringing had to be done by accurate tossing of the yarn, or by perching on huge stilts. Nowadays a kind of chair lift attached to a tractor is used.

It is important that the hops are harvested at just the right moment. If they are picked too early the crop is too light in weight; if picked too late the hops shed their seeds and have a bad colour. So hop-picking needs to be well-organized. Until recently the work was done by gangs of itinerant workers; every September whole families would move into the hop fields of Kent and other parts of the country for the picking. One of the earliest accounts of organized hop-picking is in *The Modern Husbandman* by William Ellis (1750):

> 'Esquire Whitworth . . . has a hundred acres of hop ground, in which he runs up a little hut or shed at every one or two bins, and furnishes it with wheat-straw for the pickers to lie on, and a cask of small beer, that they may not lose time in quest of drink; and to make them proceed with the greater courage, he gives each person, every morning, a quartern of gin. . . . This with a penny a bushel for gathering and a feast when the hop work is all done, makes their hearts glad . . . Accordingly he finds by such hospitality . . . they will serve him better, and before another.'

A hop-pickers' camp, photographed in 1937. Conditions were very primitive in many of these camps, but families endured them because the work provided them with vital extra money. (Reproduced by kind permission of The Museum of English Rural Life, University of Reading)

Buttered hops, that is the young shoots picked in May, cooked and steeped in melted butter, is a dish which was popular until quite recently in Kent, and there's no reason why it should not be made nowadays. Enough hops grow wild along roadsides and fields for the wild food enthusiast to pick.

Hop-picking was a task in which even young children could play their part. This tough little girl seems to be taking her job very seriously. (Reproduced by kind permission of The Museum of English Rural Life, University of Reading)

Wye College of Agriculture, near Ashford, has its own hop research centre, and has made an immense contribution to the development of hop-growing in the region. It has also done a great deal of work with apples as has the East Malling Research Station. There are 'Pick your own' signs for some of the crops grown in the college gardens and fields.

Hops.

(Illustration by Carol Fowke)

For the next 200 years or so families would travel to Kent from the East End of London and the other industrial towns, often using hopping as a holiday and a way of supplementing their income. Conditions varied a great deal and, although there are plenty of colourful stories and reminiscences about hop-picking holidays, it was in most cases very rough work. George Orwell went hop-picking in 1931 and wrote down his experiences:

'At about quarter past six in the morning we crawled out of straw, put on our coats and boots (we slept in everything else) and went out to get a fire going – rather a job this September, when it rained all the time. By half past six we had made tea and fried some bread for breakfast, and then we started off for work, with bacon sandwiches and a drum of cold tea for our dinner. If it didn't rain we were working pretty steadily till about one, and then we would start a fire between the vines, heat up our tea and knock off for half an hour. After that we were at it again till half past five, and by the time we had got home, cleaned the hop-juice off our hands and had tea, it was already dark and we were dropping with sleep. A good many nights, though we used to go out and steal apples. There was a big orchard nearby, and three or four of us used to rob it systematically, carrying a sack and getting half a hundred-weight of apples at a time, besides several pounds of cobnuts. On Sundays we used to wash our shirts and socks in the stream, and sleep the rest of the day. As far as I can remember I never undressed completely all the time we were down there, nor washed my teeth, and only shaved twice a week. Between working and getting meals (and that meant fetching everlasting cans of water, struggling with wet faggots, frying in tin-lids, etc) one seemed to have not an instant to spare.'[1]

The actual picking would start with the cutting down of the bines with a special curved hop-hook. The leaf-covered bines were carried to the pickers clustered around large canvas-work baskets or 'bins'. (Once elaborate string

1 *The Collected Essays, Journalism and Letters of George Orwell, Volume 1*, Secker and Warburg, 1968.

frameworks were introduced the bins were moved beneath the hops so that the cut bines would drop directly into them.) The pickers stripped the hop flowers from the bines, making sure that not too many leaves got into the baskets. Then the contents of the baskets, which held seven or ten bushels, were checked by a tallyman and loaded into sacks.

Before efficient accounting systems were developed, hop-pickers were given metal tokens which represented either a certain number of bushels or a sum of money. These tokens were cashed in at the end of the season. Wooden hop tallies were also used. These were divided into two identical halves, one being kept by the picker and the other by the tallyman. As bushels were counted a notch was cut across the edge of both parts.

Hop-picking used to be done entirely by hand, but after the flooding of the River Medway into the hop fields in the middle of the harvest in 1968, the growers went over to picking the hops by machine. Since then hop-pickers have had little to do, and there's now hardly a farm in Kent that employs casual workers on any scale. Machine-picking has had an effect on the hops themsleves too. Up till the 1950s about eighty per cent of the hops grown in England belonged to a variety called the Fuggle (the rest was from a variety called Golding). But the Fuggle had loose cones, and was a fragile plant, easily shattered by heavy-handed mechanical pickers. The Fuggle was also vulnerable to *verticilium* wilt, a soil-borne fungal disease which can ruin a whole crop if allowed to spread. This has meant that the old varieties which have served so well over the years are being systematically replaced by new strains like Northern Brewer and the anonymous WGV.

Hop-stringing is made much easier with the aid of a special platform.

A hop pocket stamped with the emblem of Wye College of Agriculture. (Reproduced by kind permission of The Museum of English Rural Life, University of Reading)

Some new EEC regulations, if introduced, could change hop-growing in England quite soon. The hop is a dioecious plant, that is there are male hops and female hops, different sexes on different plants. We, in England, have always grown the male among the females, but on the continent they have outlawed the male, and their hop fields are purely female. The EEC is seeking to bring us into line, but, as Richard Boston says, the male hops will never surrender.

Before tractors and platforms were introduced, hop-stringing needed men with a good eye and the ability to toss a heavy ball of yarn high into the air and over the hope poles. (Reproduced by kind permission of The Museum of English Rural Life, University of Reading)

The Kent landscape is dominated by hop fields and by oast houses. These contain the kilns where the hops are dried after they have been picked. Hops contain a great deal of moisture which has to be removed, or they will not keep, so they are dried in oast houses before being pressed and baled into upright sacks or 'pockets'.

At the Whitbread hop farm at Beltring you will find the most famous collection of oast houses in Kent. There are twenty-five of them, a stunning sight on a bright summer's day. (Siegfried Sassoon was little short of ecstatic about them, in *Memoirs of a Fox-hunting Man*, although he apparently miscounted the number of houses.) Across the road from these oast houses is *The Bluebell*, an old hopper's pub now plushly converted with only a few choice photographs to remind you of its past.

CHERRIES

Cherries were brought to Europe and Britain from Persia around 100 AD, and the fertile soil of Kent would have quickly nurtured the saplings which grew from cherry stones thrown away by Roman soldiers. The cherries that are cultivated today are the descendants of two species which still grow wild in many parts of the country. The sour cherries all derive from *Prunus cerasus*, and the best of these is the Morello with a dark skin and dark flesh. There are also some varieties of red sour cherry, such as *Flemish* and *Kentish Red*, often known collectively as *Amarelles*. These have red flesh and can sometimes be sweet enough to eat fresh, although they are mainly used, like Morellos, for cooking, canning, bottling and for making cherry brandy.

The second group are the sweet or dessert cherries; cherries for eating fresh. They are much more fastidious about their soil, climate and growing position, and consequently only thrive in a few parts of the country – mainly in Kent, Buckingham, Berkshire, Gloucester and Hereford – where the conditions are exactly right for the trees. All the sweet cherries cultivated today stem from the

The cherry fair used to be one of the most passionate and joyous celebrations in the calendar during the Middle Ages. One of the last remnants of this festival was Cherry Pie Sunday celebrated in Buckinghamshire at the beginning of August, after the harvest of the Black Bucks cherries. 'The Plough' at Cadsden used to sell large cherry turnovers or 'bumpers' to customers on that day, to eat with their beer.

Cherries picked at East Malling, being packed into boxes before being sent off for canning. (Reproduced by kind permission of John Topham and The Museum of English Rural Life, University of Reading)

On June 17th. 1788, Gilbert White made a note about the cherries growing in his garden at Selborne in Hampshire. In his Naturalist's Journal he wrote: 'Cherries turn colour, and begin to be eatable; but are small for want of moisture: are netted.'

Mazzard or *Gean* (*Prunus avium*), which is still grown commercially in Devon and other areas where the more recent varieties fail. (The varieties of sweet cherry have names like *Frogmore, Early Rivers, Kent Bigarreau, Napoleon* and *Roundel Heart.*)

One of the great springtime sights in the Weald of Kent is the cherry blossom. It rivals the explosion of the pink and white flowers in apple orchards in the Vale of Evesham. Although all kinds of fruit are grown in Kent, cherries have a particular importance and a number of local dishes and products have made use of them.

CHERRY BATTER

The idea of combining cherries with batter must have come to Kent with the Normans, and is a reminder that this was one of the first counties to be colonized by the invaders. Very similar dishes called *clafoutis* are still made in some regions of France.

'Clafoutis' consist of rounds of thick pastry topped with black stoned cherries, cooked and sprinkled with sugar. They are eaten hot or cold.

BREWERIES

SHEPHERD NEAME LTD

Faversham Brewery, 17 Court Street, Faversham, Kent.

The best bitter and the ordinary bitter must rank as two of the finest beers in southern England. They are both light, slightly sweet and very hoppy – *too* hoppy for some palates. There is also a sweet draught mild and an old (Old English Stock Ale), which is usually available only in the winter months. One of their bottled beers, a light ale called The Bishop's Finger, is known locally as Nun's Delight.

There are plenty of good Shepherd Neame pubs in east Kent, Sussex and Greater London. Among the Kent pubs *The Brewer's Delight* in Canterbury boasts a bat and trap game; *The Crown* at Sarre, sometimes called 'The Old Cherry Brandy House', is famous for its home-made cherry brandy; in Faversham itself *The Mechanics Arms* is used by employees of the town's two breweries (Whitbread are here as well); in *The Queen's Head* at Mereworth you can often get home-made bread; and at *The Joiner's Arms* in West Malling you can simply drink good beer in good company.

Shepherd Neame is one of the few independent breweries with its own hop farm, not suprising since it is on the edge of the most important hop-growing areas in the country. Queen Court Farm was purchased by the brewery in 1944. (Reproduced by kind permission of Shepherd Neame Ltd)

MARKETS

Markets flourish throughout Kent and they accurately reflect the character of the region. Good quality fruit and vegetables are the main items to look for, especially in the summer and autumn. WI stalls and markets also have a good reputation in Kent.

ASHFORD

General market, *Tuesday and Saturday*
WI market stall at the general market. *Tuesday morning*

CANTERBURY

General market, Market Hall. *Wednesday*
WI market stall at the general market. *Wednesday morning*

FAVERSHAM

General market *Wednesday, Friday and Saturday*
WI market, The Minor Hall, East Street. *Wednesday morning and Friday afternoon*

MAIDSTONE

General market, *Tuesday*
WI market, Dunk Memorial Hall, Church Street. *Friday morning*

TONBRIDGE

General market, *Saturday*
WI market (extensive), Scouts HQ, River Walk. *Friday morning*

The WI has a distinguished history of market selling and still provides the general public with high quality home-grown and home-made produce. The Crowborough stall, on the edge of the Weald, displayed a good variety in 1933. (Photograph reproduced by the kind permission of the National Federation of Women's Institutes)

Cherries. (Postcard from the Knight Series)

There are two methods of making the cherry batter. First a stiff batter can be made, which is then fried as a fritter, and served on a pile of hot, baked, stoned cherries. Or a batter pudding can be made. In this case, some ripe stoned cherries are put into a pudding basin and covered with the batter. A cloth is put over the basin and the contents boiled for an hour or so. The pudding is turned out and easten hot, strewn with sugar.

CHERRY HUFFKINS

In 'Good Things in England' (Jonathan Cape 1932), Florence White mentions that huffkins were commonly found in Maidstone and Elham, near Canterbury.

Huffkins were once very popular in Kent, though they are not sold these days in shops. They were simply flat oval cakes, a kind of tea-bread which has variations in many other parts of Britain, from 'Cornish splits' to 'Hawkshead wiggs'. Kentish huffkins had a hole in the middle which could be filled with hot stoned cherries and eaten as a hot dessert.

CHERRY BRANDY

It was inevitable that sooner or later someone would exploit Kent's marvellous crop of Morello cherries to make an alcoholic drink. That man was Thomas Grant, a Victorian businessman who moved from Dover to Maidstone in 1853, after a portion of the Dover cliffs fell on the distillery and warehouse that he owned. Once in Maidstone he began to experiment with a whole range of liqueurs – sloe gin, cherry whisky, ginger brandy, and, eventually, cherry brandy. Ripe Morello cherries would be delivered from the orchards in the Weald to his distillery in August; they were pressed and pulped, and the stones were cracked and added to give the mixture a delicate almond flavour. Then the whole lot was left to steep in French brandy for two months. Finally sugar syrup was added and the brandy was left to mature in oak vats.

Ever since the reign of Queen Victoria, who incidentally thought so much of the liqueur that she allowed her likeness to appear on the label, Grant's cherry brandy has been enjoyed and praised by millions.

The Crown at Sarre not only sells good beer, but home-made cherry brandy as well, and, at one time, they served special Sarre cakes to eat with the liqueur.

Cherries are used in a variety of other ways in Kent: look out for locally-produced cherry jam, cherry wine, baked cherries, pickled cherries and cherry cheese.

OTHER FRUIT

Although cherries have a special place in the food of Kent, there's hardly a popular type of fruit that isn't grown in the region. There are plums, apples, pears, strawberries, blackcurrants, gooseberries to name but some. Look out for colourful displays in farm shops, on roadside stalls and for signs saying 'Pick Your Own' – a cheap way of obtaining fresh fruit, as noted earlier.

A group of fruit pickers on a farm near Sevenoaks in the 1930s. Their baskets are filled with fruit including cherries and plums. (Reproduced by kind permission of The Museum of English Rural Life, University of Reading)

Redcurrants. (Postcard from the Knight Series)

England's most famous cooking apple, the Bramley, is grown in great quantities in Kent, although it was not originally raised in this area (see p.154). The Bramley is one of the late croppers, large, with a shiny, green skin, it is crisp and acid and cooks superbly.

The name 'filbert' is an anglicized version of noix de Philibert, ie St Philibert's nut. Philibert was a French abbot who lived in Normandy in the 7th century. His feast day is August 22nd, too early for English filberts, although in France the nuts ripen around this time.

Cobnuts.

(Illustration by Carol Fowke)

Greengrocers and fruiterers in all the towns and villages of the Weald are well-supplied with the various fruits as they come into season, although they often get their produce not from local growers but from Covent Garden.

COB-NUTS AND FILBERTS

There is always some confusion about the difference between cobs and filberts; but, botanically, in structure and appearance, they are different. The difference lies in the shape and length of the outer husk; cobs are round nuts with a short husk, while the filbert (*Corylus maxima*) is much longer and the husk tapers and completely encloses the nut. Both are species of *Corylus* and are related to the common hazel nut (*Corylus avellana*).

The confusion doesn't end there, however. The most popular commercial variety grown in Kent is called the Kentish Cob *or* Lambert's Filbert. First raised by Mr Lambert of Goudhurst in Kent around the year 1830, this is actually a filbert and not a cob, and its clusters of light-brown nuts make excellent eating. Other varieties are grown, mainly in gardens, but the Kentish Cob is by far the most common.

To get a good crop of cobs or filberts, it is necessary to prune the trees very carefully and thoroughly. If you look round a nut orchard you will see that the trees are normally shaped like wide open cups or basins, which makes harvesting easier as well as increasing the yield and the size of nuts from each tree. The nuts are usually harvested in two sessions, the first when they are fully formed, in August, then the main crop when the nuts have changed colour from green to brown in September and October. They appear in fruit and vegetable shops in the autumn and if you keep a look-out when you are driving around you will see roadside signs outside farms and plantations where the nuts are grown.

Wild hazel nuts are ready in the autumn too; you can pick them from the hazel copses dotted around woodland in the Weald and from the hazel hedges growing alongside roads and lanes. September is the best time, when the nuts are full-flavoured and woody-brown. Go carefully when you pick because a ripe hazel nut is easily dislodged and can fall to the ground with the slightest encouragement. Actually it's worth searching beneath hazel trees for fallen nuts, if the ground cover isn't too tangled or impenetrable. I've seen children in Kent foraging for the nuts in the way that children in other parts of the country hunt for conkers. Indeed, before the horse chestnut was introduced into this country, hazels made tiny, marble-sized 'conkers' for good sport.

Keep a nutcracker in your pocket if you are in Kent during the cob season, unless you are confident about the strength of your teeth. If you collect more than you want to eat straight away, take your nuts home – they will keep well in their shells, provided they are in a warm, dry spot. With patience, you can shell enough to make hazel nut bread, or vegetarian nut cutlets; you can also put them, chopped, into Jerusalem artichoke soup or make a turkey stuffing with them.

Filberts.
(Illustration by Carol Fowke)

MEAT

Sadly butchers' shops in the Weald don't offer a great deal to interest people in search of regional food. That isn't to say that the meat they sell is not worth buying. Often, if you locate a small butcher, his meat will come from local farms, and it will be slaughtered locally and treated with proper care and knowledge.

Lamb (and possibly mutton as well in one or two places) is particularly good in this part of the country and seems to be most prominently displayed in the shops. This is no doubt a reflection of the large herds of sheep grazing on the downs and also on the marshes around Romney. Romney Marsh sheep are particularly famous for their size and sturdiness, and they flourish on the salty rich marsh grass. Then there are Southdown sheep, the best for lamb, which graze on the turf of the chalk downs. It is worth enquiring about the lamb sold in the butchers' shops to find out whether it is locally produced or imported.

Traditionally lambs from these downland breeds had their tails cut off, unlike mountain sheep which kept theirs, so it's no surprise to learn that 'lamb's tail pie' was once made in Kent. The tails had to be used fresh, hence the pie was only made at lambing time. They were scalded, skinned and jointed and stewed with a few root vegetables (such as those the ewes had been feeding on). The mixture was packed in a pie dish with green peas and chopped hard-boiled egg, covered with short-crust pastry and baked. Sometimes the lambs' tails would be packed into the pie dish and covered with a thick parsley or mint sauce before baking.

Sausages are also good in Kent. Plenty of butchers make their own, and they are well worth buying. (This applies to all home-made sausages, wherever you find them. You may have to pay a little more for them, but they are far more exciting than the standardized specimens produced by the big companies.) One small firm which produces sausages in Kent advertises them as 'Kent Korkers', as opposed to 'bangers'. Some of the finest I have tasted in the area came from a small butcher's shop in Offham, near West Malling.

Pigs used to be quite common on farms in Kent. No doubt, like their brothers in the Vale of Evesham, they dined well on windfalls in the apple orchards of the county.

FISH

The Weald is situated neatly between London's markets and the south coast, and it is well-off for fish and fish shops. There is plenty of fish to choose from, although much of it is imported from other parts of the country. I've seen Manx kippers and Arbroath smokies in a small fish shop in Tenterden, and other shops selling small grey mullet and squid, and in Maidstone I saw my first smoked saithe (coley) fillets, which could *almost* be mistaken for smoked salmon.

In the southern part of the Weald a higher proportion of fish comes locally from Rye bay and the towns of the south coast. Dover soles and other flatfish are particularly good.

You can buy fish straight from the beach in many of the towns of the south coast, such as Hastings. The tall, timber beach huts are a special feature of the town. They were originally constructed as net-drying huts.

BAKERS, BREAD AND CAKES

Most of the old Kent specialities like 'huffkins' have disappeared, at least from shops and markets, and bakers in the area now produce little that is truly regional. But there is always a demand and a real enthusiasm for home-baked bread and cakes, and bakers who have remained independent do a very brisk trade.

Below are three items that were once features of Kentish cooking, although they are rarities now.

FLEAD CAKES

These were once made in almost every farmhouse in Kent after pig-killing, and were rather like very simple lardy cakes (see p. 93). They provided a way of using up the 'flead' or 'flare' of the animal – that is the inner membrane of the pig's inside, full of particles of lard. This was beaten into flour with salt using a special beater, and some recipes substituted sugar and spices for salt to make a sweet cake for tea.

Although flead cakes may still be made in one or two Kent kitchens, flead itself is harder to come by as less home pig-killing is done and the cakes aren't sold in shops or on markets stalls.

WAFERS

The word 'wafer' comes from the French 'wafre', but the name was originally 'gaufres', from the French 'gofer', to flute or crisp. This is another example of the influence of French cooking on the food of Kent.

Wafers were being made in England in the 12th century and remained an English speciality in Kent and other southern counties until the early years of this century. They were made from very fine flour, sugar, butter and milk often flavoured with nutmeg or even rose water. The wafer batter was mixed and put into warm wafer irons or tongs. These were circular or sometimes square, the size of small plates, and fitted with long handles so that they could be held over a red-hot fire. Beautiful designs were cut into the inside of the irons which left imprints on the wafers.

Now, sadly, gone, the famous firm in Tunbridge Wells called Romary, set up in 1862, used to make biscuits and wafers from old English recipes and even had the distinction of making them 'By Appointment' for Queen Victoria and subsequent sovereigns.

Romary's shop in Tunbridge Wells was famous in Victorian times and was blessed with royal patronage. (Reproduced by kind permission of Rowntree Mackintosh)

BIDDENDEN CAKES

These are made each year and distributed on Easter Monday to people in the village of Biddenden as part of an ancient custom called the Biddenden Dole. One account of the origin of the Dole says that it was founded by Eliza and Mary Chulkhurst, two sisters born in 1100 and joined together by ligaments at their shoulders and hips. When one of them died aged 34, the other refused to be separated from her sister, claiming that they should go together, as they had been born together. Six hours later she too died. The sisters bequeathed a plot of 20 acres called the Bread and Cheese Lands for the provision of bread, cheese and beer to the poor. This was the Biddenden Dole.

Although the beer in the Dole disappeared for some reason during the 17th century, the bread and cheese is still handed out, and in addition each deserving person gets a Biddenden cake, nowadays also passed round to visitors who come to watch the ceremony. Biddenden cakes are not actually cakes at all, but hard biscuits, sometimes too hard to be edible. They are symbolic tokens rather than food to eat.

Imprinted on each 'cake' is an unusual picture showing two female figures standing side by side, so close together that they appear to be joined on one side with apparently only one arm apiece. The names of the sisters appear above the heads and on the apron of one is the number 34 inscribed – their age at death. Most people, however, now agree that even if the legend itself is based on truth, the dates are wrong and the sisters lived and died in the 16th century.

The word 'dole' implies a share or portion and often refers to charitable distributions of one kind or another. Nowadays financial handouts are more valuable than donations of food or drink.

CIDER

It is only natural that a county like Kent with its many apple orchards should also have its cider-makers. One of the best that I know is Bob Luck, who produces cider from his farm at Benenden. It is sold locally, in a number of off-licences and shops, but as it is made in quite small amounts its distribution is limited to east Kent. (See also p.114).

(Reproduced by kind permission of Bob Luck)

WINE

The chalky slopes of the Downs have proved well suited to growing vines and are not unlike many of the wine producing areas of Champagne. Kent has a number of established vineyards including Marriage Farm at Wye, Kentish Vineyards at Wateringbury and Biddenden Vineyards at Biddenden. English wine is more extensively covered on p. 50.

A Kentish apple orchard packed with barrels. Surprisingly the contents of these barrels is not cider at all, but pulped plums ready for despatch to a jam factory. (Photograph by R. Weston, reproduced by kind permission of The Museum of English Rural Life, University of Reading)

ENGLISH WINE

(Reproduced by permission of New Hall Vineyard)

English wine is something of a joke only to the ignorant; and it is not, as many believe, a fairly recent innovation. Certainly the qualities of English wines are different from those of, say, France or Germany; they tend to be much 'younger' and are usually drunk a year or two after bottling, but they have a pleasant flavour and are almost *too* easy to drink. English wines have a northern character; they are mostly dry, light and white and pale greenish-yellow in colour. (A small amount of rosé is made as well.) But it's the clean, fruity taste that is their most distinctive quality.

English wine is a drink with a very long history, stretching back something like 2000 years. Even before the Romans arrived wine was reaching southern England from France, but, once the Roman occupation was under way, vineyards were planted in many parts of lowland Britain. In AD 280 the Emperor Probus authorized Britain to cultivate the vine and make wine,

monasteries, although some landowners did plant their own private vineyards as well. By the end of the 13th century the Vale of Gloucester had the highest reputation for its grapes, but subsequently English wine went into decline – the monasteries were dissolved, and the Wars of the Roses made the vineyards a risky proposition. From then on vineyards were kept more as a hobby by a few adventurous gentlemen; this continued until the 19th century. One of the great problems was a blanket prejudice against *English* wine, aptly summed up by Charles Hamilton, the owner of a vineyard in Surrey, who wrote in 1789 that:

(Reproduced by permission of Hambledon Vineyard)

and evidence of wine-making has been found in places as far apart as Boxmoor in Surrey, Silchester and Gloucester. By the early medieval period, viticulture, or vine-growing, had been taken over by the

(Reproduced by permission of Pilton Manor)

'Many good judges of wine were deceived by my wine, and thought it superior to any Champagne they ever drank; but such is the prejudice of most people against anything of English growth, I generally found it most prudent not to declare where it grew till after they had passed verdict on it.'

Pilton Manor, one of the west country's best known vineyards. (Drawing by Griffin, reproduced by kind permission of Pilton Manor)

New Hall Vineyard. (Photograph by S. W. Greenwood)

The real question has always been: why produce wine in England at all, when, in most cases, the vines come from Germany, and the resulting wine has to compete, at similar prices, with produce from Europe which has a good reputation and a flavour to match?

And the answer is that English wine and wine-growing *is* practicable, it *does* have a flavour of its own, and there's an identifiable connection between its flavour and the region where the grapes are grown. If the vines are cultivated at the extreme limits of their growing

An English vineyard in winter. (Photograph by Trevor Wood)

Bill Greenwood of New Hall Vineyard, showing his local M.P. a sample of his Huxelrebe grapes.
(Photograph by Geoff Baker, reproduced by kind permission of New Hall Vineyard)

Kentish Sovereign
English Table Wine

Kentish Vineyards
Cherry Hill
Nettlestead
Kent

Produce of U.K. 70 cl.

(Reproduced by permission of Kentish Vineyards)

zones the fruit ripens more slowly, and, if the conditions are right, the flavour develops gradually. The example of German grapes grown in England reflects exactly this.

Throughout the southern half of England, and even in one or two places further north, small vineyards are now producing English wine in varying quantities. Over 500 acres are under cultivation now; some vineyards are well-established, produce large amounts and have an organized distribution and promotion network set up to make their wine available to the public. Others are on a much smaller scale. One of these is Marriage Farm situated on the outskirts of Wye in Kent. Its vineyard covers about an acre and a half on

The small winery at Marriage Farm in Kent. (Photograph by Trevor Wood)

a beautiful Downs slope; and the grapes are German – Muller-Thurgau and Scheurebe. Michael Waterfield, who runs the vineyard, reckons that it could produce 3,000 bottles each year. The vineyard is now only three years old, and it achieved 2,000 bottles in the marvellous summer of 1976, but, naturally, the yield is very dependent on the weather, especially at the beginning of July when the vines come into flower.

Marriage Farm may not be one of the oldest or largest English vineyards compared with places like Adgestone in the Isle of Wight. Even so it's a fine example of the kind of working enterprise that characterizes so much of English regional food and drink. But where does the wine end up, after it has been blended and bottled? Walk down from Marriage Farm into the village of Wye and visit *The Wife of Bath*, Michael Waterfield's restaurant, where he sells his wine, to sample a bottle of aptly-named Marriage Hill.

(Reproduced by permission of Adgestone Vineyard)

The place to drink Marriage Hill wine is The Wife of Bath restaurant Wye. (*Photograph by Trevor Wood*)

(Reproduced by permission of The Merrydown Wine Co)

As well as grape wines there are a number of companies now producing what might be called English country wines, that is elderberry, apple, gooseberry and so on. Probably the most well-known is the Merrydown range, which are very pleasant. But there are others who are not always as successful in their activities!

(Reproduced by permission of Felsted Vineyard)

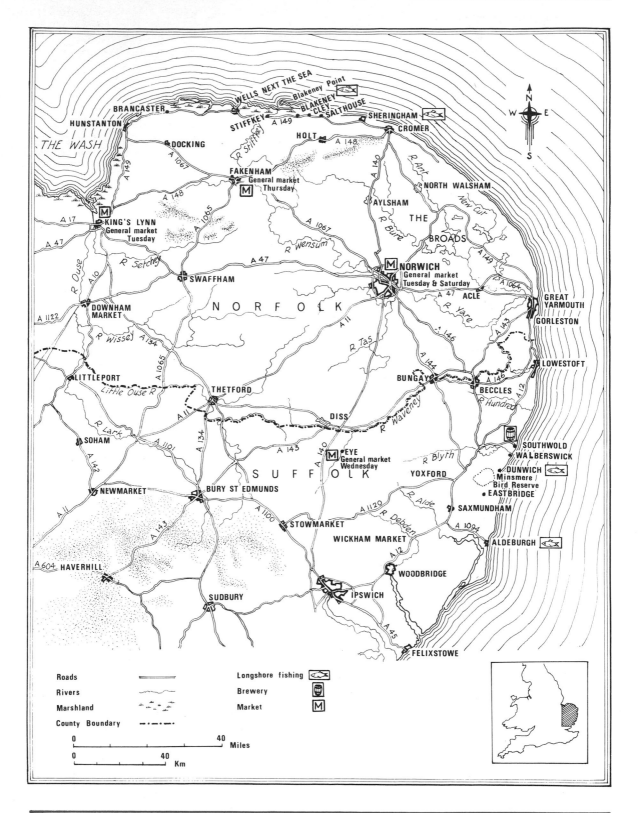

The Wash

HUNSTANTON
BRANCASTER
DOCKING
STIFFKEY R. Stiffkey
WELLS NEXT THE SEA
Blakeney Point
BLAKENEY
CLEY
SALTHOUSE
SHERINGHAM
CROMER
HOLT
A 148
FAKENHAM
General market
Thursday
A 148
A 1067
A 149
A 1065
KING'S LYNN
General market
Tuesday
A 17
A 47
R Ouse
R Setchey
SWAFFHAM
R Wensum
A 47
A 140
AYLSHAM
R Bure
THE
BROADS
NORTH WALSHAM
New Cut
R Ant
NORWICH
General market
Tuesday & Saturday
A 47
ACLE
R Yare
GREAT YARMOUTH
GORLESTON
A 1064
A 149
A 146
LOWESTOFT
A 143
DOWNHAM MARKET
A 1122
A 10
R Wissey
A 134
NORFOLK
A 11
R Tas
A 144
BUNGAY
BECCLES
R Hundred
A 12
A 146
LITTLEPORT
Little Ouse R.
A 1065
THETFORD
A 11
DISS
R Waveney
SOUTHWOLD
WALBERSWICK
R Lark
SOHAM
A 142
A 1101
A 134
A 143
EYE
General market
Wednesday
A 143
A 140
R Blyth
YOXFORD
DUNWICH
Minsmere
Bird Reserve
EASTBRIDGE
SAXMUNDHAM
SUFFOLK
NEWMARKET
A 11
BURY ST EDMUNDS
A 1100
STOWMARKET
WICKHAM MARKET
R Debden
R Alde
A 1120
A 1094
ALDEBURGH
A 143
HAVERHILL
A 604
SUDBURY
IPSWICH
WOODBRIDGE
A 12
FELIXSTOWE
A 45

Roads
Rivers
Marshland
County Boundary

Longshore fishing
Brewery
Market

0   40   Miles
0   40   Km

THE EAST ANGLIAN COAST
HERRINGS, SHELLFISH AND SHORELINE PLANTS

If you take a walk along a stretch of East Anglian coastline and turn your head inland to look over marshes and heathland as far as you can see, then you are on the 'littoral', or 'the lands near the coast'. The area is hard to define more exactly than that, but it is a unique mixture of land and sea. Local food, work, customs and traditions all depend on the ancient links that exist on the littoral.

On one side of this littoral is the sea, which implies fishing; on the other, the land, with its fields of sugar beet and barley. Between the two, right on the shoreline, there is a rich selection of wild plants that for centuries have been gathered as food. Out on the mudflats shellfish are gathered too, just as they were in prehistoric times. John Seymour called this work 'fishing on dry land', and, in fact, shellfish are collected rather like plants. The men who go out to the flats use the language of land farmers; they talk of fields and valleys, hills and ditches. Just as there are landgrown foods to be gathered, so there are sea harvests to match them. And until very recently there was no better example of the link between the land and sea in this part of the country than the seasonal movement of men who worked inland harvesting corn, and then moved out towards the coast when the barns were full. Through the winter months they would take another trade, fishing, harvesting the East Anglian herring.

In all, this area of country is still a curious hybrid, with fascinating details everywhere: shellfish gathered like plants, sheep grazing on marshes almost at the water's edge, land and sea foods in odd combinations – herrings and dumplings or cockles and bacon; men finding their work with others on boats and in fields.

Some of these details are pure history now, but there is still a great feeling of gathering and hunting for food in the region; men, women and children still work the area with buckets, nets, spears and rakes. Even if it is no more than a holiday pastime, it is a dedicated search, often bordering on obsession. It is also solitary work, even if many people are together. For anyone who is a gatherer of food in the end relies on his own eyes, his own knowledge and experience; only when the work is done, when the crops are in, does he relax. Only then does he talk and celebrate with his friends.

Look out for home-cured bacon, particularly in Suffolk, where it is often steeped in a mixture of salt, brown sugar or treacle and beer. It is almost black on the outside and deliciously sweet. Suffolk hams, cured in a similar way, appear in shops expecially around Christmas time.

HERRINGS
No one is quite sure when men started fishing for herring off the East Anglian coast. Although the craft of fishing was well developed in prehistoric times, it was with lines, hooks, bone spears and traps. The vast shoals of herring that migrated each autumn to the waters off the coast of Norfolk and Suffolk,

BREWERIES

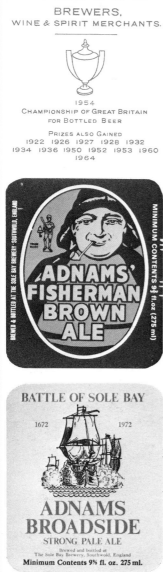

ADNAMS & Co LTD
BREWERS,
WINE & SPIRIT MERCHANTS.

1954
CHAMPIONSHIP OF GREAT BRITAIN
FOR BOTTLED BEER
PRIZES ALSO GAINED
1922 1926 1927 1928 1932
1934 1936 1950 1952 1953 1960
1964

ADNAMS' FISHERMAN BROWN ALE

BATTLE OF SOLE BAY
1672 1972
ADNAMS BROADSIDE
STRONG PALE ALE

ADNAMS & CO. LTD
Sole Bay Brewery, Southwold, Suffolk

Adnams beer completely dominates east Suffolk, and you can now drink it in Norfolk as well, which is good news for that county which is without a single independent brewery. The bitter must surely be one of the most pleasant and easy to drink in the country. There is also a dark mild, a stronger Old (brewed in the winter), and a Christmas draught barley wine – Tally Ho. The formidable Broadside – a bottled strong beer, first brewed in 1972 to commemorate the tercentenary of the Battle of Sole Bay – is also worth trying. It regularly lives up to its potent reputation. Nearly all the pubs in Southwold are worth a visit; *The Lord Nelson* is my personal favourite and hard to beat for friendliness and atmosphere. Further afield, bird watchers can call at *The Eels Foot* on the edge of Minsmere Reserve; Blythburgh *White Hart* has a fine selection of food, including smoked fish and crab; Wenhaston *Star* and Middleton *Bell* are both useful village pubs. It is an intriguing local tradition that the name of the pub is always preceded by the name of its village.

In Norfolk quite a number of free houses and hotels sell Adnams, one good example being *The Manor Hotel* in Blakeney.

*Before the days of motorised transport, the horse was essential for travel and deliveries. Adnams still use horses for local work and claim that it is up to 30 percent cheaper for deliveries in Southwold itself.
(Reproduced by kind permission of Adnams Brewery)*

needed to be caught in strong drift nets, and such nets were beyond the knowledge of these early fishermen.

But by the 12th century, Great Yarmouth had become the centre of the herring trade. It was ideally sited: there were salt workings nearby, which were vital for the curing of the fish (see p. 74); it was convenient, near to the shoals; and, even before the town was built, it was a meeting place for fishermen and buyers every autumn. This continued as the Free Fair which lasted from Michaelmas to Martinmas (September 29th to November 11th), the period of the autumn herring fishery.

The full story of the East Anglian herring fishery is really outside the scope of this book, and a great deal has already been written about it. *The Herring and its Fishery* by W. C. Hodgson (Routledge 1957), is easily the best account of the subject.

It is astonishing how much people in East Anglia relied on the herring for their food. The fish were so cheap and plentiful, and nutritious as well, that farmworkers would survive almost entirely on a diet of turnips, potatoes and herrings, while the men who worked the fishing boats were allowed ten each for breakfast. The fish were slit along the side in several places ('snotches' these were called) and fried: 'When you picked hold of the fish and got hold of a piece it would come clean away.' That is still the finest way to cook a really fresh herring.

But things changed in 1951. The herring catch suddenly dropped, and has continued to drop until today. The once great ports of Lowestoft and Yarmouth have been taken over by the big processors of frozen fish with their

The town of Great Yarmouth was once an important centre for the herring trade, but in recent years it has been taken over by the large frozen food manufacturers.
(Photograph reproduced by kind permission of Great Yarmouth Maritime Museum)

BILLY MANN, AN OLD-TIME FISH SALES-
MAN, WHO SOLD FISH ON THE BEACH NEAR
THE JETTY.

*(Engraving reproduced by kind
permission of Great Yarmouth
Reference Library)*

huge factory ships. No one knows why the herring vanished; perhaps it was
over-fishing, perhaps some change in the feeding habits of the herring or
thermal changes in the sea water. (The situation is so bad that there is now a
complete ban on herring fishing in the North Sea.)

Apart from making these marvellous fish scarce, the collapse of the fishery
has meant that two famous types of smoked herring, the red herring and the
bloater have also become a rarity.

RED HERRINGS

These were the great mass produced food of the middle ages; herrings heavily
salted without splitting or gutting, dried and heavily smoked until they were
hard, dry and highly coloured. The process would take several weeks. This

*These red herrings were cured
at Sutton's smokehouse in
Great Yarmouth. Fish smoking
in a traditional smokehouse is
an elaborate business
demanding complete accuracy
as well as a mixture of
intuitive skills and long
experience.
(Photographs by Trevor Wood)*

treatment was essential because the fish were very perishable and caught in vast numbers, and they simply would not keep if shipped abroad or carried inland since transport was slow or non-existent.

It was a highly organized trade which created a close-knit, working community of craftsmen – coopers, basket-makers, carpenters, rope makers, weavers – all of whom depended on the herring for their living. Without the supply of autumn herring the trade could not survive. Only the autumn herring with its fat content of about 15% is ideal for the production of 'reds'; other herring, like those from Scotland, have a much higher fat content, of something like 20%, which is all right for kippers, but no good for reds.

So, you will have to search hard to find any reds today. They are still cured and sold in Great Yarmouth and Lowestoft; they are less dry and salty than their forebears, and they are 'golden' rather than red. Even so, they still taste strong and salty. Reds need to be soaked in most cases, and one hour in a mixture of milk and water should make them palatable after which they can be heated under the grill. Ironically, most of the heavily cured reds from firms like Suttons of Yarmouth are exported to Africa where they will keep even in tropical conditions.

BLOATERS

When I buy a red herring, I don't normally soak it; I buy it intentionally for its strong taste. If I want a less salty and dry fish, I buy the mild relation of the red, the Yarmouth bloater.

It seems that, in 1835, Mr. Bishop, a fish curer from Yarmouth was annoyed to find that his workers had gone home one day leaving a batch of fresh herring unattended. Determined not to let them go to waste, he threw salt over them,

Mrs. Kathy Dowe and Mrs. Doreen Bailey 'riving speets' at Sutton's in Great Yarmouth. After the herrings have been brined, they are threaded onto rods before being hung in the smokehouse.
(Photograph by Trevor Wood)

One of Lowestoft's best known curers, Reggie Reynolds, retired recently. He recalls how when he was demobbed he found a batch of red herring that he had cured before the war; they had kept perfectly. They had mould and cobwebs on them, but once cleaned were quite fit for eating.

Carts like this one were used to take herrings from the fishing boats to the smokehouses dotted around Great Yarmouth.
(Reproduced by kind permission of Great Yarmouth Reference Library)

left them for a short while and finally took them to his smokehouse. He went home tired and angry with his lazy workers. But the next morning he was amazed to find that the herrings in question had a very unusual aroma, and he determined to cook one and try it. What he tasted, it is said, was the first bloater.

It's an intriguing tale, no doubt modified and distorted over the years, but it may well contain the seeds of truth. Certainly, bloaters, as we know them, originated in Yarmouth and have always been associated with that town, but it is likely that they were made as a purely local speciality well before the beginning of the 19th century.

It was not just a speciality of the coast either. Many families inland had their own smokehouses. Bob Spindler, a fish-trader from the village of Wenhaston in Suffolk, about six miles from the coast, talked to George Ewart Evans about curing at home shortly before his death.

In 1599, Thomas Nashe, a man born in Lowestoft, and one of the great working writers of the Elizabethan age, wrote a pamphlet called 'Lenten Stuffe: in praise of the red herring'. It is worth reading for its colourful description of the 'discovery' and uses of the red herring.

'Fish-curing was hard work: we had a rough time. I've seen my mother standing, what they call speeting *herren, that is putting them on sticks to make bloaters, and when she had finished she had to lay down. And they'd pull her dress off her, and it was frozen stiff. I had to cart water for her. They were hard days. There were no easy days, those days. We cured all our bloaters and kippers, at one time. Of course, they've got out of all recognition today, but three a penny fresh herren were at that time. We had two big smokehouses in the garden. We could put 10,000 fish in one. We used to put these herren up for red-herren during the winter, and we'd probably put three lots or consignments. But we always put one particular herren what we called October blue-nosed herren because they never wasted when they were hung up to be smoked. They came down almost as big as when they went up. And they used to be like ham. They used to be sent to London and various places; and when we'd done all that we got four shillings a hundred for them. And in one house we used to do 30,000 or more – we'll call it 30,000 – in three hangings.*

'The herren all came in barrels. My father used to go and buy them at Lowestoft. We used to curse them when we see 'em coming: we knew what we had to do: to get in and go to work.' 1

1*The Days That We Have Seen* by George Ewart Evans. Faber 1975

MARKETS

Norwich market is outstanding for its fish. There are plenty of stalls where you can buy fresh fish, smoked fish and crab, and there are some good shellfish stalls as well.
(Photograph by Trevor Wood)

(Labels reproduced by kind permission of Colman's Foods)

The towns and villages of the East Anglian coast cannot boast about their markets, and indeed, they are not usually very profitable places for the local food enthusiast. But there are exceptions: for instance, among the half dozen stalls on Southwold market you will find a lady selling Cromer crabs throughout the summer.

There are, however, some worthwhile markets within driving distance of the coast.

EYE

General market. *Wednesday*
WI market, Assembly Rooms, White Lion Hotel. *Wednesday morning.*
Eye is also locally popular for its Sunday market.

FAKENHAM

General market. *Thursday.*
WI market, The Old Cattle Market. *Thursday morning.*

KING'S LYNN

General market, Town Square. *Tuesday.*
Particularly useful for fish.

NORWICH

General market. *Tuesday and Saturday.*
Easily the most extensive and interesting market in the region and the fish stalls (which sell samphire) are very good.

(When in Norwich it is worth calling at The Mustard Shop, set up by Colmans. It is devoted to the history and uses of mustard, and is a museum as well as a shop.)

This postcard was sent on the 7th September, 1908 from a Mr and Mrs Tozer to their son, Harold. Part of it reads: 'The fish salesmen would make you laugh; hundreds of thousands of herrings in the market this morning, principally from S. Shields and Peterhead.'

Bloaters (the name comes from the Old Norse *blautr*, meaning soft, and implying swollen or plump) are left whole and ungutted, lightly salted and smoked for a short while. They have a silvery sheen to them and a quite unmistakable gamey flavour because they are cured ungutted. You will often see them hanging in rows 'on the spit', in fish shops. These will have come straight from the smokehouse and are the best to buy. But whatever bloaters you buy, you should use them within 24 hours as the mild cure does not preserve them for more than a few days at the most.

Bloater paste used to be closely linked to the Yarmouth area and a number of firms produced their own versions of it. The paste was not packed in glass jars, as we know it now, but in storage pots. (Reproduced by kind permission of Great Yarmouth Maritime Museum)

The simplest method of cooking is to grill the bloaters and eat with a pile of creamy scrambled egg; they can also be baked in foil in the oven; they can even be used raw, like pickled herrings, cut in strips and made into salads.

Bloater paste is another local speciality. Yallop's Bloater Paste, made at Runham Vauxhall, near Yarmouth, and packed into pots, was once famous.

KIPPERS

These, the most popular type of smoked herring, are mentioned in detail on p. 74. Although they did not originate in East Anglia, good kippers can be bought in most fish shops in the area.

The word 'kipper' comes from the Dutch 'kuppen', meaning to spawn. It referred originally to salmon that had spawned and were in poor condition. These fish were of little use fresh but after drying and smoking they could be made reasonably palatable.

Almost every Friday this pub in Suffolk serves kippers. It's an established event now, although it grew simply out of the landlord's craving for a fish at closing time one evening. It's a good example of the strong links between land and sea in these parts, for the village is deep inland, far from the coast. (Photograph by Trevor Wood)

SPRATS

These small silver fish, members of the *Clupeidae* or herring family, are in season between October and March, and are some of the best fish to be had in East Anglia. They are very cheap and are best bought on the beach, straight from the boats at Dunwich, Aldeburgh or Southwold.

The best local way of cooking sprats is to put them in a very hot pan with a good sprinkling of salt, but no fat. The salt draws out the fat from the fish and they cook in this. Fry them quickly, a couple of minutes each side is all they need, and leave them whole. Don't take off the heads or the tails, for you can then hold the fish between your fingers and 'lick the flesh off the bone', as one fisherman described it to me.

Where there are fresh sprats, there are likely to be smoked sprats too. Aldeburgh and Southwold are the places to look. In 1724, Daniel Defoe saw sprats 'being made red' (i.e. smoked) in Southwold. And Aldeburgh smoked sprats are mentioned in a number of 19th century books such as *The Art and Mystery of Curing, Potting and Preserving* by A Wholesale Curer of Comestibles (1864). They are quite easy to cure and many fishermen still smoke part of their catch. But they tend to be kept within the confines of the town; it is a matter of being in the right pub at the right time, of finding the man with the fish.

They are, like their fresh counterparts, delicious and cheap. Eat them with brown bread, butter, and wedges of lemon. Nothing else, except some white wine, or Adnams beer to quench the thirst they provoke.

*Dab-spearing needs a hawk's eye, a steady hand and lightning reflexes, as well as a long bamboo pole. These men are spearing along the coast near Stiffkey.
(Photograph by David Cleveland)*

DABS

Nearly everyone has a special memory of fish eaten straight from the water, an aftertaste that is hard to forget. For some people it is mackerel or young cod, others remember freshly-caught trout or salmon, but my own favourite is the dab. As boys, we would take these flat fish, which are rather like rough-skinned flounders, from the shallow water of Blakeney channel on blazing hot summer afternoons, and eat them with our regular pickings of marsh samphire. We didn't skin the dabs, but simply cut off their heads and cleaned them, before frying them gently in a pan of butter.

I've had few meals to match those simple feasts, and I can recall the taste even now.

EELS

Thirty years ago the Norfolk Broads was still an area worked by eel-catchers, who would leave the land after the hay harvest and tend their 'setts', as the elaborate arrangements of nets for catching eels were called. They would work right through the winter, and it was a profitable trade. But the Broads are different now; pleasure boats and holiday-makers have radically changed the ecology of the area.

But in the marshy creeks and dykes along the Suffolk and Essex coast, men still go out on dark, still nights when the moon is not visible to catch eels with all manner of nets and traps. Summer and early autumn are the best times, but you won't hear much talk about their work. It's a closed, secret trade.

In many coastal villages and towns in East Anglia, you can regularly buy fish straight from the boats or from fishermen's beach huts.

OTHER FISH

Several other types of fish are available from the fish huts on the beaches of

Southwold, Dunwich, Aldeburgh, etc. and from fish shops throughout the region. The season for locally caught fish varies: whiting appears in October and November, followed by cod through the winter until February; flat fish like plaice and Dover sole are best during the spring and summer months, so too is skate. (Of course, all of these fish are normally sold throughout the year in shops.)

CRABS

Crabs are a north Norfolk speciality, and those from Cromer are the most special of all. Whether they actually grow better in the water off this little seaside town is open to question; but the skill and persistence of the local crabmen in fishing out the best is not. Cromer lies on a stretch of coast notorious for its submerged rocks and unpredictable tides, and its fishermen and lifeboatmen have a reputation for venturing out in conditions most other men would baulk at.

The tiny crab boats work by setting down long lines of baited pots (basically wooden or iron cages covered with tarred string) on the rocky ground just off-shore, picking them up the next day, removing the crabs and re-baiting. The pots themselves (which were originally made in nearby Sheringham) are collectively so valuable that the fishermen daren't risk leaving them uninspected for more than a day at a time – which helps ensure a regular supply of fresh crabs.

Most fishermen cook and sell their own catch, so, from April to early October look out for the chalked or handprinted boards outside their houses along the coast roads. Don't be put off by the fact that lugworms (for fishing bait!) are often advertised alongside.

'Crab is a slut to carve and a wrawde wight (perverse creature)'. That is what 'The Book of Nurture' (c. 1460) has to say. It refers to the fact that crab was often served hot at formal meals in the past. The meat was packed into the 'broadshell' after long picking, but by that time it had gone cold, and had to be returned to the kitchen to be warmed up.

*Improvised stalls, like this one in Salthouse, are common to the flint cottages of the north Norfolk coast.
(Photograph by David Cleveland)*

When you prise open a crab, this is what you will see. Look carefully for the 'dead men's fingers' in particular. (Illustration by Edward Arnor)

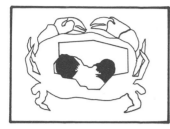

The feathery appendages, marked in the diagram, must all be removed, as they are poisonous.

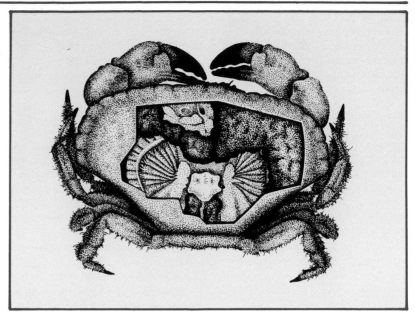

All the crabs sold in north Norfolk will have already been cooked (killed and then immediately boiled for about 20 minutes). Some will also have been 'dressed' or prepared, but it's worth trying an undressed one if you have the time. It will almost certainly be fresher and moister, and you will not miss the fun of seeing how much flesh you can extricate from the skeleton.

No self-employed crabman would want a case of food-poisoning blamed on him, and it is quite exceptional for a doubtful specimen to slip through. But you can double check as you start to dismember the crab for eating. Lay it on its back, and prise out the body so that you can see the brown meat. If the crab is unhealthy, if it is too old or the shell is cracked, the meat will be discoloured (grey or greenish), runny or foul smelling. If it is none of these things you need do no more than break off the head, remove the little stomach bag just beneath it, and find and throw away the dozen or so feathery, greyish 'dead men's fingers' on the top of the body. The rest you can eat.

One of the great delights of the crab is that it is a truly portable meal, contained in biodegradable packaging that is an adventure all of its own to unravel. The full complement of crab-eating irons would comprise a spoon for the soft meat, a pair of nutcrackers for the claws, and a skewer for the more obscure cavities. But if you are overtaken with a compulsive desire to eat your crab out of reach of such sophistications, wonders can be done with penknives, pencils, and even a combination of gentle stamping and vigorous sucking. A shingle beach is the very best place to eat one, with the sea winds providing the most perfectly scented condiment. Add a bottle of wine and a crisp new loaf and you have a feast that will last an hour. A pebble will do to crack the claws, and the corkscrew, if necessary, for cleaning out difficult corners. In some ways the more drawn-out the extraction, the more you will enjoy the different textures in the meat: the creamy brown flesh in the centre of the back, changing to an almost cheesy hardness at the edges, the long moist fibres in the claws, and the drier, fluffier white meat hidden in the complex honeycomb of the body.

Crab meat can be devilled, made into soups, omelettes or mousses. (One crab mousse we had in Wiltshire had preserved, like strata in the jelly, the different consistences of the meat.) And if you prefer longer-lasting and more convenient containers than shells, Wests of Sheringham do a fine potted crab.

Buttered crab:

2 good-sized crabs
2 anchovy fillets
1 cup white breadcrumbs
½ bottle dry white wine
3 tbs butter
pinch of nutmeg
salt, pepper

Shell the crab, extract all the brown and white meat, mix well and put to one side. Mash the anchovy fillets and blend with the wine. Add to this mixture the breadcrumbs, nutmeg and seasoning and heat for 5 minutes in a saucepan. Mix the crabmeat with the butter and add to the hot wine mixture. Cook for 4 minutes and serve with hot buttered toast.

SHRIMPS

As children, we used to have our holidays on the south coast. There I would go shrimping, pushing a half-size shrimp net (which was all I could manage) through the flat sandy shallows. We would take home shrimps by the bucketful. I preferred not to witness the actual boiling in salt water, but was quite prepared to eat my share once they were cooked.

Unfortunately those early evening trips to the water won't yield many shrimps along the East Anglian coast. You need a boat and a fine-mesh net to catch them. But from June until January (depending on the weather) there will be heaps of brown shrimps or their larger pink relatives, in the fish shops, with beer mugs sitting on top of them. For you buy things like this by the pint, not by the pound. And if you enquire in the local pubs you may be able to track down a fisherman who is prepared to sell some of his catch at a good price.

East Anglia doesn't have a strong tradition of potted shrimps or shrimp paste (although there are one or two local 18th century recipes); you would have to go to north-west England for those treats (see p.186). In Suffolk or Norfolk you buy them to eat straight from the bag. I always find that there is a real urgency about shrimp eating: heads and tails are nipped off, shells are peeled with speedy fingerwork. Sometimes, if the shrimps are small, you will crunch up the whole body after taking off the head and tail. The pace and activity are in great contrast to the contemplative mood of the man with a bowl of winkles and a pin.

MUSSELS

In his *History of the English Church and People*, written in AD 731, Bede mentions the rich supply of shellfish around our coasts.

> *'There are also many varieties of shell-fish, such as mussels, in which are often found excellent pearls of several colours, red, purple, violet and green, but mainly white.'*

It was, however, the delicious flesh of this popular mollusc which had drawn men since prehistoric times to the shores and estuaries of East Anglia and many other parts of Britain. These men were nomadic food-gatherers who existed on what they could pick, trap or glean from the wild. They would eat their mussels raw, or roast them until they opened on stones heated by bonfires on the shore. It was the fact that these – and indeed other shellfish – were fresh, at a time when nearly all other fish had to be eaten dried or salted, that made them so attractive and sought after right up to the 19th century when over-picking made them less common and more expensive. But by that time supplies of fresh fish could be eaten everywhere, thanks to railway transport, the use of ice as a preservative and better fishing methods.

Nowadays mussels are once again cheap and plentiful, and there are quite a number of mussel beds around the East Anglian coast, especially in north Norfolk. But it is more practical to buy them rather than try to gather them yourself. (Read the general notes about gathering on p.12 before you start dealing with mussels or indeed any shellfish.) Trust your fisherman or fishmonger, and find someone who has a good reputation and a regular supply. Clean and scrub the mussels well and let them stand in cold water, changed several times, for a few hours. Pull off the 'beard' or 'byssus' and check that each mussel is closed and undamaged before putting them in a saucepan with just enough boiling water to cover them. As soon as the shells open the mussels are ready. Don't be tempted to overcook them or they will shrink and become leathery. That is the simple way with mussels, but there are many other recipes, from *moules marinieres* to mussel pie, in most cookery books. Remember,

Both Scotland and Ireland had traditional and ingenious recipes for cooked mussels held in portable, edible containers which acted as replacements for their shells. Hot bread rolls were used in Scotland; the crumb was pulled out and the mussels packed in its place. In Ireland the container was a potato baked in its jacket and then hollowed out. The whole meal could be wrapped in a cloth and taken to work in a man's pocket.

Avoid East coast mussels altogether during the spring and summer. They are susceptible to the yearly 'red tides' which signal outbreaks of the protozoa Gonyaulax tamarensis (see p. 12) But don't panic, because the Ministry of Agriculture, Fisheries and Food keeps a vigilant watch on all local shellfish harvesting and selling.

Women returning home from cockling on the flats at Stiffkey at the turn of the century. Disguised with layers of clothing to protect them from the treacherous weather, they moved slowly with their loads and did not speak to each other.
(Reproduced by kind permission of The Radio Times Hulton Picture Library)

One use for clean cockle shells (and scallop shells too) in East Anglia: they were turned into containers for small sponge cakes called appropriately 'cockle cakes'. Some old fashioned baking trays for cakes were designed with the same ribbed appearance as shells.

too, the prehistoric fisherman's methods: put the cleaned mussels in hot ashes until they open, slip in a little butter with crushed garlic and chopped parsley, and eat them straight from the fire.

COCKLES

The village of Stiffkey in Norfolk is known for the sexual activities of its rector in the 1930s and for Stookey (Stiffkey) Blues. These are cockles, large ones with grey-blue shells that live in the mud and sands on that stretch of coast. The Norfolk coast, especially that area around the Wash, is now one of the three main fisheries for cockles. (The others are around Leigh-on-sea in the Thames estuary, and in south Wales.) Life is easier for the cockle gatherers these days. They set out from Boston, King's Lynn or Heacham and work the sands with their short-handled rakes, but they do not have to carry back their pickings. If you want to gather cockles yourself, it is easy. Walk out at low tide onto the flats around, say, Blakeney or Stiffkey, with a bucket and a rake. Look for the signs in the sand: a rich vein of mud or a streaky film of green plankton over the sand usually indicates the presence of cockles. You may even see the two marks of their airholes glinting in the sunlight. Failing that, a sample scratch or dig will tell you if cockles are there, for they collect in patches. Your short rake will dislodge them quite easily where they lie a few inches below the surface. (I've even gathered them with my bare hands in the soft mud.)

Follow the basic rules of shellfish gathering (see p. 12), handle the cockles carefully so that the shells don't crack, and don't bother with very small specimens. When you get home wash the cockles free of sand and mud, and let them clean themselves in cold water for a few hours. Then throw out any that are damaged, and put the rest in a saucepan of boiling water for a few minutes until they open. Strain them, pick them out of their shells and let them cool down. Eat them well peppered and moistened with vinegar.

Cockles, like mussels, can be put into soups, there is a famous cockle pie made in Wales (see p. 240), joints of lamb used to be slashed and stuffed with them before roasting, but my own favourite is a dish of cockles and bacon, a worthy combination of the best from land and sea. Fry some fat streaky bacon, lift it out of the pan when it has yielded plenty of fat, then toss in the cockles and cook them until they have browned lightly on the outside. Serve them on toast with the rashers of crisp bacon.

Cockling today is men's work, and they travel to and from the beds by boat. The brute labour has gone from the job, but the skill and close knowledge of the sands still survives. (Crown Copyright: Her Majesty's Stationery Office)

Boats like these work all the year round bringing back whelks from the waters off Wells and nearby Brancaster. (Photograph by David Cleveland)

4,000 whelks were served as a garnish for salted sturgeon at the enthronement feast of the Archbishop of Canterbury in 1504. People used them in quite different ways then: a salad listed in 'The Second Part of The Good Huswive's Jewell' (1597) consisted of 'alexander buds cut longways, garnished with whelks'. What better combination for the food hunter in East Anglia!

WHELKS

Wells whelks are almost as famous as Cromer crabs. In fact about 80% of the whelks eaten in this country are caught off Wells-next-the-sea and to a lesser extent nearby Brancaster. The big coiled shell of *Buccinum undatum*, the common whelk, is unmistakable and its edible body is a feature of shellfish stalls throughout the country.

Wells fishermen go whelking all year round in their converted crab boats or old lifeboats and they need to travel at least 10 miles off-shore before they can begin to fish. They use special iron pots which are baited with herring, attached to a rope to form a 'shank', and then shot against the tide. The pots are lifted each day, emptied, re-baited and stowed until the whole shank has been recovered. (Fishermen around Margate often use pots made of potato or fruit baskets, while at Eastbourne metal milk crates covered with net have been used.) Once landed the whelks are taken to the sheds to be boiled.

Net bags of whelks, each containing 'a wash' (an old measure, equivalent to 1/8th of a bushel) are boiled for about 10 minutes in large open coppers filled with sea water, and then cooled and packed in sacks. (Photograph by David Cleveland)

Whelks from Wells are sent all over the country, especially to London and the Midlands – a fine example of a food from a very localized source being eaten on a national scale. But it is odd that few whelks are actually consumed in East Anglia itself, except during the holiday season in Wells, Great Yarmouth and Lowestoft. Many more go to the fishermen who use them as bait for long lines during the winter cod fishing season, and you can see piles of shell fragments on the quaysides of many East Anglian towns when the fishing is under way. Raw whelks are used, the shells are smashed open and the meat threaded on the hooks. It is a tiring, messy job, strictly for well-seasoned hands.

SAMPHIRE

Marsh samphire (*Salicornia europea*) is an odd-looking succulent plant which grows on coastal marshes and mud flats in many parts of Britain. But it is particularly common and well-known in East Anglia where it grows in vast patches like badly kept lawns. The north Norfolk coast from Brancaster to Cley and Salthouse is the richest source, but you can also find it on the Blyth estuary around Walberswick and Southwold.

The only way to learn about samphire is by searching for it and picking it yourself. The hot days of July and August are the best, when the plants are just about to flower and are at their most tender. Wait for low tide and then walk out to the mud flats, armed with a sharp pair of scissors or a fish-gutting knife and a bucket or an onion net. You will have to jump over muddy creeks and watch for hidden gulleys that can easily twist an ankle, so it is best to know the ground or take someone with you who does. The samphire nestles along the edges of creeks or spreads across huge areas of bare mud flats, competing for space only with the Spartina grass planted here and there to stop erosion. These are the places to look, and locals will tell you that the very best samphire must be washed by every tide.

Once you have found a good patch you can settle down to gather. Bend or kneel depending on the ground, and cut the plants just above the base. Bend and cut, pack a handful into the net, move on a few yards, bend and cut again. It can be exhausting if the sun is hot and the east wind is streaking across the marshes. When your net is full, wade out into one of the creeks and give the

Samphire is actually pronounced sam-fer. It is also called glasswort, saltwort, pickle plant and crab-grass – all appropriate and evocative names.

They tell a story in Blakeney about a giant specimen of samphire. After the great flood of 1953, a plant, 6ft tall, was found growing in a creek. It was strapped to a bicycle, taken back to the pub and hung, like a fish, above the bar. Whether this story is true or not, samphire has now become an object of folklore guaranteeing a free drink to the teller, and it will no doubt grow from 6ft to 6 metres with further telling over the years. (Cartoon by Geoffrey Dickinson)

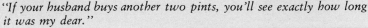
"If your husband buys another two pints, you'll see exactly how long it was my dear."

Sea Beet

crop a good wash. Then homeward with the harvest. Sore hands, aching back, reddened face and an immeasurable thirst. Time for a pint before the samphire is cooked. (Incidentally, if you do not intend to eat the samphire straight away, you must rinse it well and spread it out to dry in the sun to avoid rapid decay. Don't store it in water or it will quickly turn soggy.)

Samphire is used in many ways. Eat it crisp and raw if it is very young, or boil it briskly for five minutes in unsalted water, drain it and eat with melted butter, drawing the stems between your teeth. It can also be pickled. The old way was to pack the samphire into jars with vinegar and store them in bread ovens which were cooling down on Friday night after the baking was finished. The jars were left until Monday morning. It is difficult to imagine what this treatment did for the samphire, but it seems to have been highly valued.

In Blakeney, samphire is everywhere. Picking demands patience, tough hands and a certain knowledge of the places to look for the crop. (Photograph by David Cleveland)

Traditionally, samphire is eaten hot with mutton or lamb. This combination dates from the time when sheep were kept on the marshes and grazed on the samphire (a sub-species of the plant is actually called 'sheep-samphire'). It was the custom to serve meat with the food on which the animal had fed. Even better, now that the marshes are deserted, is samphire with a freshly caught dab fried in butter. (see p. 64).

You can buy samphire in quite a number of fish shops and stalls in East Anglia, usually in company with cod and cockles rather than with 'land' vegetables. Fish shops in places like Blakeney and Holt sell it, and so do the stalls on Norwich market. But hotels and restaurants in the area are only now beginning to make use of the plant. Any East Anglian restaurant that claims to have an interest in local and regional food should have samphire on its menu, but many do not. They forget that much of the real fibre of country cooking derives from items like samphire which literally have their roots in the landscape. However, one restaurant in Blakeney has turned samphire into a garnish as a replacement for the common sprigs of watercress or parsley which usually decorate fish and meat dishes.

EDIBLE SHORELINE PLANTS

Scattered amongst creeks and shingle banks around the East Anglian coast are many other plants which are still regularly gathered by local villagers. Some have even been taken into cultivation, and have played their part in the complex genetic ancestry of staple garden vegetables like beetroot and celery.

Coastal plants are neither more nor less edible than any others. But there are good reasons why many of them have been amongst our most popular wild foods. Manured by estuarine silt, rich in minerals from the sea, and often fleshy and succulent from the water they hoard against dehydration by salt winds, they make, as a group. a more satisfying mouthful than most inland weeds. Like marshland sheep, they are, in effect, farmed by the sea.

Seakale is an object lesson both in these ingenious adaptation processes, and how *not* to harvest wild plants. Although it grows in bare shingle, you can tell it is a cabbage immediately from its flowers and floppy foliage. But look more closely at the leaves and you will see that they are as thick and heavy as rubber sheeting. In fact it is only the very young leaf-stalks that are eaten, blanched, boiled and buttered like asparagus. When seakale became popular as a vegetable in the early 19th century, huge quantities were transplanted from the wild into gardens. So the Norfolk coast, where it was once abundant, was almost stripped bare. There are only a handful of plants left, and they should be treated with great respect.

Much commoner on the drier land between beach and saltmarsh is scurvy grass (*Cochlearia officinalis*). According to Charles Johnson, it used to be boiled up with watercress and Seville oranges '*as a health-giving draught for children in the vernal season. It is probable that the fresh leaves, eaten as a salad, are far more beneficial than any such nauseous compound; they certainly form the most beneficial and probably one of the most effectual anti-scorbutics.*' [1]

A pleasanter source of Vitamin C is wild spinach or sea beet, which grows in bushy clumps along the sea walls. The leaves, picked between May and October, and cooked with just a little butter and sugar, make cultivated spinach seem bland by comparison. Sea beet is the direct ancestor of many of our cultivated beetroots and chards, and indeed of the sugar beet that will often be growing in vast prairie fields only yards away from its ancient forebear.

Another sea-wall speciality is alexanders, a pot herb bought to this country by the Romans, and cultivated in gardens until the 19th century. All parts from the root to flower buds were once used, but for our tastes the young white stems, boiled quickly and served with butter, are probably the most acceptable. They have a pleasantly soft texture and a slight fragrance of angelica. (The plant is known as 'angelica' in some parts of East Anglia.)

Along banks and waysides near the sea you should also look for fennel. It is unmistakable with its feathery green foliage and spicy aniseed fragrance, which makes it a perfect foil for fish dishes in these parts.

Sea Purslane

Seakale

(Illustrated by Carol Fowkes)

Asparagus, a shoreline plant in the wild, is cultivated extensively in East Anglia and is almost as widespread here as in the Vale of Evesham

1*The Useful Plants of Great Britain*, 1862.

KIPPERS

oak fires to smoke for about 12 hours. He had invented kippers, and they quickly replaced the much more salty and dry red herring that had been the staple diet for hundreds of years. Now, kippers, with Finnan haddock and smoked cod fillet, make up about 90% of the smoked fish eaten in this country.

Kippers are so common in fish shops in almost every town in the British Isles that you may think they have lost all regional or local connections. But there are four main areas where really fine kippers are produced: along the north-east coast of England around the original site at Seahouses, in the Isle of Man, along the western coast of Scotland around Loch Fyne, and, to a lesser extent, around Great Yarmouth, that famous East Anglian herring town, where incidentally John Woodger also set up a curing works.

To prepare good kippers the curer needs a supply of very fresh fat herring. The big summer Scotch or Norwegian herring are used in the north; in the Isle of Man they use a much smaller fish caught in the waters off the north-west coast of England. But the East Anglian autumn herring is no good for kippers – it has too little fat – although it is perfect for bloaters and reds, so most of the kipper curers in East Anglia use herrings from other parts parts of Britain, especially Scotland.

It is claimed that the first kippers were prepared at Seahouses in Northumberland early in the 19th century. The story goes that John Woodger, a fish curer from that area, began to experiment in 1843 with a new way of smoking herrings. He knew that salmon had been 'kippered' as long ago as the 14th century, and he wanted to try the same method with herrings. So he split the fish down the backbone, gutted them and soaked them in brine. Then he hung them up over

Herrings being split and gutted before being put into brine, which is the first stage in preparing kippers. The fish are always split so that the backbone lies on the left-hand side. (Photograph by Trevor Wood)

A spit of kippers fresh from the smokehouse.(Photograph by Trevor Wood)

When you go out to buy kippers there are a few points you should look out for. First of all the fish should be plump and oily. Size isn't really important; the largest kipper I have ever eaten was a fish 35cm (14ins) long and 15cm (6ins) across when opened out. It was superb, but it was equalled in flavour by a Manx kipper less than half its size. A kipper should be a whole, split fish with head and bones intact; it should be silvery-golden in colour and have a mild smoky smell. If the kipper you buy has all these attributes it will eat well.

Don't be tempted by packets of kipper fillets, which are seldom completely free of bones despite what the advertisements say, and avoid tinned kippers. Only a whole fish, chosen straight from the fishmonger's slab, will give real satisfaction. Then you have to decide how and when to eat the kipper. For me the great kipper-eating time is Sunday morning, a fine breakfast after a long Saturday night. Grilling is the easiest way to cook the fish, although it can be poached in a shallow pan of water or 'jugged' – that is put head first into a large jug of hot water and left for 5–10 minutes. They can also be fried singly or in pairs, sandwiched together flesh to flesh in butter.

I am a great believer in boning a kipper completely before eating any of the flesh. The method I use is quite simple and as good as any other.

When the fish is ready you can spread the flesh with butter and a little mustard, give it a sprinkling of black pepper and enjoy a meal without equal.

A smokehouse in Lowestoft, Suffolk which produces kippers as well as a range of other smoked fish. (Photograph by Trevor Wood)

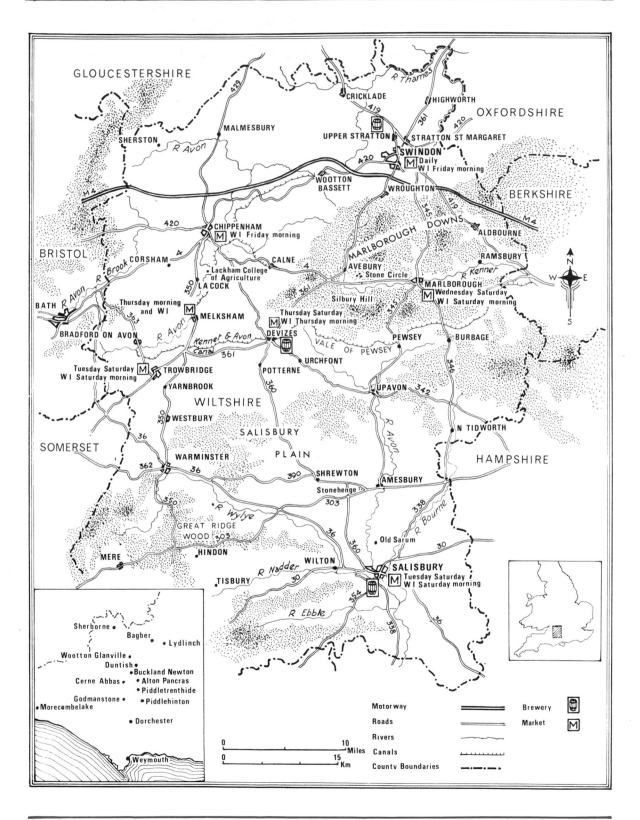

GLOUCESTERSHIRE

R Thames

CRICKLADE

HIGHWORTH

OXFORDSHIRE

MALMESBURY

SHERSTON

R Avon

419

361

420

420

UPPER STRATTON

STRATTON ST MARGARET

SWINDON
Daily
WI Friday morning

WOOTTON
BASSETT

WROUGHTON

BERKSHIRE

M4

M4

345

419

MARLBOROUGH DOWNS

ALDBOURNE

420

CHIPPENHAM
WI Friday morning

RAMSBURY

BRISTOL

R Brook

CORSHAM

4

CALNE

4

AVEBURY
Stone Circle

R Kennet

MARLBOROUGH
Wednesday Saturday
WI Saturday morning

Lackham College
of Agriculture

LACOCK

350

361

Silbury Hill

343

N

BATH

R Avon

363

Thursday morning
and WI

MELKSHAM

Thursday Saturday
WI Thursday morning

PEWSEY

BURBAGE

BRADFORD ON AVON

R Avon

Kennet & Avon
Canal

361

DEVIZES

VALE OF PEWSEY

346

Tuesday Saturday
WI Saturday morning

TROWBRIDGE

URCHFONT

POTTERNE

UPAVON

342

YARNBROOK

WILTSHIRE

340

R Avon

N TIDWORTH

350

WESTBURY

SALISBURY

SOMERSET

36

PLAIN

HAMPSHIRE

362

WARMINSTER

36

390

SHREWTON

AMESBURY

Stonehenge

338

R Bourne

350

R Wylye

303

36

360

Old Sarum

30

GREAT RIDGE
WOOD

303

HINDON

MERE

TISBURY

R Nadder

30

WILTON

SALISBURY
Tuesday Saturday
WI Saturday morning

354

338

36

R Ebble

Sherborne

Bagber

Lydlinch

Wootton Glanville

Duntish

Buckland Newton

Cerne Abbas

Alton Pancras

Piddletrenthide

Godmanstone

Piddlehinton

Morecombelake

Dorchester

Weymouth

0   10
          Miles
0   15
          Km

Motorway

Roads

Rivers

Canals

County Boundaries

Brewery

Market

M

WILTSHIRE
THE KINGDOM OF THE PIG

When you come to Wiltshire, reflect first of all on the name Swindon. Nowadays the county's biggest industrial centre, it had a quite different role in the past, when it was called Swine Downe. Around 1800 BC the Beaker People moved in from the continent and began to colonize the undulating chalk hills of the area. They created some of the first settlements in England and depended on pasture and pigs for much of their livelihood. The Beaker People left behind many symbols of religion, worship, and superstition: burial mounds and barrows, stone circles like the one at Avebury, the mysterious Silbury Hill, and even Stonehenge itself. Today, all these landmarks stand on ground still inhabited by flocks of sheep and pigs – the very animals which were part of the everyday life of those early sun-watchers.

The association of the county with the products of its pastures has continued since those first settled days. In the 18th century the people of Britain recognized Wiltshire for its wool, its cheese and its bacon. But the wool trade has declined, and Wiltshire cheese has vanished altogether; only bacon still holds its place in the county. The pig and all its products, in fact, are more important here than in any other part of Britain. Fresh pork, bacon, ham and a whole range of by-products fill the butchers' shops. Restaurants serve it; markets sell it; even factories are geared to the food uses of it. The pig is supreme.

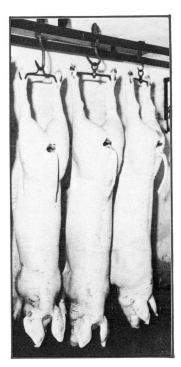

(Reproduced by kind permission of The Meat and Livestock Commission)

THE PIG

In the last century, in the days before mass-produced food, farm workers were able to provide for themselves. Although most of them were literally tied to the land they were very *self-efficient*; they used their supplies wisely and they did not waste food unnecessarily. The family pig was an important asset; it was tended throughout the year, growing fat on potatoes and greens grown in the plot behind the cottage, and in the autumn it was turned loose to root out acorns, windfalls and grain left in the fields after the harvest.

Then, once the weather had turned and it was nearing winter, once all the spare food had been used up and the animal was almost unable to walk, it was time for the killing. This was a great occasion, a celebration of food and provisions; for hundreds of years autumn slaughter had sustained families through the harsh, scarce months of winter. Originally it was a way of overcoming the lack of winter fodder for animals but even when this problem had been solved, the cottage pig remained because it was part of a system of 'domestic economy' that worked; it gave the year a structure and a focus for a family and its food.

Pig killing wasn't confined to Wiltshire. This slaughter took place in Lincolnshire in the winter of 1945, but it is a scene that could equally belong to the Middle Ages. The men are washing the animal and scraping the bristles from the carcase. The pig is laid on a special stretcher so that it can be moved easily. (Reproduced by kind permission of The Museum of English Rural Life, University of Reading)

The killing was a savage, messy business, but it was essential; a family that could not kill its pig would likely starve. The animal was their insurance, their food bank, and they used every part of it.

This practice, of course, wasn't confined to Wiltshire; it occurred in every part of the country where there were land workers. But you have only to walk round any Wiltshire town today to see how much the food still reflects the virtues of the pig. There is no better example of the way traditional foods can survive and flourish, even when they have ceased to have a close and important function in local and family life.

FRESH PORK

Not much of the cottager's pig was eaten fresh; most of it was salted down so that it would last through the winter. But there were pieces of offal and also blade bones and spare ribs; what a feast they must have provided while they lasted – roast meat after months of old bacon and vegetables.

As the family sat round their table, gnawing the bones from their first meal of fresh pork, they might reflect that they had succeeded in their work; they had looked after their pig and now it would, with luck, fill their stomachs over the coming months.

We can eat fresh pork throughout the year, thanks to better farming methods, breeding and refrigeration, and any butcher's shop in the country will be well stocked with pork. But Wiltshire has a few special surprises. Look in any butcher's window and you will see pork everywhere: rows of heavy legs hanging on rails, loin and collar joints often boned and rolled (like meat in the Scottish highlands which is prepared in this way for boiling in the pot rather than roasting in the oven). This is most characteristic of Wiltshire, and it must

MARKETS

Markets throughout Wiltshire are particularly well-stocked with local and regional food. There are good meat stalls, often completely devoted to pork and pork products, which rival the best butcher's shops in the area. Mobile cheese shops visit Wiltshire from nearby Somerset and the local WI markets have plenty to offer. Devizes market, while not the grandest market in the county, is the most interesting for the food hunter, with Marlborough as a close second.

CHIPPENHAM

WI market, Neeld Hall. *Friday.*

DEVIZES

General market, Market Square. *Thursday and Saturday*
WI market, Market Square. *Thursday*
(Without doubt the best market for local food.)

MARLBOROUGH

General market. *Wednesday and Saturday*
WI market, High Street. *Saturday*

MELKSHAM

General market including WI stall. *Thursday morning*

SALISBURY

General market. *Tuesday and Saturday*
WI stall. *Saturday*

SWINDON

General market. *Daily*
WI market, Victoria Road. *Friday morning*

TROWBRIDGE

General market, Market Hall. *Tuesday and Saturday*
WI stall. *Saturday morning*

A friendly atmosphere and good quality produce are a hallmark of the over 330 WI markets throughout the country. (Photograph reproduced by the kind permission of the National Federation of Women's Institutes)

The Malmesbury Vale Honey Company Limited

Pure Wiltshire Honey

1lb. (454g) net

The Old Coach House Bristol Road Malmesbury

Pork butchers in Wiltshire and surrounding areas are well-stocked with all types of pork products: sausages, black puddings, faggots, pigs' heads, pigs' feet cooked and sold with jelly surrounding them, hog's pudding (rather like a long, straight mealy pudding) and many other items. (Photograph by Trevor Wood)

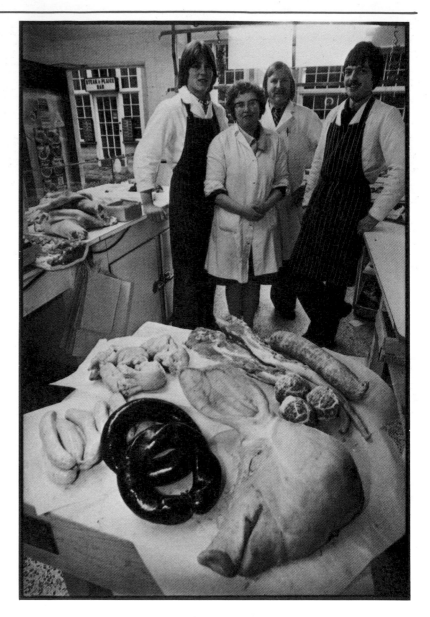

Buy some pig's tails – they are very cheap – and use them like tiny oxtails. You can cook them slowly in a casserole, or boil them in stock and eat them with pease pudding. You can even add them to an oxtail stew to make a dish that is sticky beyond belief; the juice is like glue on your lips and fingers.

be important since good butchers always reflect the eating habits and cooking customs of the people they serve.

Then there are the 'extremities', that is pig's heads, ears, trotters, tails and so on. You can usually buy these anywhere if you are persistent, but it is a marvellous surprise to see them actually displayed in shop windows, as they are in places like Marlborough.

PIG PRODUCTS

Once a pig had been killed, the kitchen was busy. All the bits and pieces that could not be salted or eaten straight away were made into sausages, pies, faggots, black puddings and brawn, and the animal's lard was rendered down and stored for the coming months. All these items are still commonly made throughout the country; some have strong links with other regions, but here, with the pig, is where they really belong.

Faggots:

Sometimes called 'savoury ducks', these rich balls of mixed meat, breadcrumbs and herbs are popular almost everywhere, but you are unlikely to find any better than Wiltshire faggots. Recipes vary from area to area, but usually include pig's liver, lights, fat and onions with breadcrumbs and plenty of herbs. Each faggot is wrapped in a piece of caul fat (the lacy, fatty membrane surrounding the stomach and guts of the pig) and cooked slowly in the oven until it looks 'like a small penny loaf'.

The word faggot means 'a bundle' – originally sticks bound with twine – and that is exactly what it is, a bundle of meat, bits and pieces bound together with caul fat. Remember this when you go looking for faggots, for the caul helps to hold the faggot together and the fat prevents it from drying out when it is being cooked. But often nowadays faggots are prepared without caul and with extra cereal to bind them together, so they tend to be much too dry and lacking in richness.

The best way to eat faggots at home is hot, with peas; not fresh garden peas, but dried or processed marrowfat peas, cooked until they start to go mushy. If you are out in the town, however, eat faggots cold, straight from the shop, as you go on your way.

You will find excellent faggots in other areas, especially in South Wales (when apples are often included in the recipes), Leicestershire and Lancashire.

Black pudding:

'Small otemeale mixed with blood, and the liver of either sheep, calf or swine, maketh that pudden . . . whose goodness it is in vaine to boast because there is hardly to be found a man that doth not affect them'.

That is what *The English Housewife's Booke* of 1600 had to say about the black coils which hang in butchers' shops across the country. 'Blood puddings' they used to be called, when they were made after the pig killing; a bucket of carefully drawn blood would be taken to the kitchen with lengths of intestine which were washed and formed into skins. The blood was mixed with oatmeal or barley and lard and stuffed into the tough, natural casings. That was proper household economy.

Wiltshire, being the county of the pig, has a good reputation for black puddings although nothing on the scale of Lancashire and Yorkshire – where they hold contests, award prizes to the proud champions, and polish the pudding skins as if they were glass (see p. 182). No, in Wiltshire, black puddings are less spectacular, but commonly sold by the best butchers in the area.

They are still prepared from pig's blood, oatmeal or some other cereal, pork fat and a lot of spicy seasoning. Cook them by boiling them whole, or by slicing them and frying in bacon fat.

White puddings:

These are black puddings without the blood. They are made from oatmeal and pork fat with sometimes a little minced lean pork too, and plenty of salt and pepper. They are quite common in Wiltshire, and you will also find them in Oxfordshire (Oxford market is a good source of supply), in the Midlands and in Scotland, where they are called 'mealy puddings' and are first cousins to the haggis.

They are best boiled and then browned quickly in bacon fat.

Brawn:

One of the 'handsomest' foods of England. 'Brawn and mustard' (it has always been served that way, and I hope always will be), was featured in the first

A recipe for Wiltshire faggots:

450 gr (1lb) pig's fry
2 onions
75 gr (3oz) breadcrumbs
1 egg
1 tsp dried sage
1 tsp dried mixed herbs
salt and pepper
a piece of caul fat

Soak the caul in tepid water for a couple of hours until it softens. Mince the onion and pig's fry, add the breadcrumbs, beaten egg and seasoning, and blend to a smooth paste with a fork. Divide the mixture into small balls each weighing about 50 gr (2 oz). Cut the caul into a number of small squares and wrap one square around each faggot. Place in a greased tin so that each faggot touches the next. Bake for 30 minutes in the oven at 350°F (Gas Mark 4).

Although brawn is usually made on a small scale and packed in tubs or pots, many large food producers, like Harris, use cans to contain this marvellous concoction. (Reproduced by kind permission of C. & T. Harris, Calne, Ltd.)

printed cookery books of the 15th century, and the 16th century farmer and writer of verses, Thomas Tusser, expected to see brawn on his table at Christmas time:

> Good husband and huswife now chiefly be glad,
> Things handsome to have as they ought to be had.
> Good bread and good drinke, a good fier in the hall,
> Brawne, pudding, and souse, and good mustarde withal . . .

'pudding' = black pudding
'souse' = pieces of pork,
usually belly, pickled in
brine.

There is no need here to give elaborate details of the way a pig's head is transformed into brawn, a brief summary will suffice: the long simmering with herbs and spices, the separation of the meat from bone and gristle, the chopping of the meat, the reduction of the stock until it is thick and sticky, the setting of the mixture in its tin, and then after a day or two, the release of the solid, glistening brawn onto a plate, and the cutting of the first slices.

When you buy a brawn remember the time taken to prepare it, and remember the history too. It is a shining example of the fact that people are still prepared to spend time on food.

One reason why less brawn is made nowadays is that pig's heads are no longer shaved with the rest of the animal when it is slaughtered. So desperate measures are needed if you buy a head covered with bristles. Here is one lady's solution to the problem.

(Cartoon by Geoffrey Dickinson)

'Will there be anything for the weekend, sir?'

They make fine brawn in Wiltshire, and in many other areas too. The sight of home-made brawn in shops is a good indicator of a healthy atmosphere; it tells you that there is likely to be plenty of interesting regional food in the area.

(Brawn is often called 'head-cheese' and as such it is often confused with 'pork cheese', which is made from lean pork finely minced, not roughly chopped. To add to the confusion, brawn is sometimes made from cow-heel, especially in North East England, from sheep's head in Scotland, and even rabbit.)

Lard:
The rendering of lard from the pig was an important task because lard itself was essential in the kitchen. It was a cooking fat, it was spread on bread instead of butter, it went into black puddings and the pastry for pies and tarts, and it was also used as an ointment to be rubbed on chests when coughs were about.

One of the main sources of lard was the 'flead', 'flare', or 'leaf' of the pig – that is, the inner fatty membrane surrounding the kidneys and loin of the

The flead of the pig was put on a special lard table and softened with a steel beater. It would often take two men a whole day to beat the lard from one pig. Flead cakes would also be made on the lard table. (Reproduced by kind permission of The Museum of English Rural Life, University of Reading)

animal. The other was the solid layer of back fat. Flead cakes were made in many areas, particularly in southern England, until quite recently, by beating together flead, flour and salt. The ingredients had to be beaten, not mixed by hand, and there were special lard tables and beaters for the job. These cakes were the ancestors of the lardy cakes so common these days (see p. 93).

Once lard had been rendered there would be crisp morsels at the bottom of the pot; these 'scratchings' were not wasted. Dorothy Hartley in *Food in England* describes tarts packed with chopped scratchings, apples, brown sugar and spices, with a dash of home-made wine to moisten the tarts and give them extra flavour.

A bag of scratchings warmed in the oven until they are crisp, and then sprinkled with salt makes a thirst-provoking snack.

You will see huge white blocks of lard in butchers' shops. It is still a valuable substance. It goes into the pastry for the pasties sold in Chippenham (see p. 91) and the covering for the sausage plaits sold by the WI at Devizes market, and it is of course essential for lardy cakes themselves. In fact lard gives the cooking of this area an unmistakable richness.

Sausages:

Plenty of butchers make their own sausages, but you will have to hunt. It is worth the trouble because most of the pink, pasty sausages produced these days are not worth eating. Good Wiltshire sausages, and those of nearby Oxfordshire, are made of roughly chopped pork, highly spiced, with fresh herbs added to them. They look dazzling, with green specks and a marbled pattern of red meat and white fat; they don't need to be bulked out with cereal; they don't shrink when they are fried, and the taste is little short of a revelation to anyone brought up on factory bangers. But remember that they will need long, slow cooking.

The plait was like a huge sausage roll, but the criss-cross pattern of the pastry allowed you to see the filling inside.
A food hunter's lunch in Wiltshire: sausage plait; a bunch of watercress; a piece of farmhouse cheese and 2 bottles of Wadworth's beer.

An 18th century recipe for Oxford sausages.

'Take a pound of lean veal, a pound of young pork, fat and lean, free from skin and gristle, a pound of beef suet, chopped all fine together; put in half a pound of grated bread, half the peel of a lemon shred fine, a nutmeg grated, six sage leaves washed and chopped very fine, a teaspoonful of pepper and two of salt, some thyme, savoury, and marjoram shred fine; mix it all well together, and put it close down in a pan: when you use it, roll it out the size of a common sausage, and fry them in fresh butter of a fine brown, or broil them over a clear fire, and send them to the table as hot as possible.' – 'The Art of Cookery Made Plain and Easy' by Hannah Glasse, 1747

When you are in butchers' shops look out for *haslet* – a big brother to the faggot, the size of a large granary loaf and normally cut in slices. Also *chitterlings* – pig's intestines – which are cleaned, boiled and allowed to set in a jelly. They are often eaten with vinegar and hunks of bread, or they can be grilled and eaten with hot vegetables.

PIG CURING
The farm

Once a cottager's pig had been killed, the fresh meat had been eaten and the trimmings were in the kitchen, the rest of the animal was prepared for curing. Two sides or 'flitches' would be all that remained, but once salted and smoked these provided bacon and ham through the winter and into the spring.

For bacon, the sides were taken to a cool dry shed and laid on stone slabs or in big troughs. They were rubbed and covered with salt and saltpetre (which 'fixes' the pink colour of the meat, otherwise it would turn grey-brown). Other ingredients were added too: some families used treacle or molasses, others favoured tipping beer over the meat or rubbing herbs and spices into it. The meat was tended and turned as the curing progressed, more salt was rubbed in, and the brine and juices that formed had to be drained off. It was patient work that took days or sometimes weeks to complete, but eventually the pork became bacon, the sides could be divided up and the pieces hung from ceilings or walls until they were needed. They were sometimes known as 'countrymen's pictures', although curing was hardly a decorative art. To keep longer, some pieces might be smoked over smouldering oak fires, or hung high in the chimney for weeks until they had a beautiful dark sheen, but this process must have made very dry, tough, salty meat.

Oak sawdust is piled into neat heaps before flitches of bacon and hams are smoked. Once the fires are lit it is almost impossible to see inside the smoking chamber. (Reproduced by kind permission of J. Sainsbury Ltd.)

PIG CURING

The factory

Wiltshire's association with commercial bacon curing is largely a geographical accident. The county stands neatly between Bristol and London, and in the 18th century, before the Great Western Railway was built, Irish pigs were driven along the main road that cuts through the county, in particular the town of Calne. The drovers rested here; the pigs were fed and watered, and the men refreshed themselves at one of the pubs in the town, like the *Butcher's Arms*. Just down the street – in Butcher's Row – was a shop owned by the Harris family. Sarah Harris, who sold fresh pork, pies and sausages, would meet the men when they reached town and buy up some of their pigs for her shop.

The business grew quickly, a second shop was opened by Sarah's son, John, and by 1808 both had started to cure and sell bacon. But the real turning point came in 1847 when John's son, George, visited America. There he saw bacon being cured throughout the year, even in the hottest weather, thanks to ice-cooled curing houses. So ice was the key; it could transform curing from a task limited to the coolest seasons of the year into a continuous process. By 1856 the Harris family had installed their first ice-house. In hard winters, when the water froze, ice was cut from local ponds and from the Calne canal; it was stored in specially-built thatched barns, alongside the houses that kept the wood chippings and sawdust for smoking the bacon. The trees of nearby Savernake forest were no doubt a good source of fuel for the smokehouses.

John Harris was running a small shop in Calne in 1805. Here the firm's reputation for sausages and other pork products began. (Reproduced by kind permission of C. & T. Harris, Calne, Ltd.)

By the 1860s the Harris family had almost perfected their bacon cure; because they could work through the year, they did not have to use such a strong cure as most people did, as the meat was unlikely to spoil in the cool atmosphere. In 1888 the two businesses merged to become the factory that stands in Butcher's Row – or Church Street as it is now called – alongside the Calne canal. The icehouses and sawdust stores have gone, but if you go round the factory its history is still apparent. Much of the building has been modernized, but the old roof with its wooden beams and rafters is intact, and decorative pig's heads carved out of stone adorn the walls, latter-day

When Thomas Harris and Sons ran the bacon factory in Calne in 1887, you could see live pigs waiting in pens before they went to the slaughter. (Reproduced by kind permission of C. & T. Harris, Calne, Ltd.)

This scene was photographed in 1910, but pig slaughtering and butchering is still a barbaric business – only for strong stomachs. (Reproduced by kind permission of C. & T. Harris, Calne, Ltd.)

In Devizes Museum there is a horn-handled 18th century fork that was discovered when the foundations of the Harris factory were being dug.

misericords that remind one of the wooden carvings in medieval churches which also celebrated the animal.

Today, bacon pigs come from all parts of the country to the Harris factory. The so-called 'Wiltshire cure' begins with slaughter, scalding and butchering. There is a certain smell and atmosphere around each stage of curing that reflects what is going on; here it is hot, steamy, noisy and rather unnerving. But move on with the pigs (now reduced to sides or flitches) into the brining chamber and it is suddenly quiet and cool. Here the sides are injected with brine (so that the salt can diffuse through the meat quickly and evenly), stacked in huge white tanks and left to steep in brine for four days.

Next the sides are moved to the maturing cellar where they are stacked and left for the flavour to develop. Some of this bacon – less than half these days –

The Harris factory is a fascinating piece of Victorian industrial architecture. In the brine curing cellar there are huge tanks and a network of metal rails for conveying carcases round the building. (Reproduced by kind permission of C. & T. Harris, Calne, Ltd.)

In 1910, bacon smoking at the Harris factory was a primitive business. The sides of salted pork were cut up on wooden benches before being despatched to the smokehouses. (Reproduced by kind permission of C. & T. Harris, Calne, Ltd.)

goes on to the smoke chambers, where it is warm and there is a recognizable and reassuring 'bacon' smell in the air. The rest is sold as 'green' or unsmoked bacon.

It is not worth comparing factory and home-cured bacon; both have their virtues, but they are essentially two different foods. Factory bacon is not very salty, not very dry, and does not keep for long. It is produced under strictly controlled conditions, and such standards are necessary in this kind of large scale technical process; the home-curer applies his own standards based on experience and good sense.

Harris and other companies are always working on new cures; the trend is clearly towards very mild flavoured, rindless rashers with a small amount of fat. Their 'Sweetcure' bacon is the best example of this; it is, as the name

The sides of pork are sprinkled with dry salt when being packed into the tanks for brining. Only the workers' clothes have changed since this photograph was taken. (Reproduced by kind permission of C. & T. Harris, Calne, Ltd.)

Harris' bacon and ham are famous throughout the world, and in the export packing department they would send them to such places as Mombassa and Peking. (Reproduced by kind permission of C. & T. Harris, Calne, Ltd.)

suggests, a sweet cure using dry salting rather than brining, and is very mild and unsmoked. In fact this bacon will not keep unless it is vacuum-packed as well. But that is the paradox of today's factory bacon; it is regarded as a perishable food.

The name of Harris isn't solely associated with bacon, however; the factory produces pies, sausages, faggots and black puddings (like their neighbours Bowyers at Trowbridge). And in the tradition of pig killing and curing they use as much of the animal as possible; even the lard goes into their pie pastry.

Small vans like this one were a common sight before Harris introduced large refrigerated lorries to deliver their produce. (Reproduced by kind permission of C. & T. Harris, Calne, Ltd.)

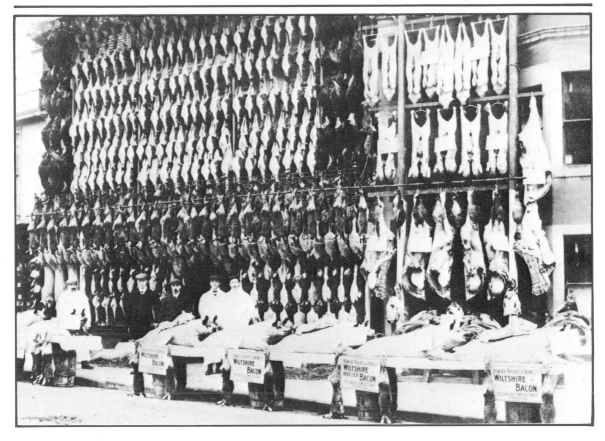

BRADENHAM HAM

A few miles west of Calne, at Chippenham, there is the Royal Wiltshire Bacon Company, which, apart from bacon, produces one of the finest English hams. Bradenham ham didn't begin life in Wiltshire; it migrated from Bradenham Manor in Buckinghamshire in the 19th century. The story is that the butler there fell out with his employers, moved to Wiltshire and took the recipe with him. He set up the Bradenham Ham Company in 1871 on the site where the present factory stands. This ham is made nowhere else, and the process is secret. There are no written recipes and details are released to no one outside the factory. So the men at the factory have special knowledge which is passed on from one curer to the next; but they are prepared to divulge a few pieces of information: the hams are soaked in molasses flavoured with juniper berries, coriander and other secret spices, leaving the outside unmistakably black - hence the name, Coal Black Bradenham. After smoking, the hams are left to mature for months. They say it takes up to six months to produce a good quality Bradenham ham.

Look in any butcher's window in Chippenham, particularly around Christmas time, and you will see signs advertising the ham; they are appropriately jet black with white lettering. Ham curers usually send a leaflet with their products, and the Bradenham is no exception. You are told to soak the ham for at least 72 hours before boiling it in water, or a mixture of water and treacle, giving it 30 minutes to the pound.

WILTSHIRE TRACKLEMENTS

Britain hasn't the tradition of regional garnishes for meat that you will find in France for instance. Dressings and condiments are either made quickly and

Display at Bowyers (Reproduced by kind permission of Bowyers of Trowbridge)

Abraham Bowyer, a founder member of the family firm of Bowyers. (Reproduced by kind permission of Bowyers of Trowbridge)

BREWERIES

J. ARKELL & SONS, LTD
Kingsdown Brewery, Upper Stratton, Swindon
A small, localized brewery that has moved over to draught beer. Most of the pubs are within a five-mile radius of Swindon. Arkells brew two very good bitters: an ordinary bitter, and a slightly stronger BBB (Best Bitter Beer), which is bottled as well. Also strong Kingsdown Ale.

(Reproduced by kind permission of Arkell's Brewery.)

One of the best pubs is *The Borough Arms* in Wootton Bassett; apart from the excellent beer it has an extraordinary collection of chamber pots and other conveniences. Between Wootton Bassett and the M4 is another pub, *Sally Pussey's Inn*, worth a visit for its name alone.

KINGSDOWN BREWERY · Griffin 72

GIBBS MEW & CO, LTD
Anchor Brewery, Milford Street, Salisbury

GIBBS

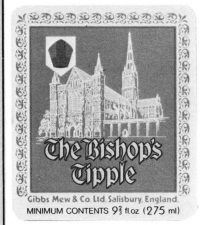

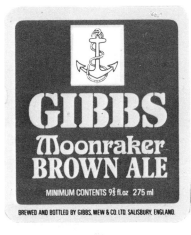

Another small family brewery that has recently recognized the trend towards draught beer. The Bishop's Tipple, introduced in 1976, is a very original beer, brewed to a formula that has no sugar; just hops and malt. It is deceptively strong.

Several pubs in and around Salisbury sell Gibbs Mew: *The Swan* at Harnham, *The Hogshead* and *The Conquered Moon* on Bemerton Heath.

(Reproduced by kind permission of Gibbs Mew and Wadworth's Brewery.)

WADWORTH & CO, LTD
Northgate Brewery, Devizes

Has always been on the side of draught beer, and is by far the most widespread in Wiltshire, with many good pubs. Mild, ordinary bitter (IPA), and 6X (a heavy, strong bitter) are worth trying. If you are in the area in the winter, look out for Old Timer, strong, fruity beer; also bottled. Try *The Pheasant* near Chippenham; good pub food (their pasties of lamb and potato covered with a suet and lard pastry are large and memorable). In Devizes, *The Pelican*, almost opposite the brewery, is a small, crowded and unpretentious drinking house. Go there at lunchtime on market days.

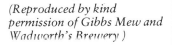

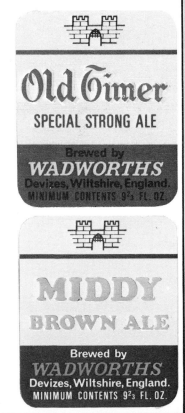

In the Wiltshire Tracklements shop in Calne you can buy a whole range of their mustards, herb jellies, pickles and vinegars. It is a colourful and friendly place to visit. (Photographed by Peter Lowry, reproduced by kind permission of Wiltshire Tracklements)

Although Urchfont mustard is mainly associated with pork, there is no reason why it should not be used with other meat, such as beef.

simply at home, like mint sauce, or manufactured as a nationally recognized accompaniment to a particular dish, like horseradish sauce for roast beef. Indeed, the ancient generic term for such garnishes – 'tracklements' – is pure cottage English, and you will not find it in many orthodox dictionaries.

Wiltshire Tracklements, which is tucked, appropriately, as snug as an apple at the side of Harris's great pork factory, is consequently a cottage industry in more than one sense of the word. It has successfully revived many traditional British household garnishes and prepares them on a scale which ensures that quality can be maintained.

The story of its origin is typical of many local food enterprises. William Tullberg was a refugee from the pork trade, and a mustard fanatic to boot. Disillusioned with the limited range of mustards to be found in Wiltshire, he began making his own in an electric blender. His first marketplace was the local pub in Urchfont (the village after which the mustards are now named), where his latest blends were put to the test with sausages by the Saturday lunchtime drinkers. They passed this test, the sternest there is for any mustard, and aware of having tapped a real public hunger, Mr Tullberg went into business.

Urchfont mustards have a distinctive flavour and 'nose', largely because the mustard seeds are not ground into a powder, but just lightly split, so that their volatile oils are retained. As well as the strong, ordinary mustard, there are milder varieties flavoured with tarragon or honey, and a sharp black mustard. All are made with fresh spices and vinegar.

In spite of the rapid expansion both of its range and its market, the firm has managed to maintain its connections with Wiltshire – and that means, of course, the pig. A range of herb jellies (available in mint, thyme or sage flavours) has now been developed especially to accompany pork and lamb.

There are plans, too, for pickled eggs, which may eventually find their way onto the Devizes pies (see below) which are still made not ten miles away.

For those used to only a single kind of mustard, confined to the edge of the plate, Wiltshire Tracklements has also published a leaflet of recipes incorporating mustards, which have been devised mostly by Wiltshire cooks. You could sample some of these dishes in another of Tullberg's enterprises, Maslen's Restaurant, next to the shop, and one, in particular – Kidneys Urchfont – at the *Bell Inn* at Ramsbury where it was invented. It is as fine and traditional a use for a mustard as you could imagine, a dish of kidneys, bacon and mushrooms braised with mustard and seasoned with Worcester sauce and port.

Wiltshire Tracklements is best known for its mustards and its fruit and herb jellies, and the labels on their jars are very distinctive, being hand-written by the proprietor, William Tullberg. (Reproduced by kind permission of Wiltshire Tracklements).

Red Currant Jelly
made to a Wiltshire recipe, in small batches, from the best available ingredients

INGREDIENTS
REDCURRANTS, SUGAR GLUCOSE SYRUP, PECTIN, FRUIT ACID.
Net Weight
1 lb - 453g
THE WILTSHIRE TRACKLEMENT COMPANY LIMITED
44 CHURCH STREET, CALNE WILTSHIRE, ENGLAND.

Red Currant Jelly
our red currant jelly contains no artificial colouring, and is splendid with lamb, hare or game

Urchfont Mustard
Made to the recipe of a private gentleman of Urchfont in Wiltshire, from freshly ground whole spices, thus preserving the essential oils.

INGREDIENTS
MUSTARD SEED, CIDER & WINE VINEGARS BY DUFRAIS, BLACK PEPPERS, ALLSPICE, CHILLIES
Net Weight
12oz - 340g
WILTSHIRE TRACKLEMENTS 44 CHURCH STREET, CALNE, WILTSHIRE, ENGLAND.

Urchfont Mustard
A robust mustard, made to complement the hams, sausages and pork pies for which Wiltshire is famous

DEVIZES PIE

Thought by many to be nothing more than a name from the past, a relic, this marvellous pie still lives on; we found it at *The Bear Hotel* in Devizes, where it is very popular, although this is probably the only place that serves it. We discovered it quite by chance, when we were walking the streets of the town, taking in the smell of Wadworth's brewery and scanning shops and menus. It was a real piece of luck.

It is a classic English pie, stuffed full of pickled tongue, sweetbreads, veal, bacon and hard-boiled eggs (even deer umbles were included in some recipes). It should be eaten cold, and it was originally garnished with pickled eggs – a brilliant, but simple and effective accompaniment that ought to be revived. These days the pie is often served with Urchfont mustard; a fine marriage of old and new local foods.

The Bear Hotel is easy to find, it stands opposite the market square in Devizes, and an ornamental effigy of a black bear is fixed above the entrance, so that there is no doubt about the identity of the place.

LARDY CAKE

In the days when women baked bread regularly, every week, they would often be left with odd bits of dough after the loaves had been moulded, and one way of using these up in Wiltshire was to make lardy cake. This was put into the ovens on Saturday after the bread had been baked, and eaten, heated up, for Sunday tea.

Rich, sticky lardy cake was originially made for tea on Saturday and Sunday, and it is still a delicious tea-time treat, spread thickly with butter. (Photographed by Trevor Wood)

Lardy Cake

450 gr (1 lb) white bread dough, left to rise for an hour

150gr (6 oz) lard

150 gr (6 oz) mixed currants and sultanas

50 gr (2 oz) candied peel

150 gr (6 oz) granulated sugar

Once the dough has risen, roll it out into an oblong, and cover two-thirds of it with half the sugar, dried fruit and lard. Fold up the bottom third of the dough to cover the filling, and bring the top third down over this. Turn the dough and repeat with the rest of the filling. After folding again, fit the dough into an oblong baking tin and leave in a warm place for 30 minutes. Then bake at 400₀F (Gas Mk. 6) for 45 minutes. Let the lardy cake stand in the tin for 10 minutes to re-absorb the fat, then turn out, upside down.

Lardy cake – sometimes called 'shaley cake' or simply 'fat cake' – is basically a mixture of bread dough enriched with lard and sweetened with sugar and dried fruit. Although it no longer has links with home-baking, it is still immensely popular in the county.

Lardy cake should be rich, fruity and sticky. It was always made into oblong or square shapes at one time, but bakers now seem to prefer thick round cakes. They are easy to recognize because they are nearly always sold upside down, showing the toffee-like layer at the bottom which is the mark of a good lardy cake. By selling the cakes upside down the baker also avoids them sticking to one another or to the display trays.

However, watch out for fake lardy cakes, even in Wiltshire. These are dry, the inside is airy and yellow instead of white and moist, and there is little or no sign of the stickiness produced by the lard and sugar. Lardy cake – the real kind

– is easy to find, all the fruitful market towns like Trowbridge and Devizes stock it, and it sells very fast. When we were in Devizes the whole stock in the bakery opposite the market square was snatched up in a few hours.

More dough cakes, similar to the lardy, turn up in Oxfordshire and other counties where there is a strong tradition of pigs and pig cookery.

FAIRINGS

Food has always been a feature of fairs. It was a chance for makers of pies, sweets, cakes, bread, beer and cider to sell their wares; it provided the people at the fair with refreshment; food was also a way of advertising the event, and was a source of gifts and cheap presents for lovers and friends. These gifts were called 'fairings'; they might be squares of gingerbread, special cakes or pies. But in Wiltshire they were crisp discs made of treacle, sugar and butter flavoured with brandy and spices. In fact, these irregular, lacy wheels were unrolled brandy snaps.

They are still made and sold in Wiltshire, mostly in baker's shops, but also at the big fairs like the Marlborough Mop, where they rival the toffee-apple as the choice fair-food. They are still much the same, although golden syrup – a product dating from the 1880s – has replaced black treacle. You can also buy bags of broken fairings to nibble as you walk round stalls and sideshows.

Mops were originally 'Hirings', meetings of farmers and farm-workers, where wages and conditions were discussed and men were hired. They were important occasions for eating, drinking, trading and gossiping. In due course these hirings became fairs, but up to the First World War men would still seek employment there. Now, although the name Mop is still used, the fairs are simply entertainments.

Wiltshire men are still sometimes called Moonrakers, and the name is also perpetuated in at least one brand of locally-produced butter and one of the bottled beers produced by Gibbs Mew in Salisbury.

Wiltshire Moonrakers

The origin of this title is explained in a legend connected with the days of smuggling, when the excise officers were kept busy night and day in endeavouring to frustrate the designs of those who believed in free trade – at least in spirits. It appears that the scene was enacted "up north" near Devizes. A publican had engaged several vokels to bring home some smuggled kegs of brandy in a trap, during the night, and whilst nearing their destination the donkey bolted, and the trap coming into collision with a bridge, was upset, the kegs of brandy rolling out into the stream underneath. Whilst trying to rescue the kegs with some hay rakes they found close at hand, the cry of "Zise-min" was raised. Asking what they were about, one of the vokels told him they were raking for a cheese which had rolled into the water. At this the exciseman, laughing to see the vokels raking at the shadow of the moon rode off, leaving the grinning countrymen at liberty to rescue the kegs of spirits and carry them off. Not so very soft, were they ?.

Boletus edulis, one of the most common and delicious of the edible ceps. (Illustration by Edward Arnor)

SAVERNAKE FOREST

Savernake Forest, like all ancient woodland, is rich in fungi living off the complex underground network of roots and centuries of accumulated leaf litter. Savernake has a history which can be traced back to the Middle Ages. In Norman times it was a Royal Hunting Forest; in the 18th century, the site of extensive new beech plantations; now, its 2,000 acres are managed by the Forestry Commission, and many of the mature hardwood trees have been cleared to make way for conifers. But along the tracks and rides (where there is public access) strips of the old forest have been kept, and here in autumn you may find edible species like ceps, chanterelles and blewits.

THE HUNT FOR BLUE VINNY: A DETECTIVE STORY.

The picture painted by most reference books was bleak. Blue Vinny was once a famous cheese, made exclusively in Dorset, but now perhaps extinct. Yet we had heard that it could still be found, so, before embarking on the hunt, we had to learn more about it.

We knew that much of the information would be written between the lines of tales and local customs, and so it was. The 'Vinny' of the name is a corruption of 'vinnid' or 'veiny', referring to the mass of blue veins that run through the cheese. The milk for the cheese would come from cows that grazed around Sherborne and other parts of the county, and it would be hand-skimmed, since mechanical skimming takes away too much cream from the milk.

The creation of the blue in this otherwise dull and heavy cheese was another matter. We read about working dairies, unhygienic by today's standards, where cheeses were left for months while the mould grew in them. These dairies were cold, damp places with the smell and atmosphere of the fields. In such conditions the spores of *Penicillium roqueforti* would grow, slowly, gradually, and in time the blue mould would spread inside the cheeses and they would begin to vein up. In some dairies, farm-hands would dip harness leathers in the milk churns when the day's work was over, and they might leave mouldy bread or old boots in the cheese room too. (This has a sound scientific basis, since the mould grows well on leather.) The final trick was to store the cheese at the bottom of a vat of cider; it might take months, but eventually the cider would clear and the cheese would ripen. What a harmonious and practical partnership between two foods.

Could such a craft survive amid today's strict health regulations, mechanical skimming methods and the economic pressure to sell cheese before it has had time to ripen? We would surely find the answers once we reached Dorset. At least we knew what the cheese would look like if we did discover it: traditionally six inches high and eight inches in diameter, weighing ten to twelve pounds with a thick rind riddled with cracks and crevices. Inside it would be almost white with the blue running through it.

That was the knowledge we took with us when we finally went to search for 'the vein of truth'.

We began at the old centre of the Vinny country, Sherborne. Our first call was a notable provisions shop, aptly named Mould and Edwards, and there, high on the shelves, was a cheese. But it was labelled Dorset Blue. This puzzled us, so we enquired. It was indeed Dorset Blue, the legal and 'clean' version of Vinny sold these days. But even this cheese was surrounded by an air of secrecy;

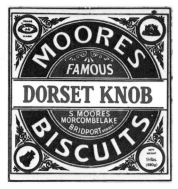

In 1978, the Moores' Bakery decided to limit their production of Dorset Knobs. They will no longer be made between May and December, the peak period for the bakery, and are likely to be much harder to find in Dorset and elsewhere. (Reproduced by kind permission of Moores' Goldencap Bakery)

the assistant knew that there was a regular supply, but did not know where it came from – or at least he wasn't prepared to tell us.

Were there two different cheeses still in existence? Had the Vinny been completely replaced by this Dorset Blue? Indeed was the Dorset Blue an authentic cheese, or a bastardized version of something else? Why the secrecy even among people who dealt with the cheese? We already knew some of the answers. The conditions and methods used in those damp dairies for producing the distinctive mould in the cheese would not be accepted by today's health inspectors. So it would be illegal to sell a cheese made in this way. If Vinny was still being made in the old manner it must be part of a 'cheese underground' kept close within the confines of a few families, never coming onto the open market. So we must expect secrecy, suspicion and vagueness.

We turned south off the main roads and onto the narrow twisting lanes that thread their way around the edges of fields and through tiny villages—the country of Thomas Hardy's *Woodlanders*—lanes thick with mud, lined with patches of coppiced hazel and, wandering in the wet fields, dark-coated Dorset sheep. The feeling of a past way of life carrying on in the present was so strong we could sense, at least in our imagination, that across a waterlogged field, behind a barn door, Vinnys were even now growing their special infestation.

Reading the village names, we travelled on: Bagber, Lydlinch, Glanvilles Wooton, Duntish, Buckland Newton. We stopped for a drink. The pub was quiet, so we talked to the landlady about Vinny. She was a newcomer to the area, impressed with the mystery surrounding the cheese. 'Sherborne,' she said, 'and Dorchester and perhaps Cerne Abbas too.' After checking the map, we set off again: Alton Pancras, Piddletrenthide, Piddlehinton, Cerne Abbas. We found a grocer's shop with some very sad-looking wedges of blue cheese on the counter. 'Not Vinny,' snapped a very suspicious lady, who claimed there was no such thing. Clearly she knew something, but she would not tell.

Lunchtime. We elected to adjourn the hunt while we refreshed ourselves. We also decided to cheat in a small way, and opened the envelope we had brought with us which contained the name of a supplier of Vinny. It directed us westward, to Bridport. Was it likely that there would be a place there selling Vinny? Would it simply be more Dorset Blue?

We reached *The Smith's Arms* at Godmanstone. The landlady there doubted the existence of true Vinny, although she had lived in the county for thirty years. But she knew the Bridport shop. Before making the journey we made a detour into Dorchester. There again was the same Dorset Blue, and the same vague responses. It seemed that Bridport would be our last hope.

We found the shop and there in the window were the cheeses – Dorset Blue again, but fine-looking specimens, worth buying. We wanted to talk to the dairyman at the shop, but he was called out to his cows by the vet before we had a chance to speak to him.

The cheese we had in our hands was indistinguishable from the first specimen we had seen in the Sherborne grocer's shop. We had not found any Vinny, but we could make a shrewd guess about it now that we had penetrated the area. The real answer would need more time: time to get beyond the official opinions about the cheese, time to gain the trust and confidence of people who were not prepared to reveal anything to strangers.

The Eldridge Pope brewery in Dorchester produces Thomas Hardy's Ale, which is the strongest bottled beer brewed in Britain. It comes in individually numbered bottles and is naturally conditioned, so that it needs to be kept for several years before being drunk. (One bottle I purchased in 1976 was not meant to be opened until 1981.)

Dorchester is the town known as Casterbridge in Thomas Hardy's novels. In 'The Trumpet-Major' there is a passage about Dorchester beer, reproduced on the label of the Hardy Ale bottles: 'It was of the most beautiful colour that the eye of an artist in beer could desire; full in body, yet brisk as a volcano; piquant, yet without a twang; luminous as an autumn sunset; free from streakiness of taste but, finally, rather heady.'

'The Smith's Arms' competes with 'The Nutshell' at Bury St Edmunds for the title 'Smallest Pub in England'.

BANBURY CAKES

A gentle walk along that narrow street will inform you with some sense of Banbury's past. It snakes its way up the hill behind the High Street. Perhaps the most striking feature is the sign for the *Old Reindeer Inn* which hangs precariously above the centre of the road, suspended from a huge bracket, and naturally draws your eye across the street to the site of *The Original Cake Shop*, now occupied by new shops.

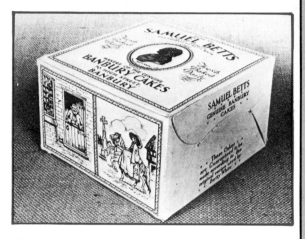

One of the boxes which were used to contain Banbury Cakes. (Reproduced by kind permission of Jon Hall and Banbury Museum)

May, 1967, was a sad month for the town of Banbury. After more than three centuries of trading *The Original Cake Shop* closed. Since 1872 the shop had been run by the Brown family, and it had a reputation for selling the best Banbury cakes of all. The people of the town still talk about 'Brown's cakes' – it is an affectionate way of remembering the family and the cakes they made. It also suggests that there were local variations made by other bakers in the area, but that they did not compare with the cakes from the shop in Parsons Street.

Betts Banbury Cake shop at the turn of the century. (Reproduced by permission of Jon Hall and Banbury Museum)

A selection of objects from Banbury Museum. (Photograph by Trevor Wood)

Banbury cakes were first mentioned in 1586 in T. Bright's *Treatise of Melancholy*: 'Sodden wheat is a grosse and melancholicke nourishment, and bread especially of the find flower unleavened. Of this sort are bag puddings made, with flower, fritters, pancakes, such as we call Banberne cakes.' Hardly a shining advertisement, even though a similar recipe printed a few years later (1615) in *The English Huswife* by Gervaise Markham suggests that they were once more like Simnel cakes (see p. 193).

In the middle of the 18th century the White family – Old Jarvis White and his wife Betty – started to bake Banbury cakes as we know them today in the back room of the Parsons Street shop. Jarvis would, it is said, spend most of his time leaning over the hatch of the shop door, but he had an enterprising sales pitch for the cakes. To emphasize how light they were he would maintain that a sparrow had flown into the shop one day and carried off a cake in its beak.

The shop changed hands a couple of times in the 19th century before the Browns took over in 1872. But this wasn't the only shop in town selling the cakes. Betty White's grandson, William Betts, opened a shop in the High Street and one of his sons in turn opened yet another shop. It was a prosperous time. In 1840, the Parsons Street shop sold 139,500 cakes at 2d each; they were exported to America and Australia, and, once the railway was established, you could buy them on the station platform. You can today, in the tea room above Banbury Station.

They are still proud of their cakes in Banbury; all the bakers' shops sell them, and you cannot miss the signs advering the fact. The cakes themselves are unmistakable: flat, oval, made of flaky pastry and covered with a crust of sugar and egg white. The filling is a dark mixture of dried fruit, candied peel, butter, sugar and rum.

The Old Reindeer Inn, opposite the site of the Original Banbury Cake shop. (Photograph by Trevor Wood)

The cakes are intended to be eaten warm rather than hot, so, put them under a very low grill allowing the heat to penetrate the cakes gradually and bring them to life – lightening the pastry, softening the filling, and melting the sugary crust. Don't be impatient, and be sure to watch the cakes the whole time. Take your eyes off them for a few seconds, and you will find that the golden coating of sugar has burnt and turned black. Try dipping the tip of the cakes into very thick cream before eating them.

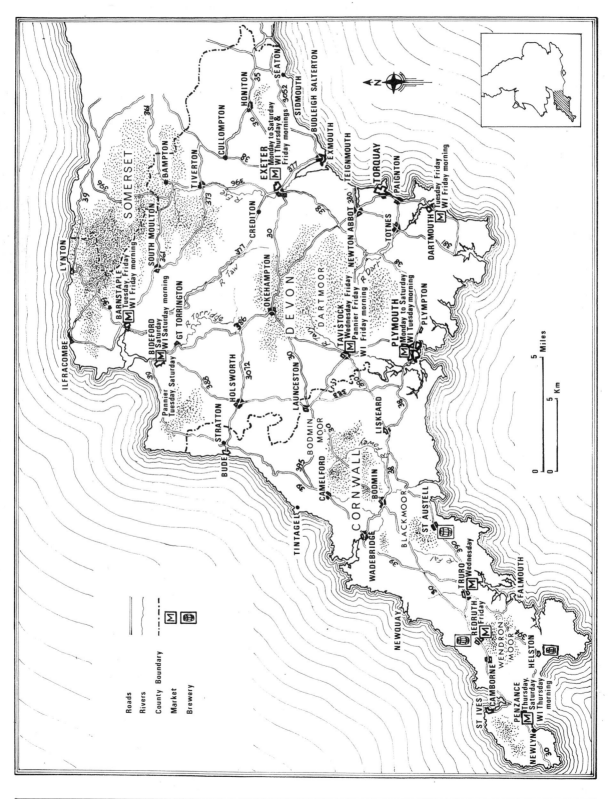

DEVON AND CORNWALL
STARGAZEY, OGGIES AND SCRUMPY

Devon and Cornwall have a rich tradition of local and regional food, and it's hard to isolate one single factor that has influenced what people in this area cook and eat. Echoes of Celtic inheritance and a style of food reflect not only the west of England, but Ireland, Scotland and Wales as well. But, above all, there is the emphasis on dairy products. When people think of Devon and Cornwall, they think too of clotted cream. It is now a food for tourists as much as anything else, but this is nothing new. There was commercial cream production in the west country back in the 13th century.

The Cornish people, in particular, are fiercely independent; they still fight for their own language and their own laws and in many Cornish kitchens dishes with odd names like 'figgy obbin', 'shenagrum' and 'likky pie' are still made. But even the strongest, most independent culture has to bend, and the fact that the west country is now one of the most popular tourist areas in the land inevitably means change. It is a pity that more tourists are not interested in the foods of this area; they know about Cornish pasties and cider and clotted cream, but are not inclined to scratch beneath the surface to discover some of the other attractive foods that the west country has to offer.

There's a deep-rooted tradition of sea-faring in these parts, dating back to pre-Christian times, when the Phoenicians are said to have traded along the coast for tin. In the 18th century west country sailors were still introducing many new foods to the area. Boats went out to fish as well as to trade, and this aspect of sea-work survived. The great pilchard fishery may have vanished but mackerel, crabs, lobsters, turbot, soles and prawns can still be caught and eaten by visitors to the west country.

CLOTTED CREAM
Eleven types of cream are produced in Britain, ranging from pasteurized single cream to the richest of them all, farmhouse clotted cream. This is one of the best-known foods of the south-west – perfect for packaging as a holiday souvenir. It had its origins in the day-to-day workings of small farms and dairies before the days of cream separators.

Clotted, or scalded cream is cream that has been heated. This helps it to keep longer than untreated cream, because heating destroys those bacteria that would otherwise turn the cream sour. Heating also gives the cream its distinctive flavour and thick granular texture.

The four breeds of cattle found in Devon and Cornwall (Devon and North Devon, Guernsey and Jersey) all yield milk with a high butterfat content. Large fat globules rise quickly to form a thick layer of cream if the milk is allowed to

Clotted cream used to be packed in stoneware pots like this, but nowadays it usually comes in small plastic tubs. On the side of the jar there is the inscription 'To be kept dry and cool not on ice or it turns fusty'. (Reproduced by kind permission of The Museum of English Rural Life, University of Reading)

Old spellings of the word clotted vary from clowtyd, clowted, clouted to clawted. The origins of the name are uncertain, but a clout means a thick patch, and may refer to the appearance of the cream as it forms.

Ordinary cream was also packed in special jars, which have now become collector's items. (Reproduced by kind permission of J. Sainsbury)

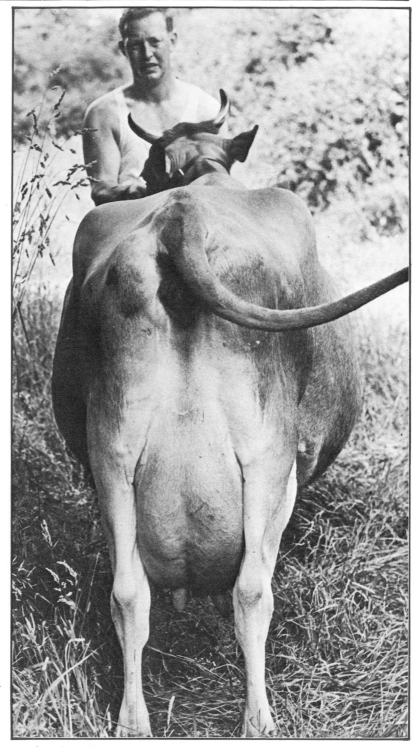

There's no doubt that this animal is a dairy cow! It is actually a very well-hung Jersey, a breed with an extraordinary capacity for producing milk. (Reproduced by kind permission of The Museum of English Rural Life, University of Reading)

stand undisturbed in the cool temperature of the dairy in large pans called 'setting pans'. Then the milk and cream are carefully heated to a temperature of 77–78°C for about 40 minutes, and allowed to cool for anything up to 24 hours depending on the weather. As the pans cool a wrinkled yellow crust forms which is skimmed off by hand and packed into cartons as clotted cream.

A great amount of clotted cream is made in the west country: the trade reaches its peak during July and August when tourists buy pot after pot to take home with them. (It is easy to transport because it is thick, and will keep well because of the way it has been made.) It appears in food shops and in souvenir shops too, alongside postcards and sticks of seaside rock. But make sure that you are buying the real thing, not a substitute.

Guernsey cattle, like this prize-winning beast, are splendid and prolific milk producers and are one of the commonest breeds in the west country. (Reproduced by kind permission of The Museum of English Rural Life, University of Reading)

In the 19th century Mrs Beeton wrote: *'This cream is so much esteemed that it is sent to the London markets in small square tins and jars, and is exceedingly delicate eaten with fresh fruit.'* If you don't make regular visits to the west country, and still want to taste clotted cream, you can order it by post. Three good sources of supply are:

Babbacombe Creamery, Reddenhill Road, Babbacombe, Torquay, Devon.
Penzance Buttery, Alverton, Penzance, Cornwall.
Wonnacotts Dairy, Lansdown Road, Bude, Cornwall.

The Penzance Buttery is one of many in the west country which produce and sell clotted cream by post. (Reproduced by kind permission of The Penzance Buttery)

The equipment needed these days for producing clotted cream is a celebration of the virtues of metallic containers. (Photographed by W. A. Saxton)

It is worth checking before you order clotted cream as it is made seasonally, and is not always available all year round.

Mrs Beeton's advice about clotted cream and fresh fruit is very sound, but in Devon and Cornwall there are other ways of using it. It is spread on little buns known as *Cornish splits*, and carefully spooned on top of junket. Clotted cream, surprisingly, can also be an ingredient of savoury dishes, such as pork and leek pie or 'lammy pie', which is a mixture of lamb, chopped parsley and cream, topped with pastry.

Cornish splits are small, plain buns made from butter, flour, yeast, sugar and milk. They are called splits because that is exactly what you do to them before loading them with jam or clotted cream. Cornish splits, clotted cream and home-made jam together make up west country cream teas.

This postcard of Devonshire Dumplings is a portrait of a dish that is rarely made nowadays.

Cornish burnt cream

This dish consists of layers of egg custard alternating with layers of clotted cream. The top is sprinkled with castor sugar and heated under the grill until the sugar becomes brown and caramelized. In other words it is a variation of *crème brulée*.

CORNISH PASTY

> *'Pastry rolled out like a plate,*
> *Piled with turmut, tates, and mate,*
> *Doubled up, and baked like fate,*
> *That's a Cornish pasty.'*

turmut = turnips   tates = potatoes   mate = meat

Quite recently a prominent British Rail spokesman commented about the poor quality of the Cornish pasties sold at Paddington Station – the terminus used by thousands of travellers to the west country. He felt that the public should be given an authentic and edible introduction to the classic regional food of the west.

This Cornish rhyme gives some idea of what a Cornish pasty should be. Of all traditional and regional foods, the pasty has been more abused than any other. The dubious specimens that appear in railway buffets, bakers' shops, supermarkets, cafés and pubs are often no more than a mixture of 90% mashed potato and 10% 'meat' – usually mince, sausagemeat, or even corned beef, enclosed in some sort of pastry.

There is no strict rule about what should or should not be put into a pasty. (In Cornwall they say that the Devil never crossed the river Tamar for fear of ending up chopped and cooked in pastry, such was the Cornish woman's habit of including anything in her pasty recipes.) The traditional mixture is, as the rhyme indicates, turnips, potatoes and meat with perhaps some chopped onion as well. Much of the flavour of a true pasty derives from the fact that the meat is put in raw and cooked *inside* the pastry cover, although the potatoes and turnips are cooked beforehand.

Although most Cornish pasties are tiny in comparison with these specimens, you can still buy giant, meal-sized pasties in Cornwall itself. (Reproduced by kind permission of Truro Public Records Office)

A recipe for Cornish pasties:

The filling –
450 gr (1 lb) chuck steak
100 gr (4 oz) chopped onion
50 gr (2 oz) chopped turnip
  (cooked)
250 gr (8 oz) sliced potato
  (cooked)
salt, pepper
pinch of thyme

Make a batch of shortcrust pastry in the usual way, being sure to use lard in the mixture. Chop the meat, after removing fat and gristle, and mix with the chopped vegetables and seasoning. Roll out the pastry and cut it into two large circles. Put half the filling in the middle of each circle. Brush the rim of pastry with beaten egg, draw the two sides of the pastry together so that they meet at the top, and pinch together along the length of the pasty. Make a small hole in the top of each one, and brush all over with beaten egg. Bake the pasties for 20 minutes at 400°F and a further 40 minutes at 350°F.

Saffron Crocus.

(Illustration by Carol Fowke)

The size and shape of the pasty also varies. We usually think of it as torpedo-shaped – the pastry seam at the top – but, looking at old photographs of people eating pasties, it appears that they were often quite flat and at least twice the size of those made and sold today. They were functional work foods in those days. The pasty (pronounced *pah*-stee) or 'oggie' was a portable meal that could be stuffed into a man's pocket as he went to work. All the ingredients for a filling lunch were sealed inside it, so there was no need for lunch boxes or paper bags. Men working in the fields, fishermen on the boats, and workers in the Cornish tin mines all survived on pasties, and, because each man's pasty was so large, and often had to be put down half-eaten, it was marked at one corner with its owner's initials. If he began eating at the opposite end to the initials, he could leave the remains and return to the pasty later, knowing that it was rightfully his. This was important because each pasty would probably contain a different mixture – each man's personal favourite.

Even though you can now buy so-called Cornish pasties anywhere in the country, the best are still to be had in Cornwall. There will always be people who say that they are not as good as they used to be, and some pasties will always be better than others, given the number that are made nowadays. So it is worth shopping around, trying out many different ones, before you decide on your favourite source of supply. It really is hard to match a large pasty washed down with beer, or, better still, a mug of cider.

SQUAB PIE

Squab is the name of a young, unfledged pigeon, and in Devon and Cornwall this pie was originally made with pigeons. (According to Theodora Fitzgibbon, young, skinned cormorants were sometimes used instead.) But, although the pie still retains its original name, somewhere along the line pigeons disappeared from the recipe to be replaced by cheaper mutton and lamb. Unlike the Cornish pasty, this pie is made in a dish, with a pastry covering over the top, and is eaten hot. Though the recipes vary, the pie usually consists of layers of mutton or mutton chops alternating with layers of chopped apples spread with honey and chopped onion, with the addition of dried fruit such as currants or prunes. The mixture is spiced with nutmeg, mace and cinnamon and moistened with mutton stock, then covered with shortcrust pastry, baked and eaten hot with clotted cream.

Pies of this type are still made in west country kitchens, and there's always a chance that an enterprising restaurant will include it on their menu. If you see it advertised, be sure to try it.

CAKES AND BAKING

In addition to the pies that were such a feature of food in Devon and Cornwall there were also many cakes, buns and breads with odd names. Most of these have disappeared, but two in particular have survived as examples of a tradition of baking that has been eroded by commercial pressures over the years.

SAFFRON CAKE

Saffron is an expensive product obtained from the stigmas of the saffron-crocus: the orange-red threads impart a beautiful yellow colour to anything they are mixed with. Saffron was introduced to England from Asia Minor, and the saffron-crocus was cultivated back in the 16th century, mainly at Saffron Walden in Essex, but also in Cornwall, particularly at Stratton in the north of the county. The Saffron Walden plantations died out in about 1770, but tiny pockets of saffron cultivation may well have lingered into this century.

Saffron cake, which is more like a sweet bread, was always eaten at Easter, like simnel cake in other parts of the country. It is still common in bakers' shops throughout Devon and Cornwall, although it is less seasonal than it used to be. Sometimes you will see it sold as a large cake, and sometimes as small buns, but in each case the recipe is the same.

Saffron cake is a close relative of Wiltshire lardy cake and Welsh bara brith, but the saffron adds a strong aroma and a distinctive and beautiful yellow colour.

HEAVY CAKE

This cake is aptly named, judging by its ingredients: flour, butter or clotted cream, beef dripping, sugar, currants and lemon peel. But, once these have been mixed together to form a stiff dough, rolled into thick slabs and baked, the cake should turn out so light it can be pulled apart with the fingers.

HELSTON PUDDING

The town of Helston in Cornwall is known for three things: the Furry or Floral Dance performed each year on May 8th, the Blue Anchor home-brewery (see p. 142), and Helston pudding. This is made with currants, breadcrumbs, suet, sugar and ground rice, mixed together and moistened with milk to which baking soda has been added. The mixture is put into a pudding basin, covered with a cloth and steamed for two hours.

The Helston Furry Dance is one of the oldest surviving examples of a communal spring festival dance. The participants dance into shops and private houses, in at the front door and out through the back, and through gardens bringing the luck of Summer to the owners and driving out the darkness of Winter.

The Helston Furry Dance, as it was forty years ago, is still a well-advertised and well-attended celebration. (Reproduced by kind permission of The Museum of English Rural Life, University of Reading)

BREWERIES

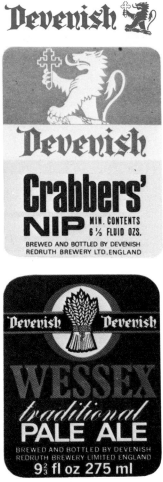

DEVENISH (REDRUTH) BREWERY LTD
The Brewery, Redruth, Cornwall

This is a subsidiary of Devenish's brewery in Weymouth. There is a strong 'Cornish' bitter, a thin, ordinary bitter and a XXX dark mild, but in a number of pubs you can only buy pressurized beer.

Many pubs, however, especially in west Cornwall, sell draught Devenish beers. *The New Inn* at Manaccan is a thatched pub which does a good range of food such as crab soup and home-made pasties. *The Hazelphron* at Gunwalloe (try saying that after a night's drinking) is worth visiting and so is *The New Inn* at St Columb Major.

The cask-filling shed at Devenish's brewery.(*Reproduced by kind permission of Devenish, Redruth, Ltd*)

(*Reproduced by permission of Devenish (Redruth) Ltd*)

(*Reproduced by permission of the St. Austell Brewery*)

ST AUSTELL BREWERY CO. LTD
St Austell, Cornwall

This brewery produces two bitters, the strong Hick's special, introduced in 1975, and the weaker, but palatable, BB. There is also a XXX dark mild. In St Austell pubs you can try the bottled Prince's Ale, a very strong barley wine.

Once again, you will find that a large number of the St Austell pubs sell only pressurized beer, though a good many in the south and west of Cornwall do sell traditional draught beers. Try *The Earl of Chatham* in Lostwithiel, *The Star* in St Just, or *The Radjell* in Pendeen.

Devon and Cornwall are cider counties. They are also overwhelmed every year by millions of tourists who more often than not demand 'safe' keg beer. Yet the area does sustain one of the few home-breweries in the country: *The Blue Anchor* at Helston in Cornwall which produces two strong bitters and special brews at Christmas and Easter.

MARKETS

Barnstaple. Pannier Market, East End.

The tradition of market selling still flourishes in Devon and Cornwall, and there are plenty of good markets selling all kinds of local produce. In some towns there are also 'pannier markets', where individual smallholders come with eggs, cream or onions — anything, in fact, that they have produced — and sell straight from the basket. This postcard shows the scene at Barnstaple pannier market (east end) in the early years of this century.

BARNSTAPLE

General market, *Tuesday and Friday*
WI stall in the Pannier Market. *Friday morning*

BIDEFORD

General market, *Saturday*   Pannier market, *Tuesday and Saturday*
WI market stall, Butchers Row. *Saturday morning*

DARTMOUTH

General market, Butter Market Hall   *Tuesday and Friday*
WI stall in the market   *Friday morning*

EXETER

General market, St George's Market. *Monday–Saturday*
WI stall in the market   *Thursday morning and Saturday morning*

PENZANCE

General market, *Thursday and Saturday*
WI market, St John's Hall. *Thursday morning*

PLYMOUTH

General market, *Monday–Saturday* (very good for dairy produce and fish)
WI stall in the market. *Tuesday morning*

REDRUTH

General market, *Friday*

TAVISTOCK

General market, *Wednesday and Friday*
Pannier market, *Friday*   WI market stall, *Friday morning*

TRURO

General market, *Wednesday*
WI market, Lemon Street. *Wednesday morning*

Throughout the mackerel fishing season, men still work hard to catch the profitable crop of fish that feed in the waters off Devon and Cornwall. (Reproduced by kind permission of Devon Library Service)

MACKEREL

Although mackerel are sold and eaten throughout Britain they are mainly fished in the south-west. They overwinter deep in the North Sea and in waters around the south-west coast. During the winter months they migrate to their spawning grounds south of Ireland and west of the English Channel – an area sometimes called the Celtic Sea. Once they have spawned they start to feed voraciously and between April and June west country fishermen catch them with drift nets. The great centre of this fishery is Newlyn in Cornwall, where it has been known for as much as half the total English catch to be landed.

In June and July the fish move inshore in small shoals, feeding on small fish rather than plankton. Now is the time for the small boats to go out loaded with hooks and lines. This fishing lasts until September, when the fish begin to disperse for their winter rest in the depths. This seasonal activity means that mackerel are at their best, both in the shops and bought straight from the boats, between April and September.

I know of one mackerel fisherman in Cornwall who smokes the fish in disused oil-drums, rather than a brick smokehouse or the whisky barrels used in Scotland, and produces superb results.

Mackerel has a beautiful texture and a strong flavour, but it must be eaten very fresh, and many of the fishing towns on the south coast of Devon and Cornwall will supply freshly caught mackerel. Because it is so common in this region, there are many people who smoke the fish on a small scale (just as fishermen smoke sprats in East Anglia). Cornish smoked mackerel is a great treat, and not too expensive either. Small fresh mackerel are best simply grilled, while the large ones can be split, filled with a stuffing and baked in foil. In Cornwall they also make soused mackerel. Normally this is mackerel (gutted and beheaded but otherwise left whole), baked slowly in a mixture of white vinegar and water, flavoured with peppercorns, bayleaves and fennel, but in Cornwall a mixture of cold tea (without milk) and vinegar is sometimes used.

PILCHARDS

The European pilchard (*Sardina pilchardus*) is a close relative of the herring, and its Latin name is a reminder that young pilchards are known by another common name – Sardines. Like the herring, the pilchard is a seasonal migratory fish, but it lacks the robustness of its common relation, being delicate and soft skinned. There was a prolific pilchard fishery off the Cornish coast during the Middle Ages and vast numbers were caught during their late summer visits to the waters off St Ives and other ports.

By the 19th century the pilchard fishery was a vital and profitable trade in the west country. Wilkie Collins observed and recorded it in *Rambles Beyond Railways* (1851) with his customary skill. It begins on the Cornish cliffs in late August. A stranger walking there might see a man:

'*standing on the extreme edge of a precipice, just over the sea, gesticulating in a very remarkable manner, with a bush in his hand; waving it to the right and left, brandishing it over his head, sweeping it past his feet – in short, apparently acting the part of a maniac of the most dangerous character. It would add considerably to the startling effect of this sight on the stranger if he were told, while beholding it, that the insane individual was paid for flourishing the bush at the rate of a guinea a week. And if he, thereupon, advanced a little to obtain a nearer view of the madman, and then observed on the sea below (as he certainly might) a well-manned boat, turning carefully to right and left exactly as the bush turned right and left, his mystification would probably be complete, and the time would arrive to come to his rescue with a few charitable explanatory words.*'

That man on the cliffs was 'the huer' and the bush he waved was a gorse branch with a piece of white linen tied to it. His job was to scan the surface of the water for the characteristic reddish stain that marked the shoal of pilchards, and to direct the boats towards the shoal with his semaphore signals.

Seine-netting was the main method used for catching the fish, with the boats working in teams. Once the men in the first boat saw the signal from the cliffs and neared the shoal, they moved quickly to surround it; a smaller boat, 'the lurker', guarded the gap to prevent the fish from escaping, and finally a third boat, 'the voyler', went inside the circle and drew the pilchards together so that the whole seine and its contents could be hauled from the water by men called 'blowsers'.

Nearly all the pilchards were salted, packed into barrels and exported. Nothing from the curing process was wasted: the oil drained from the fish went

The old name for pilchards, used in the 16th century, was 'pylcher' or 'pilchar' and it is sometimes known as the gypsy herring. Because it is a frail fish with a high fat content it travels badly and if exported it had to be preserved by salting or smoking. Nowadays it is still unusual to find fresh pilchards sold in shops at any distance from the areas where they are caught.

In the 16th century there was a great trade in smoked pilchards to Spain. They were called, in Spanish, fumados – a word which became corrupted in English to 'fair maids'.

As well as fishing for mackerel and pilchards, west country fishermen used to go out in search of herrings in small sail boats. (Reproduced by kind permission of The Museum of English Rural Life, University of Reading)

You will not see a sight like this at Brixham fish market today, but it is still a flourishing centre for fishing and fish trading. (Reproduced by kind permission of Brixham Museum and The Museum of English Rural Life, University of Reading)

It is a pity that the nearest most of us come to pilchards these days are the tins of fish swamped in tomato sauce. These pilchards are caught mainly off the coast of South Africa.

to the leather tanners and was used as an 'illuminant'; the skimmings from the water in which the fish were washed were bought by soap boilers, and any broken or damaged fish were sold off for manure.

Although most of the pilchards ended up in barrels the fishermen were able to claim some of the catch as part of their wages. The west country was a poor area and the people needed the food for the winter when there was little work, and less money. They would eat some of the pilchards fresh as a dish called 'dippy', in which the fish were simmered with potatoes and thin cream. But most of them were preserved either by salting or smoking, and, for short-term preserving, they were dried out in the sun or pickled in vinegar, which kept them from spoiling for a few days. Alternatively, the fish would simply be split open, dusted with salt, pepper and sugar, left overnight, then 'scrowled' or grilled over an open fire.

Quite suddenly, just before the First World War, pilchards began to disappear from the Cornish coast. Nobody is sure why this happened, but it put an end to the pilchard fishery. The fish still appear unpredictably and in small numbers, sometimes in the North Sea, sometimes in the English Channel, and, in ports like Brixham, you can occasionally buy them if the fishermen have been lucky. Plenty of fresh 'sardines' are sold in London and in fish shops all over the country, but these mostly come from the Mediterranean as do canned sardines which are common everywhere.

One pilchard recipe that should be preserved is *Stargazey Pie*. The name alone is intriguing: it refers to the design of the pie and the appearance of the fish. They are put in whole arranged in a geometric pattern, like spokes in a wheel. Then a pastry cover is put over the bodies leaving the heads exposed – gazing starwards. Under the blanket of pastry there might be pulp from the cider press, pickled rock samphire, pieces of fat bacon, all held together with a rich egg custard.

This design is a delightful example of culinary cunning. The heads of the fish can't be eaten, but they contain valuable oil that would be lost if they were cut off. So rather than cover the heads with pastry, which would be wasteful, they are left exposed, and the oil drains back into the body of the fish as the pie cooks.

In the past, stargazey pie was often made in a long strip, with the fish lying next to one another but separated by pastry. This method was used for pies sold in the markets; it was simple to cut the strip into any length containing the required number of fish.

CRABS

Living as I do in East Anglia, I am biased in my belief that Norfolk crabs are the best in the land. But there's no denying that Devon and Cornwall are close competitors. West country crabs generally are much bigger than those from East Anglia (see p. 65) and are the most common shellfish in that region.

Three west country crabmen with a sample of their catch. Compared with East Anglian crabs, these are monsters. (Reproduced by permission of Ken Browse)

Brixham is *the* centre for crabs, and, if you buy one, treat it exactly as described on p. 66. If you want to take it home and make a dish out of it, try buttered crab as an evening snack.

SALMON

Quite a considerable poundage of salmon is caught from the rivers of Devon and Cornwall, usually identified on local menus with its river: Taw salmon, Exe salmon and so on. And it is often prepared in ways which bring together other local specialities. For instance, poached salmon will be simmered in west country cider with herbs, and the liquor enriched with Devonshire cream.

Crab fishermen not only needed the skills of their own trade, but had to work as basket-makers as well, providing their own equipment. (Reproduced by kind permission of W. J. Brunell and Ken Browse of Brixham)

CIDER

A disused stone wheel and harness in a Herefordshire orchard. (Reproduced by kind permission of The Museum of English Rural Life, University of Reading)

First, a warning: the word 'cider' derives from the Latin *sicera*, meaning strong drink. And your first taste of true cider, the 'scrumpy' made in a few farmhouses and by a few small firms, can be devastating – the smell alone can set your head spinning.

The process of pressing and fermenting apples has gone on for centuries in those parts of Britain which are fertile and warm enough to sustain orchards. Cider-making was introduced from France in the 12th century, and, naturally enough, it was in the fertile valleys of Kent and Sussex where cider was first made in this country. The idea soon spread, and today we tend to associate the western regions of England with the drink. A healthy rivalry has grown up between the border counties of Hereford, Monmouth and Gloucestershire, and Somerset, Devon and Cornwall in the south-west.

To begin with there were no orchards, and the apples themselves were nothing like the ones we pick today. They were crab- or hedge-apples planted in hedgerows along the edges of fields. The cider they yielded was very strong, smoothed with honey and often spiced. Then in the early part of the 17th century Lord Scudamore, a man who loved and devoted his life to cider, started to experiment. Much of his estate at

Packing a cider press or 'cheese' with apples in Herefordshire. (Reproduced by kind permission of The Museum of English Rural Life, University of Reading)

The traditional method of pressing apples, still used by some cider makers. (Supplied by The Aspall Cyder House)

Kentchurch in Herefordshire was turned over to apple orchards. He planted trees scientifically, worked at grafting and after years of work produced Scudamore's Arab, the most famous redstreak cider apple of its day. Scudamore and his apples were even celebrated in poetry:

Of no Regard, 'till Scudamore' skilful Hand
Improve'd her, and by Courtly discipline
Taught her the Savage Nature to forget:
Hence styl'd the Scudamorean Plant.

(*Cyder* by John Philips, 1708)

John, Viscount Scudamore. An engraving dated 1642. (Supplied by Bulmers Cider Co)

Cider apples have a sweet juice and an acid pulp, whose malic acid content is essential for good cider. Early cider apples had marvellous, evocative names, the first of which were the Moile, White Swan, Slack-My-Girdle and French Longtail. Later there was Redstreak, Redstreak-Blackstreak, Sweet Coppin, Yarlington Mill, Kendrik Wilding, Foxwhelp and many others. These apples were literally, the fruit of years of patient labour. In recent years the scene has changed completely. Those large trees with their twisted, tangled branches took up too much room, were inconvenient for picking, and uneconomical. So they have been uprooted and replaced with squat bush-like trees that are easier to manage and to pick from and can be crammed closer together. It is all for the heaviest crop in the smallest space.

(Reproduced by permission of Coates Cider Co)

The time for cider-making has always been late autumn, between September and Christmas – 'the black end of the year', as it is sometimes called. In Scudamore's Hereford and the neighbouring border counties the traditional method has always been to crush the apples between heavy stone wheels, to one of which is harnessed a horse moving slowly, hour by hour, round the mill as the apples are loaded in. The resulting pulp is then packed into thick horsehair mats which are set into a screw press usually made of iron or stone. The juice runs out quickly into barrels or vats.

(Reproduced by permission of Gaymers Cider Co)

In 1296 one Simon de Monte was fined at Wakefield for failing to collect crab-apples for the lord of the manor, who was then short of two hogsheads of cider.

In the west country the process is rather different. Once the apples have been crushed in a similar way, the pulp is spread onto straw or wooden racks and cloths and a large sandwich or 'cheese' is made by laying these one on top of the other. Once this is set into a wooden press the juice begins to leak out, but the mechanics and

A load of apples being tipped out ready for pressing.
(Reproduced by kind permission of Bulmers Cider Co)

eggshells, milk, cream, even sheep's blood might be put into the vats to clear the cider as it was fermenting or 'working'. A man would put his ear to the cask to listen to the 'singing'.

Three hundred years ago Lord Scudamore started the idea of putting cider into heavy glass wine-bottles that were strong enough to resist bursting and the jolts of long road journeys. Today, fizzy, sweet and golden bottled cider is big business. The commercial cidermakers – Bulmer's, the Taunton Cider Company and

(Reproduced by permission of Bulmers Cider Co)

design of the press mean that it is a much slower process than the pressing in the border counties.

Cider in the vats used to be subjected to all manner of tricks. Stories of rats and other animals being dipped into the cider help perpetuate the myths about the effects of scrumpy, and other strange items like

Cider-making equipment at the Aspall Cyder House in Suffolk. (Photograph by Trevor Wood)

(Reproduced by permission of the Aspall Cyder House)

Reproduced by permission of The Taunton Cider Co)

others – produce thousands of gallons, crushing around 100 tons of apples a day during harvest time. I must admit that I find their products for the most part pleasant but innocuous. Much more interesting are the flagons produced by smaller enterprises in different parts of the country: from Luck's of Biddenden in Kent and Weston's of Ledbury in Hereford to Aspall Cyder from Stowmarket in Suffolk. Their cider is easy to find in local off-licences and pubs; it is still, clear and potent.

drinkers and even unpleasant for palates weaned on much milder stuff. Not surprisingly, it has produced a crop of rosy stories about prodigious quantities consumed – can you imagine drinking 35 pints in a day! – and of chronic after-effects. Scrumpy is still there to be tasted, but you will have to look hard, ask questions and do a fair lot of travelling. Don't forget the warning though; there's hardly a drink in the world which can produce such drastic physical effects in such a short time.

The Aspall Cyder House. (Photograph by Trevor Wood)

But the real rough cider, the true scrumpy, is harder to find. Only a few pubs still sell it, partly because it is not an economic proposition and partly because it has always been a suspect liquor – too strong for most

(Reproduced by permission of Merrydown Wine Co)

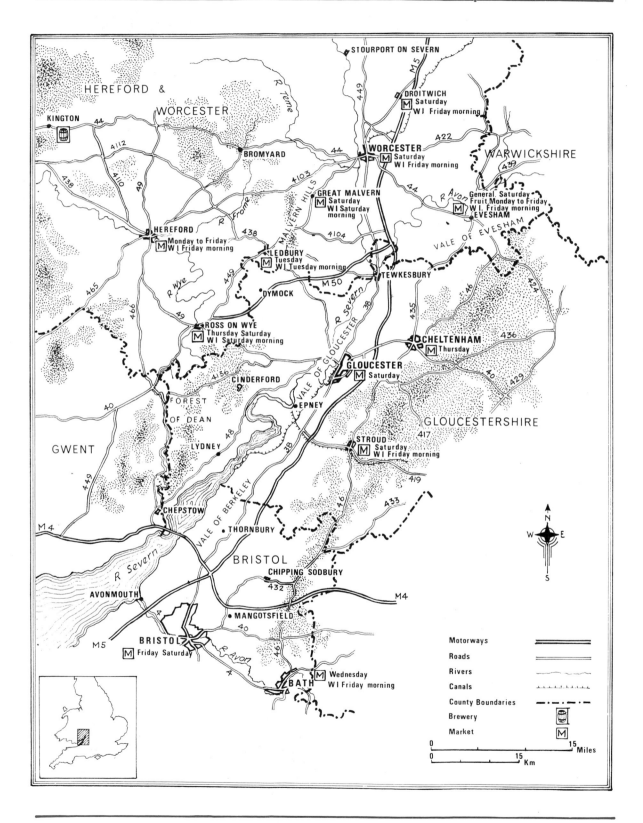

STOURPORT ON SEVERN

HEREFORD &
WORCESTER

R. Teme

M5

DROITWICH
Saturday
W I Friday morning

KINGTON

A44

449

A4112

A422

WARWICKSHIRE

BROMYARD

A44

WORCESTER
Saturday
W I Friday morning

A439

A438

A110

A49

R. Frome

A103

MALVERN HILLS

GREAT MALVERN
Saturday
W I Saturday
morning

A44

R. Avon

General. Saturday
Fruit. Monday to Friday
W. I. Friday morning
EVESHAM

HEREFORD
Monday to Friday
W I Friday morning

A438

A104

VALE OF EVESHAM

A465

R. Wye

A449

LEDBURY
Tuesday
W I Tuesday morning

A46

A424

A466

A49

DYMOCK

M50

R. Severn

A38

TEWKESBURY

A435

ROSS ON WYE
Thursday Saturday
W I Saturday morning

A436

VALE OF GLOUCESTER

CHELTENHAM
Thursday

A436

A40

A429

A136

CINDERFORD

GLOUCESTER
Saturday

A40

FOREST
OF DEAN

EPNEY

GLOUCESTERSHIRE

GWENT

A48

LYDNEY

A38

A417

STROUD
Saturday
W I Friday morning

A419

A449

VALE OF BERKELEY

A46

A433

CHEPSTOW

M4

THORNBURY

R. Severn

BRISTOL

N

W   E

S

CHIPPING SODBURY

AVONMOUTH

A432

M4

A4

MANGOTSFIELD

A40

M5

BRISTOL
Friday Saturday

A4

R. Avon

A4

A36

BATH
Wednesday
W I Friday morning

Motorways	━━━━━━
Roads	────────
Rivers	～～～～
Canals	⊦⊦⊦⊦⊦⊦⊦
County Boundaries	─·─·─·─
Brewery	🛢
Market	Ⓜ

0   15
|_____| Miles
0   15
|_____| Km

SEVERNSIDE AND THE VALE OF EVESHAM
HEREFORD, GLOUCESTER, WORCESTER, AND AVON

The apple orchards of the Vale of Evesham and Herefordshire are in full blossom during May, and provide one of the most pleasing sights in the English countryside. (Photograph reproduced by kind permission of Bulmers Cider Company and Derek Evans.)

This region is known, quite rightly, as the heart of England. It is a fertile area with a warm climate engendered by the Gulf Stream, and it is famous for its apple orchards in the Vale of Evesham, and its grazing. The river Severn, which cuts through the region, also sustains a rich crop of regional foods. It is this combination of land and river foods which characterizes the heart of England.

The rich, heavy soil is ideal for apple orchards, although it is less good for other fruit, and its fertility suits the crops of asparagus that grow in the Vale as well as the hops which are found in Hereford. Because the soil tends to be heavy it is better for grazing and pasture rather than arable farming. In the south of the region, the dairy cattle produce milk for cheese like Double Gloucester, for which this area is famous. And the locally named Hereford cattle produce some of the best beef in the country. Pigs were once put to root about in the orchards for windfall apples, and although this is less commonly practised today, the custom has left us some fine, local pork specialities like Bath chaps.

BREWERIES

This area of Britain is a brewing wilderness, which is surprising since it is not only one of the main hop-growing regions but also has a strong tradition of malting and brewing. Only one small brewery serves to provide locally-brewed beer.

PENRHOS BREWERY
Penrhos Court, Lyonshall, Kington, Hereford.
This new brewery is mentioned in detail on p.142. It is centred at Penrhos Court an ancient building complex which is being systematically restored, and the brewer produces a small quantity of excellent bitter which is available in quite a number of pubs around Hereford. Try *The Saracen's Head* in Hereford itself or *The Burton Hotel* in Kington.

One of the best places to drink Penrhos beer is The Burton Hotel in Kington. Left to right: Mr. Bert James, Ian Ferguson, Mr. Alf Price (aged 81). (Photograph by Trevor Wood)

An impression of Penrhos Court as it may have looked. It is hard to recognize today, but it may yet return to something near its original state (Reproduced by kind permission of Martin Griffiths and Penrhos Court)

Penrhos Court stands on a hill between the villages of Lyonshall and the ancient border town of Kington close to the ruins of Lyonshall Castle. The earliest part of the Court, the original cruck house with its large curving timbers was probably built about 1280 during the reign of Edward I. It is an example of a regional carpentry style found only in western Herefordshire.

The river Severn and the smaller rivers and streams are fruitful too. Every spring shoals of tiny elvers, the small fry of the eel, make their way up the river and are relished by local people. The Severn is also a fine salmon river, and the fish are often caught using traditional traps.

This part of England is also rich in food from other areas. It's central position gave the city of Bath a high reputation for the variety of its food. To the west there was Wales with its mutton and fish, to the east the Cotswolds and their soft fruit, to the south the cheese and cider of Somerset, and from Cornwall came fish and clotted cream. Today, Bath still sustains its reputation.

The Vale of Evesham is not only famous for its food. It can boast some fine cathedrals and a scenic beauty which, at best, is hard to match.

EELS AND ELVERS

Eels have one of the most complicated life cycles of any sea creature. They breed in the Sargasso sea at a depth of about 600 fathoms, and once the larvae have hatched they begin a three-year journey of thousands of miles, across the Atlantic to western Europe. As they reach the coastal waters in the autumn of the third year, they begin to change into young eels or elvers. In the following spring the elvers move into the rivers on the western coast of Britain. They form vast transparent strings or 'eel-fare' (from which we get the world elver) which are extraordinary to see. The movement of elvers in clear water has been described as the current running in the wrong direction, for they always swim against the tide, clinging tenaciously to rocks and stones and leap-frogging over each other. The river Severn is a vast funnel which takes in huge numbers of these tiny transparent eels (they are no more than two-and-a-half inches long).

A mass of frothing elvers caught from the Severn. (Photograph by John L. Jones)

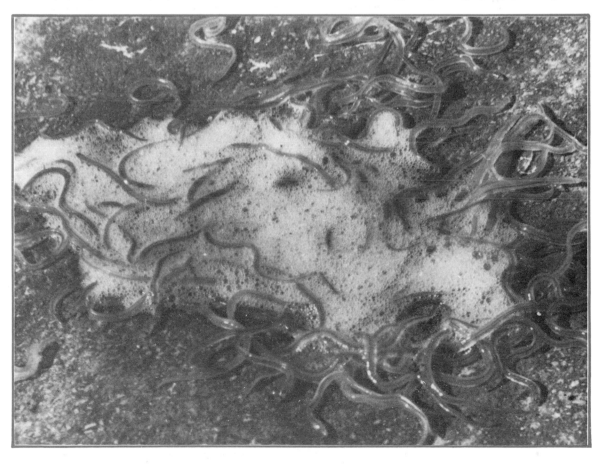

A camera-shy woman holds up a well-used elver net on the river bank at Ashleworth, one of the main elver fishing centres on the Severn. (Reproduced by kind permission of The Museum of English Rural Life, University of Reading)

After the last war the Ministry of Agriculture asked owners of waters in the Severn to take more elvers in order to increase the eel population in other parts of the country. The situation is very different today. Most of the elvers caught in the Severn are exported to Europe and Japan, where they are bred to full-sized eels. This has created something of an elver crisis and the Severn River Authority is now anxious to control catches.

Along the Severn valley elvers have been a local speciality for many hundreds of years (in the 1748 edition of Daniel Defoe's *Tour through the Whole Island of Britain*, he mentions elver cakes made at Keynsham on the outskirts of Bristol) and they are caught during the spring tides of March and April. The Elver Fishing Act of 1876 decreed that they should only be caught between March 1st and April 25th and they are unique in that they are the only fish fry which may be legally caught as food.

Elver fishing is a craft with its own language, equipment and lore. In many Severnside towns and villages like Ashleworth, Epney, Framilode and Elmore, the elver fishermen set out at dusk armed with a simple fine-meshed scoop-net usually made of cheese-cloth, two forked 'tealing sticks', a bucket, a lamp and a sack. Each man heads for a special vantage point on the bank, called 'the tump'. These tumps are highly valued, often handed down from generation to generation of fishermen from the same family. They have to be sited where the river is flowing strongly as elvers hardly ever enter slack water. The men stand on the bank until the cry of 'tide' is heard, a cry that is taken up and passed on from man to man. Then they have to wait, with their nets ready, for about an hour until the tide turns to ebb. Then the nets go into the water and the lamp is suspended above to draw the elvers, like moths, towards the light and into the net. Once in the net the elvers are tipped into the bucket. In *About Chepstow* (1952), I. Waters describes the sight of a bucket of freshly-caught elvers, '*Once in the pail the elvers froth like newly drawn beer and a few inches of elvers will quickly form an inch of foam . . .*'

You can buy the slimy, thread-like elvers during the season from Gloucester market and, if you can establish a friendly contact, from the fishermen who work the Severn valley. Take a sack or even an old pillow case to collect the elvers in, and when you get home wash them several times in salt water. There are several ways of eating elvers: first of all they can be floured and deep-fried like whitebait; in Epney they are fried in bacon fat until they turn milky white, then beaten eggs are stirred in and the 'omelette' is eaten with bacon, and a mug of cider to wash it down. Elvers can also be put into a pie and covered with hot-crust pastry, as they did in Keynsham in the 18th century, or they can be turned into a thick cheese after slow-cooking in a cloth with herbs and onions and pressing into a dish.

Easter Monday is the great day in the elver-fishing calendar. Each year, in villages like Epney and Frampton-on-Severn, there is an elver-eating contest. In 1977 on the village green at Frampton, which is the longest in England, twenty-two-year-old Keith Lane from Sandyleaze near Gloucester achieved a world record by swallowing a pound of elvers (about 700 in all) in 31 seconds.

This may strike outsiders as sheer gluttony or a criminal waste of potentially fine eels, but the elver is so deeply entrenched in the traditions of this region that it is bound to engender rituals of some kind.

Two champion elver-eaters, Liz Butcher and Gordon Pack displaying their talents at Frampton-on-Severn. (Photographs by Leslie Leach)

SALMON

In 1639, John Smyth of Nibley wrote, '*Howbeit at certain places and seasons in lakes or pools (in the Severn) any stranger may with a Becknet or Ladenet, fish.*' According to J. N. Taylor this Ladenet was probably the ancestor of the 'lave net' still used on the Severn for catching salmon. The lave net is virtually unique to the Severn (it is rarely used on the Usk and the Wye). It's rather like a very large elver net, with a Y-shaped frame and the net is slung from the two arms or 'rimes'. It is a very old method of trapping salmon, a long, and often risky occupation for one man on his own.

The fisherman needs the clean sandbanks and tidal pools of the lower Severn for his craft, not the evil mud of much of the estuary. And he has to wait until the tide has retreated before he can begin to look for the fish locked in the pools and searching for a way out. He watches for the signs of salmon, then moves swiftly, running ahead of the fish, cutting it off and scooping it out of the water with his net. This technique can only work when the sand is clean and firm underfoot, and the water clear. It is quite specific, and perfectly suited to the waters where it is used.

Sometimes a fisherman would make an artificial diversion of the main stream, and stand, with water up to his thighs, waiting with his net for hours until the salmon sped through the gulley at about 30 miles per hour. It is easy to forget that men earned their living in such precarious ways. The hours of waiting, the cold, and the constant threat of being stranded by the tide or caught in a sudden blanket of fog made it grim, unromantic work.

Between April and August another method of salmon catching is seen on the Severn: basket traps. There are two types, 'putchers' and 'kypes', both of which are large wicker funnels set up across the estuary to ensnare the fish. The putcher traps are made of willow and hazel woven into a funnel five-and-a-half feet long and tapering from thirty inches at the opening to a few inches at

A visit to Gloucester Folk Museum is essential for anyone interested in the fishing traditions of the Severn. It contains a fascinating selection of fishermen's nets and equipment, and in addition you can get a copy of J. N. Taylor's 'Guide to the Severn Fishery Collection'.

The lave net is still used on a small scale for catching salmon in the River Severn. It is a type of 'push net', once very common throughout Britain, but used less and less today because of the small number of licences issued for this type of fishing. (Photograph by John L. Jones)

the butt. Ranks of these traps set up on permanent frames are extremely effective. The principle is simple. On a fast ebb tide the salmon hurtles into the putcher and gets stuck, like a cork in a bottle. All the fisherman has to do is visit his putchers regularly and extricate any salmon that they are holding.

A 'weir' or row of putchers set up across the Severn estuary to trap salmon. (Photograph by John L. Jones)

Kype traps are much bigger than putchers and are designed rather differently, but they are just as effective for catching salmon. (Photograph by John L. Jones)

Kype traps are much bigger, wider at the opening and with two smaller sections of much finer weave fitted onto the butt end. These traps are staked in a long row across the estuary with a sea hedge of withy and hazel on either side of the row to channel the fish towards the open funnels. These kype traps will pick up anything from the largest salmon or conger eel to the smallest sprat (sturgeon have even been caught in kype traps.)

These long-surviving traditions on the Severn may not continue much longer. The fishermen cannot now get local supplies of withy needed to weave the traps; modern farming methods and new drainage schemes have almost obliterated the willow that once grew so freely in the region. And there is another, more sinister threat to the fishermen. If the proposed Severn Barrage is constructed, it will dramatically alter the conduct of the estuary. And if as a result of this barrage (intended to generate hydro-electric power from giant turbines) the ebb tides become slower and the low tides do not fall low enough, putchers and kypes simply will not work. They will end up as show pieces in Gloucester Folk Museum, deprived of their function and usefulness.

The season for the lave net fishermen is from early February to the middle of August. Traditionally they worked as farmers as well as fishermen, and the state of the river often hurried them away from their fields at critical haymaking times. Recently, the increasing popularity of silage-making has made their double-life easier. Silage-making is a much more weather-proof form of grass harvesting, and this is especially important in the unpredictable weather of the Severn estuary.

A salmon which has eluded the row of wicker traps across the Severn estuary, but is stranded in the mud nearby. (Photograph by John L. Jones)

A fine Wye salmon on display in a Hereford fish shop. (Photograph by Trevor Wood)

It is claimed that Severn salmon are moister than those from the river Wye on account of their longer spell in tidal waters, but this you can judge for yourself because both are sold in fish shops in the area. You have only to go to Hereford or Gloucester to find marvellous specimens on display. The simplest and favourite local method of cooking them is poaching. (The ambiguity of the word is well understood in these parts. As one fisherman said, 'I've never poached a salmon; they give themselves up.') But if you want to poach a salmon for yourself the way is to cook it whole, wrapped in a cloth and put into a fish kettle. Let the water come to the boil, then leave the fish to cook in the cooling water.

LAMPREYS

One of the creatures which sometimes finds its way into kype traps is the sea lamprey (*Petromyzon marinus*), which should not be confused with the

One of the old local names for the sea lamprey was 'nine-eyes'. The number nine comes from adding the seven pairs of gill slits to the two eyes proper. The lamprey was also known as 'the prid' or 'the pride', a term used by Izaac Walton in his 17th century fishing classic 'The Complete Angler'. (Photograph by John L. Jones)

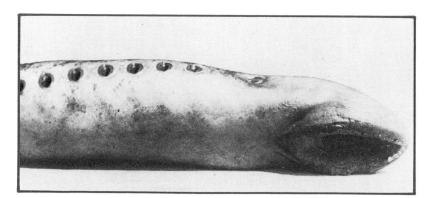

A huge lamprey pie (looking like a cake) was sent to the present Queen on the occasion of her accession to the throne. It was a traditional symbol of loyalty from the burghers of Gloucester. (Photograph by John L. Jones)

lampern or river lamprey (*Lampetra fluviatilis*). The lamprey is a primitive eel-like fish, a jawless parasite that latches onto other fish with its powerful sucker, and hitch-hikes into the waters of the Severn estuary.

It was highly prized in the middle ages, and it remained a delicacy right up to the 19th century. Although its flesh is edible, it is very rich and fatty, and best eaten during the winter months. But it isn't a fish that is sold or eaten except on rare occasions.

ASPARAGUS

The Vale of Evesham is famous for its asparagus, and this is one of the main regions where the crop is grown. The fat, green asparagus grown in Norfolk, Suffolk and Essex is just as good but is easily distinguishable from the thinner stems from the Worcestershire fields.

Asparagus has been cultivated since the time of the ancient Greeks. It came to Britain with the Romans, and has become naturalized in waste places and sand dunes. It has always been something of a luxury vegetable, partly because of its fine flavour and its treasured, brief season, and partly because of the way it is cultivated. The problem for asparagus growers is that the crop is permanent. The land it grows on can be used for nothing else once the season from May to early July is over. It is also a crop which is so delicate that it has to

The Romans cultivated asparagus with great care and were able to produce sticks which weighed three pounds each. They overcame the seasonal drawbacks of the vegetable by drying the asparagus heads, storing them, and simply boiling them in water for a few minutes when they were needed.

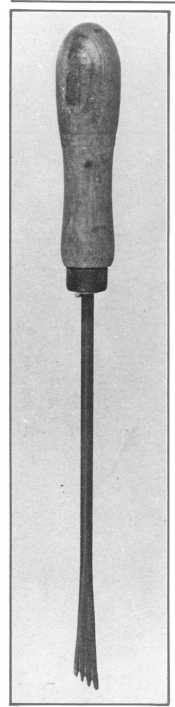

be harvested by hand with special asparagus knives. Consequently it is, in commercial terms, increasingly uneconomical, and the 2,000 acres of the Vale once covered with asparagus has now dwindled to less than 100. Many growers firmly believe that the trade will be gone in less than 15 years from now.

But while the asparagus is still grown it should be enjoyed. There's still enough harvested for bunches to turn up for sale in petrol stations and on roadside stalls. In a pub called *The Round of Grass* (i.e. the bunch of asparagus) there is a feast each year at the end of the cropping season, and local connoisseurs give their verdicts on the crop, while seeking what they call 'the oyster' – the delicious morsel lodged at the bottom of the white part of the spear, considered to be the best part of all.

APPLES AND CIDER

The sight of apple blossom in the Vale of Evesham must be one of the most beautiful in the English countryside. Like Kent (see p. 35) this area is ideally suited to fruit growing, the climate is agreeable and the soil is fertile. All types of apple are grown in the Vale, not only cooking and eating varieties, but many cider apples as well. I have mentioned this in more detail on p. 114. The area around Hereford is especially good for cider. There are the big commercial cider-makers, like Bulmers, which is based in Hereford itself; there are smaller concerns, like Weston's of Ledbury who produce farm cider for sale in shops; and there are farms here and there which produce and sell small quantities of cider and advertise the fact with scribbled boards tucked into hedges or fixed on gateways.

Commercially grown asparagus is cut with a special long-stemmed knife with a short cutting edge. (Photograph reproduced by kind permission of The Museum of English Rural Life, University of Reading)

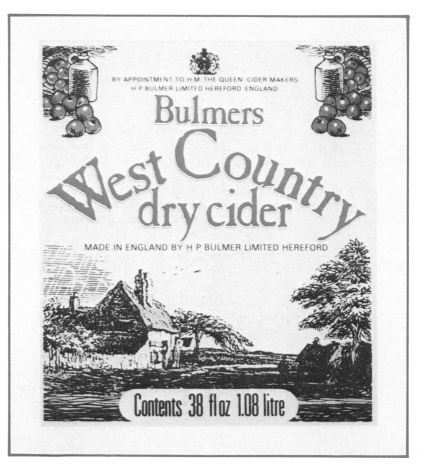

PEARS AND PERRY

Pears generally need a richer, moister soil than apples and they need a reliable warm climate. Dessert and stewing pears are grown mainly in Kent, although some are cultivated in the Vale of Evesham. But Worcester and Hereford are famous for their perry pears.

Perry is the fermented juice from certain varieties of pear which were introduced into this country around the time of the Norman Conquest. They look much less 'pear-shaped' than most of the dessert varieties and their names date back hundreds of years. There is the Yellow Huffcap, and the Thorn Pear, which was known in 1676, the Taynton Squash Pear, recorded in Thomas Andrew Knight's *Pomona Herefordensis*, and the Red Pear, which looks more like a ripe, red apple and has been known in Hereford and Worcester since Tudor times.

Unlike cider, perry is not blended but made from the juice of a single variety. Although cheap 'piriwhit' was mixed with ale and sold to labourers in the middle-ages and continued to be made alongside cider, perry has never had the popularity of its apple-based relative. In this country perry-making is a small scale activity, confined to a few farmers in the area. But there is a chance that interest in it may be revived for new perry pear orchards are now being established in nearby Somerset. In years to come, perry may once again become a more nationally popular drink.

Perry pears.

(Illustration by Carol Fowke)

(Reproduced by kind permission of Bulmers Cider Company)

HOPS

Next to Kent, Hereford and Worcester are the most important hop-growing areas in the country, and hop fields are a common sight throughout the region. But sadly this has not led to the survival of independent breweries, apart from Penrhos Court (see p. 120).

OLDBURY TARTS

These 'tarts' are actually pies. They are hand-raised with hot-crust pastry, like a pork pie, although the filling is not meat, but gooseberries sprinkled with Demerara sugar. The pies are covered with a pastry lid, baked and served warm or cold with a jug of cream.

Although Oldbury tarts seldom appear in public, they are sometimes featured on the menu at Thornbury Castle. (Supplied by Kenneth Bell)

Oldbury tarts are sometimes served in the grand surroundings of Thornbury Castle. The restaurant here, although best known for its French cooking, does feature a few local Severnside dishes as well.

CHEDDAR CHEESE

Cheddar cheese was first made in the area around the Cheddar Gorge in Somerset in the late 15th century. (Reproduced by permission of The Museum of English Rural Life, University of Reading)

CATTLE AND CHEESE

HEREFORD CATTLE

Hereford beef is arguably the best in the country, and the grazing in this part of the country is well-suited for beef production. The distinctive cattle, with their white faces, red markings and down-pointing horns, are a common sight in the meadows of Herefordshire and nearby counties. They thrive off grass, need very little in the way of cereals, and they mature early.

If the large joints of Hereford beef are hung properly, – for at least two weeks – the meat will be well-flavoured, tender and 'marbled' with areas of fat *among* the lean, which helps to prevent drying out during cooking.

GLOUCESTER CHEESE

Cheese has been made in Gloucestershire from earliest times, and developed into a cottage industry during the 17th century. On the level, heavy lands around the Severn Valley, the land was difficult to cultivate, so it was practical to turn it into grassland pasture and concentrate on dairy farming.

Until 1945, Gloucester cheese came in two forms: Single Gloucester and Double Gloucester. In *The Rural Economy of Gloucestershire* (1783), Marshall gives a long account of cheese-making in the area. The difference between the two types was mainly a question of the milk used. Double Gloucester cheese was made from the morning's milk with part of the evening's milk; the cheeses were made between May and September and weighed 15–25 lbs. Double Gloucesters needed to be ripened for several months. Single Gloucesters, on the other hand, were made from the morning's milk or from the skimmed evening's milk; they were much smaller (weighing 9–12lbs) and did not need much ripening. They were eaten mainly on the farm, while the Double Gloucesters ended up at the cheese fairs at Berkeley, Gloucester, Lechlade and Stow-on-the-Wold.

One of the most fascinating aspects of the old cheese-making was the way the cheeses were stored and matured in cheese chambers. The floors and shelves in these chambers were rubbed with bean tops, potato haulm, in fact any

A Hereford bull among a herd of Hereford cows, grazing in the Herefordshire countryside. (Reproduced by kind permission of The Museum of English Rural Life, University of Reading)

Many Gloucestershire farms still have items of traditional cheese-making equipment, presses, moulds and boxes, and also relics of cheese-chambers. There are also some fine examples in Gloucester Folk Museum and in Blaise Castle in Bristol.

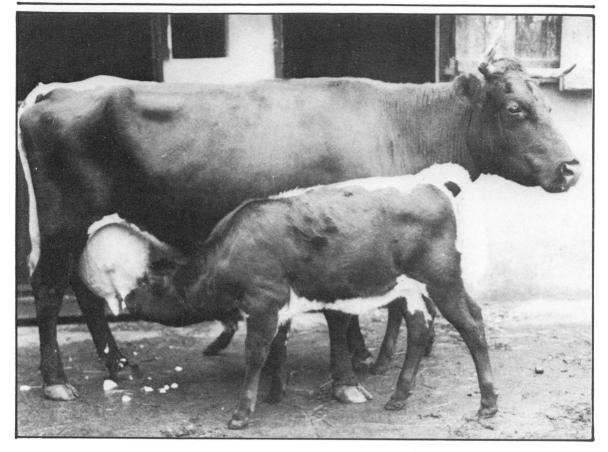

Shermanwood Primrose II, one of the Old Gloucester cattle owned by Charles and Monica Martell, mothering a calf. The success of the Martell's farming enterprise is that their herd of Old Gloucester cattle has increased to a commercially viable size. (Photograph reproduced by kind permission of Charles and Monica Martell)

One of the great sights of the 19th century on the Thames was the procession of barges piled high with bright red Gloucester cheeses on their way from Lechlade to London. In those days the outside of the cheese was painted with a mixture of India-red or Spanish-brown mixed with beer.

succulent vegetation that could be spared. The boards ended up black in colour and were then ready for the cheeses. Every two weeks the floors were scrubbed with fresh herbs to encourage the development of a blue coat on the cheeses. This would also have helped to keep the atmosphere moist and humid, and so prevent the rinds from drying out and cracking.

Single Gloucester cheese is not made these days, but Double Gloucester is still immensely popular. Until recently it had lost touch with its origins, for in Marshall's time the cheese was made from a breed of cattle called Old Gloucester. These cows, with black faces and a white streak running down the back, had almost disappeared from dairy farming until the Gloucester Cattle Society was re-formed. The champions of the society are Charles and Monica Martell, who not only breed the cows but have started to make authentic Gloucester cheese from the milk at their farm in Dymock. The milk from these cows is special because it has very small fat globules which give the cheese a fine texture.

I like this kind of enterprise. It is a serious-minded and enthusiastic attempt to restore some of our finer traditions of food and farming. The Martells care, and they want people to share not only their concern, but also their excitement about the cattle and the cheese made from the milk.

Double Gloucester is a fine cheese; it is silky and creamy with a rich delicate flavour. It is ideal for toasting and marvellous when eaten on its own – in a large piece. But when you buy it, make sure you are getting Gloucester because it is rather confusingly dyed orange like Leicestershire and red Cheshire.

CHEESE-ROLLING

It was once the custom in Randwick, Gloucester, to celebrate the advent of spring by decorating three large Gloucester cheeses with flowers and carrying them through the streets of the town to the church, where the cheeses were taken off their litters and rolled three times round the church before being eaten.

This ceremony no longer exists, but in some places cheese-rolling is still a traditional entertainment. One of the best-known sites is Brockworth in Gloucestershire, where, every Spring Bank Holiday Monday, Cooper's Hill is crowded with visitors who have come to see the event. A cheese packed in a strong wooden case is rolled down the precipitous slope of the hill, and the competitors run after it, rolling and tumbling on their way. The person who negotiates the tussocks and pot holes and wins the race, keeps the cheese.

It is said that cheese-rolling on this hill is an ancient custom, performed each year as a necessary ceremony for the maintenance of grazing rights on the common, but now it is simply a precarious challenge for the competitors and good entertainment for the spectators.

In the 19th century cheese-rolling sometimes accompanied the occasional scouring of The White Horse at Uffington. A cheese was rolled down the very steep slope of the coomb known as the Horse's Manger. Unlike the annual event on Cooper's Hill, the Uffington cheese-rolling has long since disappeared.

WORCESTERSHIRE SAUCE

In 1823, Mr William Perrins, a chemist from Evesham, formed a partnership with Mr John Wheeley Lea, who owned a similar shop in Broad Street, Worcester. It was the beginning of an association which is now world famous. To begin with it had nothing to do with sauce. In 1835 Lord Sandys, returning to Worcester from India, where he had been Governor of Bengal, walked into Lea and Perrins' shop with a recipe that he had acquired during his stay in the East.

'A First Introduction to Lea and Perrins.' No doubt the sauce was as enthusiastically received in the 19th century as it is today. (Reproduced by kind permission of Lea and Perrins)

There is a cupboard full of bottles in the board room of Lea and Perrins. It contains all the sauces produced by the company in various parts of the world. Some of the examples date back to the 1860s. My favourite is a bottle retrieved from a shipwreck in 1898. A tiny mollusc had drifted into the bottle, grown inside it, and consequently become too big to escape through the narrow neck. When the bottle was salvaged and the water removed the mollusc died, but its chalky remains are still at the bottom of the bottle. An imitation sauce made by a Japanese company in 1908 had the unlikely recommendation that it could be used in 'Hot and Cold Nrats, Roups, Ragouts, Btets, Cops, Steas and Pier Cutlets, Grayies and all Palad Dressing.'

The chemists duely made up the sauce, and, being curious men, made a few extra gallons for themselves. But it tasted so unpleasant that they took the stone jars down to their cellar and forgot about them. Much later, they found the jars, tasted the contents again and realized that the sauce had matured and was now superb. Lea and Perrins knew the original recipe and they knew how long the sauce needed to mature. In 1838 they started to manufacture it on a commercial scale, but were very careful to keep the essential details of the process a secret.

I don't think it is merely coincidence that Worcestershire Sauce should have been established in this area. Back in the Middle Ages crab-apples were planted in Worcestershire hedgerows and used to make verjuice; this was later replaced by a vinegar industry, linked with hop-growing, malting and brewing. And there were important salt-workings nearby as well. Two of the essential ingredients of the sauce (salt and vinegar) were already on hand. The necessary spices could be obtained from their own chemist shop. All that was needed was a suitable recipe for an independent local industry to emerge.

For 150 years Lea and Perrins have kept their secret, and the real details of the sauce are known to perhaps half a dozen employees in the factory. I have seen the door that conceals the mysteries of the sauce, but I have not seen beyond it. Some of the aspects of the process, however, don't need to be concealed. After the mixing of the ingredients the concentrated sauce is stored in oak-casks for a certain length of time (they do not even reveal whether it is a matter of weeks, months, or even years!) It is then processed, filtered and sterilized. (A mixture of salt, vinegar and acid should be 'self-sterile', no bacteria should be able to grow in the sauce, but recently workers at the factory have found that one bacterium has become immune. It is a 'lactobacillus', related to the bacteria which cause milk to go sour, and has been affectionately named *Lactobacillus Lea and Perrinus*!) After sterilization the sauce is ready

MARKETS

Quite a number of the most important foods from Severnside and the Vale of Evesham do not appear in the markets at all, for example cider and, at the other extreme, Worcestershire Sauce. Nevertheless the markets are worth visiting, especially those at Gloucester, Bath and Hereford.

BATH

General market,   *Wednesday*
WI market, Rivers Street   *Friday morning*

BRISTOL

General market, St Nicholas Market.   *Friday and Saturday*

CHELTENHAM

General market,   *Thursday*

DROITWICH

General market,   *Saturday*
WI market, Sacred Heart Parish Room, Worcester Road,   *Friday morning*

EVESHAM

General market,   *Saturday*
Fruit market,   *Monday – Friday*
WI market, Bewdley Street.   *Friday morning*

GLOUCESTER

General market,   *Saturday*

GREAT MALVERN

General market,   *Saturday*
WI market, Lytleton Rooms, Church Street.   *Friday morning*

HEREFORD

General market, Butter Market.   *Monday – Friday*
WI market, St Peter's Church House.   *Friday morning*

LEDBURY

General market,   *Tuesday*
WI market, St Katherine's Hall.   *Friday morning*

ROSS-ON-WYE

General market,   *Thursday and Saturday*
WI market, Edde Cross Street.   *Saturday morning*

STROUD

General market,   *Saturday*
WI market, The Shambles.   *Friday morning*

WORCESTER

General market,   *Saturday*
WI market, St Albans Church Hall, Deansway.   *Friday morning*

This isn't a brewery but a cool cellar at the Lea and Perrins factory where the sauce concentrate is stored in oak casks 'for a certain length of time'. (Photograph by Trevor Wood)

The sign above the original Lea and Perrins shop (Reproduced by kind permission of Lea and Perrins)

for bottling in those characteristic bottles with long narrow necks. The shape is important because the sauce forms a sediment and needs to be shaken before it can be used. So the bottles are only filled up to the neck, leaving a good space for shaking. Many of the fake Worcestershire Sauces neglect this detail.

Worcestershire Sauce has a long association with hangovers. Locally they make a 'prairie oyster' by flavouring a beaten egg with the sauce and there are many other variations, all claimed by their inventors to be the perfect cure. But the classic partnership is tomato juice and Worcestershire Sauce. Lea and Perrins actually produce a tomato juice cocktail, which originated at a brewing exhibition in 1938. Such occasions tend to produce a heavy crop of hangovers, and the Lea and Perrins stall was crowded each morning with requests for the classic cure. So the first commercial tomato juice cocktail was produced.

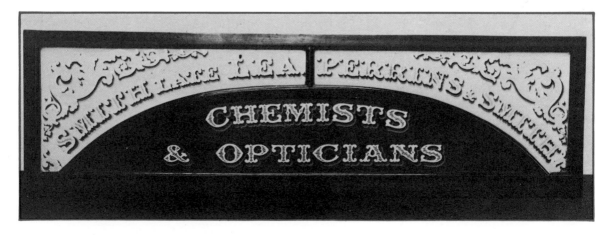

THE CITY OF BATH AND ITS FOODS

Bath, surely one of the most beautiful and elegant cities in England, has been famous ever since it was the Aquae Sulis of Roman times. It is known for its baths and its mineral water – long believed to have marvellous therapeutic qualities. And it is a good place for food too. It has produced more local specialities than any other English city other than London, and there's no sign that these will disappear in the near future.

BATH CHAPS

These are the cheek pieces of the pig, salted and smoked like hams, in fact they are sometimes cured alongside hams. They became well-known in Bath in the 18th century, because this city was near enough to the important pig and bacon countries of Wiltshire and, to a lesser extent, Gloucestershire to receive supplies regularly. Bath chaps were originally produced from Gloucester Old Spot pigs, which were long-jawed animals that fed on windfalls from the apple orchards in the area.

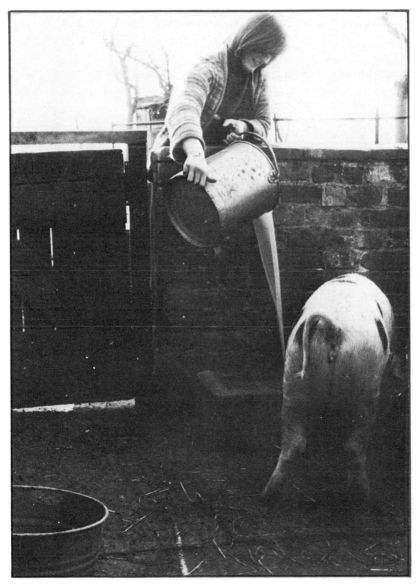

Although Bath was an important town in Roman times, it was relatively small. It occupied only 23 acres, whereas Roman London at that time spread over something like 330.

Gloucester Old Spot pigs were until quite recently a dying breed, mainly because they were not bred lean enough for today's butchers. However thanks to the efforts of Rare Breeds Survival Trust they are being reintroduced at least on a small scale.

Gloucester Old Spot pigs don't only feed on apple windfalls. Like all of their kind they are very adaptable. This animal is about to enjoy a feed of whey left over from cheese-making. (Reproduced by kind permission of Charles and Monica Martell and 'Farmers' Weekly')

(Reproduced by kind permission of The Meat and Livestock Commission)

The cheek pieces are first dry salted and then pickled in brine for about two weeks. Finally they should be smoked, although most of the Bath chaps I have seen in the west of England are sold unsmoked. Sometimes you can buy them uncooked, but normally they are already cooked and covered in breadcrumbs. Although the difference should be obvious to anyone, it is still worth checking with the butcher if the chap has been cooked or not.

Bath chaps can be eaten cold in slices with pickles, strong English mustard and potatoes, or eaten hot with broad beans or pease pudding and freshly made parsley sauce.

A pair of large Bath chaps, cooked and ready for carving. (Photograph by Trevor Wood)

BATH OLIVERS

Drunkenness and overeating were common in the 18th century among people rich enough to indulge themselves. And it became fashionable to visit spa towns like Bath to recuperate by drinking the mineral water and eating simple food. It was Dr W. Oliver, founder of the Bath Mineral Water Hospital, who in 1750 invented and gave his name to Bath Olivers. These are biscuits or crackers made from flour, butter, yeast and milk and they are delicious with a hunk of English cheese. The biscuits are pricked all over with a fork before baking, and authentic Bath Olivers have an imprint of their inventor's face on one side of each biscuit.

The firm of Fortt's produces Bath Olivers in very distinctive packets with a creamy-white label that echoes the colour of the biscuits inside. You can buy them everywhere in Bath, as well as throughout the country.

Bath Olivers were thought to be as beneficial in their own way as the celebrated Bath mineral water. (Photograph by Trevor Wood)

It is easy to identify a Bath Oliver because each biscuit is marked with a print of Dr. Oliver's face. (Reproduced by kind permission of Fortt's)

BATH BUNS

Dr Oliver is said to have been associated with another famous Bath food, the Bath bun. These are made from butter, flour, yeast, eggs and milk. They are a beautiful yellow colour when cut open and are always decorated with crushed-up lump sugar. Although Bath buns should not include currants, a few are often put on top with the sugar as an extra decoration.

A Bath bun, a cup of coffee and the tranquil atmosphere of the Pump Room in Bath. (Photograph by Trevor Wood)

In an attempt to emphasize its local connections, the restaurant in The Pump Room at Bath has 'carrots cooked in Bath mineral water' on its menu!

The place to eat Bath buns is The Pump Room in Bath. This peaceful hall has an unnerving atmosphere. The past is completely preserved here, and, although tourists flock in and out, it seems completely detached from the outside world. Bath buns on silver trays, chandeliers, a palm court trio of aging musicians playing as the people drink morning coffee; these are the features of The Pump Room.

SALLY LUNN CAKES

There is a spot in Lilliput Alley in Bath which many people believe was once the house and shop belonging to Sally Lunn, an 18th century woman who sold cakes in the streets of the city. No doubt she did really exist, but it seems likely that she cried her wares in West Country French: 'Solet Lune' – a good description of these cakes or buns which are round with a flat top and golden-yellow inside.

Sally Lunn cakes are made from a sweet yeasted dough, put in baking rings and allowed to rise for two hours. (In the past the dough might be left overnight.) The tops of the cakes are brushed with beaten egg yolk and baked in a hot oven until they are golden brown, well-risen and light. The traditional way to eat the cakes is to split them open while they are hot and stuff them with sweetened whipped cream.

In 'Modern Cookery for Private Families' (1845), Eliza Acton gives a recipe for 'solimemne' – a rich French breakfast cake – which is very like the recipes for Sally Lunn cakes that we know.

These cakes are still made in small numbers in Bath, especially at the Red House shop and restaurant. They are quite large, perhaps larger than you would expect, something like four inches across and six inches high.

Sally Lunn cakes in the snow. In the background is one of Bath's classic, elegant crescents. (Photograph by Trevor Wood)

HOME-BREWING

The John Thompson Brewery at Ingleby, Derby. (Reproduced by kind permission of John Thompson)

One of the side-effects of the recent revolution in British beer-drinking is that a number of pubs now serve their own beer, that is beer brewed on the premises, often by the landlord himself. Ten years ago it looked as if traditionally brewed beer might disappear altogether. Keg had arrived, and there were only a handful of commercial home-brewers grimly hanging onto their skills and their customers. But now the list is growing almost by the month; a tremendously hopeful sign for anyone who values variety in beer – differences in taste, flavour, strength and the effect on the drinker.

The tradition of brewing and the selling of beer goes back to the Middle Ages. At the beginning of the 14th century, for instance, London had 1,334 beer houses brewing their own beer; the term 'brewery', in fact, originally implied a place where beer was not only brewed but sold as well. These local breweries survived, and indeed thrived, so long as they supplied close-knit communities and while transport, or the lack of it, made the distribution of beer a costly and

The Miners Arms in Priddy, Somerset. (Reproduced by kind permission of Paul Leyton)

impractical business. But by the 19th century the big breweries in London, Burton-on-Trent and elsewhere were beginning to take over. Home-brewing took time, you could only produce small quantities of beer, and the business of running a pub as well made it much easier simply to fall in with the large brewers and let them take responsibility for brewing and supplying their own products.

By 1974 only four home-brewers were still in business in England: *The All Nations Inn* and *The Three Tuns*, both in Shropshire, *The Blue Anchor Inn* in Cornwall (where the beer they brew is called 'Spingo'), and *The Old Swan* at Dudley in Worcestershire. Then, in 1975, the tide turned and there are

Inspecting the vats in the brewhouse of The Masons Arms. (Reproduced by permission of The Masons Arms)

House Specialities

Mendip Snails
Priddy Paté
Seafood Mousse in Pastry Shells
Home Smoked Loin of Pork
Onion Soup with Cheddar Cheese Straws

Baked Severn Salmon with Shrimp Sauce
Priddy Oggy
(Pork sirloin and smoked pork in a
cheese pastry)
Fillet Steak Theodora
(cooked in butter, brandy and herbs with
peach and sweetcorn)
Chef's Steak and Kidney Pie
with
Mushrooms and Red Wine
Liberated Eve
(Pork from the Ribs, kidney and apple sauce)
Rabbit Pie with Pickled Pork

Miners' Delight
Chocolate Whisky Cake with
Drambuie Cream
Orange Conserve
Rum and Cherry Meringue

The Miners Arms offers a good range of regional food as well as its own beer.

now at least a dozen home-breweries scattered throughout the country. Some brew their beer just for the pub while others supply free-houses in their area. Some are not pubs at all, in spite of the name. *The Miner's Arms* at Priddy in Somerset, for example, is a restaurant whose owner, Paul Leyton, collects snails which he prepares and cooks himself. These, together with the beer, are the specialities of the place.

The Mendip snail is actually no more than the garden snail. In the west country they are described as 'wallfish'. (Illustration by Edward Arnor)

The flavour and potency of good home-brewed beer are quite unlike those of even the finest beer from the independent breweries. The beer brewed at Penrhos Court in Herefordshire, for instance, is very clean-tasting, thin, hoppy and deceptively mild. It's easy to imagine that you could drink a large number of pints with very little effect. But you quickly appreciate its strength as it produces a light-headed intoxication, not unlike the the effect of champagne.

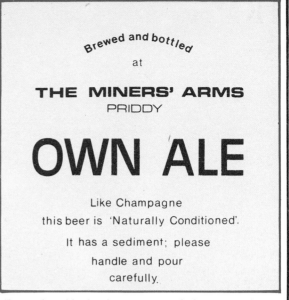

Brewed and bottled
at
THE MINERS' ARMS
PRIDDY

OWN ALE

Like Champagne
this beer is 'Naturally Conditioned'.
It has a sediment; please
handle and pour
carefully.

(Reproduced by kind permission of The Miners Arms)

Penrhos is a recent and quite unusual addition to the list of commercial home-breweries. It's not actually linked to a pub, but supplies a small number of pubs in and around Kington in Hereford – a county with no

Part of the brewery set up in one of the outbuildings at Penrhos Court. (Photograph by Trevor Wood)

An old wagon parked among the trees outside Penrhos Court. (Photograph by Trevor Wood)

other surviving brewery. The brewery uses its own spring water (which must surely contribute to the quality of the beer) it makes use of local hops (Hereford is the second largest hop-producing county in England) and it mills its own malt. Its beer is brewed for a small locality. But Penrhos brewery has made another contribution to the county. Penrhos Court to the outsider looks like a ruin; the main house and its outbuildings stand in a quadrangle around a cobbled area with a duckpond in the middle; but it is being restored. The main building is an early cruck house, parts of which date back to about 1280, and it has features belonging to a style of regional architecture peculiar to Herefordshire. The whole building complex is gradually being brought back to life. The tall

PENRHOS ALE

Jones's First Brew
brewed at
The Penrhos Brewery Kington

Part of the original Penrhos Court which is being systematically restored. (Photograph by Trevor Wood)

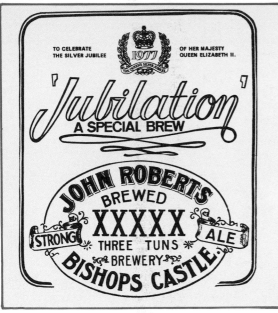

usefulness is vital and strong here; the regional architecture, the beer brewed in the old buildings and the tradition of hop-growing and brewing in the region are all linked together by one enterprise.

A barrel being transferred to the cellar at Bishop's Castle.

barn is already fitted out with brewing equipment which usually operates twice each week; another barn houses a restaurant and an outlying meadow is now a small market garden. The sense of locality and local

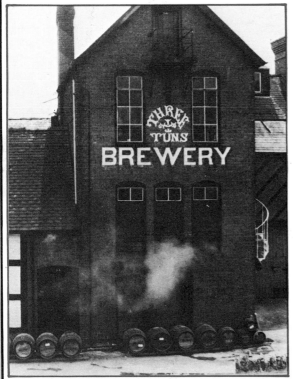

Part of The Three Tuns Brewery at Bishop's Castle

At the time of writing there are a dozen home-breweries in England and Wales, but the list is bound to increase.

Eliza Lewis, *All Nations Inn*, Coalport Road, Madeley, Shropshire.
Shirley Jones, *Blue Anchor Inn*, Coinagehall Road, Helston, Cornwall.
Godsons, Atherden Works, Lower Clapton Road, London E 5.
John Thompson, John Thompson Brewery, Ingleby, Derby.
Monty Raczkowski, *Fighting Cocks*, Corby Glen, Grantham, Lincolnshire.
Tom Litt, *Masons Arms*, South Leigh, Witney, Oxfordshire.
Paul Leyton, *Miners Arms*, Priddy, Wells, Somerset.
Gerry Lane, *Miskin Arms*, Pontyclun, Glamorgan.
Alan Mawdsley, *New Fermor Arms*, Rufford, Ormskirk, Lancashire.
Doris Pardoe, *Old Swan*, Netherton, Dudley, Worcestershire.
Peter Milner, *Three Tuns*, Bishop's Castle, Shropshire.
Martin Griffiths, Penrhos Court, Kington, Hereford.

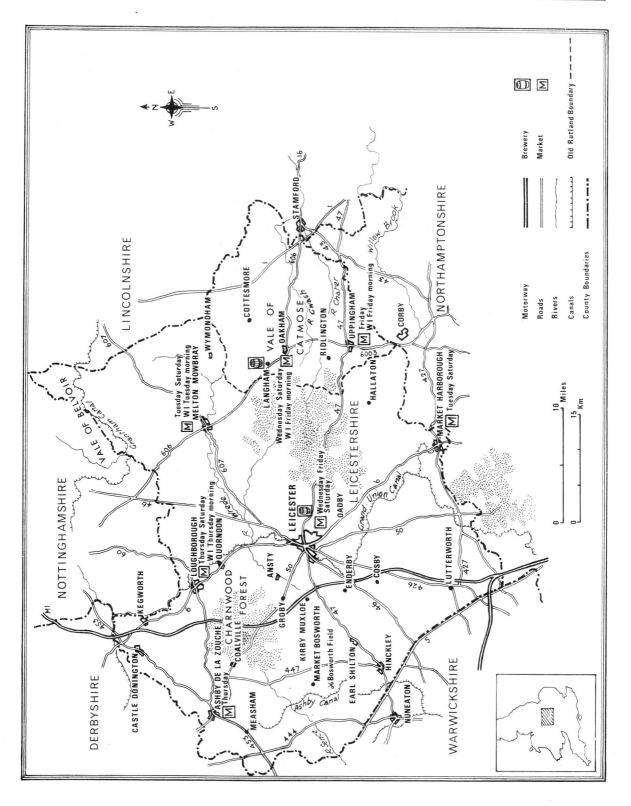

THE SHIRES
HUNT BREAKFASTS AND BRAWN SUPPERS

There is no strict geographical boundary to The Shires; it is a region defined by the customs and activities of one group of people, fox-hunting men. Roughly it is an area of the south and east midlands that always includes at its heart Leicestershire and the county once called Rutland. Its limits may extend to parts of Northamptonshire to the south, and Lincolnshire to the east, but it is essentially the territory of the Belvoir, Cottesmore, Quorn, Fernie and Pytchley – the Shires' Hunts.

It is a landscape that might have been made for riding and hunting; few trees and large rolling fields with low hawthorn hedges. Perfect steeplechase country, in fact. Yet it was not always like that. In the Middle Ages the fields were divided up into strips which were cultivated by villagers. By the end of the 15th century, however, some villages had been abandoned and the fields

The regional food associated with the Shires is mainly concentrated in Leicestershire and Rutland. The neighbouring counties of Northamptonshire and Lincolnshire are linked because of fox-hunting, and there is little in the way of traditional food to connect them.

(Reproduced by kind permission of Dickinson and Morris)

around others were being enclosed and transformed by landowners into more profitable pastures divided by hedges and ditches. This happened something like 200 years before the famous Enclosures Acts of the 18th century. But while the purpose of the land was altered the pattern of its past remained, and ridged fields are still one of the great features of the landscape. It was over these fields that the first organized fox hunts set off in earnest in the 1770s. The extra fences that had appeared during enclosure served only to provide greater challenge and excitement for the riders and horses.

No other sport has had such strong links with food as fox hunting in The Shires. Melton Mowbray alone, the centre of Quorn country, can claim to be the home of at least three great foods: the Melton Mowbray pork pie, Red Leicester cheese and Stilton cheese. The fields that were so suitable for hunting also made fine pastures for cattle, whose milk was turned into butter and cheese, and the whey from cheese-making was fed to pigs, whose sweet meat eventually found its way into pies.

The walls of many hotels in the Shires are bedecked with pictures and prints of fox-hunting and great huntsmen of the past, and the links between the sport and the food associated with it are still very strong.

The hunt breakfast was the great meal of those days; vast, time-consuming, and strictly for men with iron constitutions. How anyone could go out riding after such a feast of pies is astonishing. This tradition only survives now in occasional, formal Hunt Breakfasts put on by some hotels in the region once a year. But there is still great enthusiasm for, and popular concern with, food. You have only to listen to the talk in a Melton pub on market day to appreciate the fact. The locals have simpler feasts now, at the other end of the day; you might, for instance, hear a man joyfully inviting friends – and strangers too – to a brawn supper he is planning. And the grand pies and cheeses of the past are now the property of everyone.

MELTON MOWBRAY PORK PIE

'A season approaches, well nigh one and indivisible, for pork pies and fox hunting, that justly celebrated Meltonian edible.' Those words from *The Leicester Journal* of 1855 sum up two of the features of Melton Mowbray. Although pies had been made in farmhouse kitchens in the area for centuries the development of the trade in the town itself only dates from about 1831, when a small bakery and confectioner's shop began to make pork pies. (Bakers, rather than butchers, are normally the pie-makers, although butchers subsequently sell many of the pies.)

The trade grew quickly in the 19th century; the pies were well publicized and attracted a great deal of interest. In 1863 an American farmer named Elihu Burritt, on a walking tour of England, decided to investigate the Melton pie:

The Dickinson and Morris pie and bakers shop in Nottingham Street, Melton Mowbray, has remained virtually unchanged – at least outside – since the 19th century. (Reproduced by kind permission of Dickinson and Morris)

'From Oakham I walked to Melton Mowbray, a cleanly, good looking town in Leicestershire, situated on the little River Eye. I spent a quiet Sabbath in Melton; attended divine service in the old parish church and listened to two extemporaneous sermons full of simple and earnest teaching and delivered in a conversational tone of voice. Melton Mowbray has also a very respectable individuality, it is a great centre for the scarlet-coated Nimrods who scale hedges and ditches in well-mounted squadrons after a fox, preserved at great expense and care, to become the victim of their valour. But this is a small and frivolous distinction compared with its celebrated manufacture of Pork Pies. It bids fair to become as famous for them as Banbury is for buns. I visited the principal establishment for providing the travelling and picnicking world with those very substantial and palatable portables. I went under the impulse of that uneasy suspicious curiosity to peer into the forbidden mysteries of the kitchen, which generally bring no satisfaction when gratified and which often astonishes a man not only to eat what is set before him without any question "for conscience sake" but also for the sake of the more delicate and exacting sensibilities of the stomach. I confess that my first visit to this, the greatest Pork-Pie factory in the world, savoured a little of the anxiety to know the worst instead of the best in regard to the solid materials and lighter ingredients which entered into the composition of this surprisingly cheap luxury. There were points also connected with the process of their elaboration which had given me an indefinable uneasiness in the refreshment rooms of a hundred railway stations. I was determined to settle these moot points once and for all. So I entered the establishment with an eye of as keen a speculation as an excise man searching for illicit distillery, and came out of it a more charitable and contented man. All was above board fair and clean, the meat was fresh and good, the flour was fine and sweet; the butter and lard would grace the neatest housewife's larder, the forms on which the pies were moulded were as pure as spotless marble; the men and boys looked healthy and bright, their hands smooth and clean, their aprons white as snow. Not one smoked or took snuff at his work. I saw every process and implement employed in the construction of these Pork-Pies for the market, the great tubs of pepper and spice, the huge ovens and cooling racks; the packing rooms, in a word every department and feature in this establishment. And the best thing I can say of it is this, that I shall eat with better satisfaction and relish hereafter the Pie bearing the brand of Evans of Melton Mowbray than I ever did before.'[1]

J. E. Brownlow's monograph, 'The Melton Mowbray Pork Pie Industry' (Leicestershire Archaeological and Historical Society, Vol. XXXIX, 1963–4) is a fascinating piece of local history, worth reading. It also contains this extract from Burritt's 'Walk'.

1 *A Walk from London to John O'Groats* by Elihu Burritt, (1864)

Once the pie dough has been raised, the cases are filled with the meat mixture, lids are fitted on them and trimmed with a pastry cutter. Then they are ready for the oven. (Photograph by R & D Studios)

In nearby Nottinghamshire a sweet, fruity raised pie used to be made in much the same way as a Melton pie, but with gooseberries not meat as the filling. Green gooseberries were used with clear apple jelly around them, and a hot-crust pastry slightly sweetened, with sugar replacing the usual salt and pepper. These pies were once very popular at Mansfield Fair.

After the pies have been baked they swell around the base and develop 'a belly'. This is a sure sign that they have been hand-raised. Judging by the grin on the pie-maker's face, this must be a good batch. (Photograph by R & D Studios)

This is a classic piece of food hunting. It captures perfectly the excitement of visiting an area, of settling in before the search; the curiosity and anxiety all of us feel when about to witness the making of a manufactured food. Mr Burritt also reminds us that food hunting is a serious business, though not without its lighter moments.

What of the pies themselves? Melton today has two principal pie-makers, Suttons in Burton Street, where pies have been made since about 1860, and Dickinson and Morris in Nottingham Street, which was a bakery in the 17th century and began pie-making in 1851.

The beauty of the pies is their simplicity, and the makers score over most of their competitors with an unrivalled skill for preparing and baking hot-crust pastry. They also use pure pork – no ground rind or rusk – and the meat is roughly chopped, not minced. The final trick is the hand-raising of the crust with a wooden mould. I was able to watch the chief 'raiser' from Dickinson and Morris at work, and what astonished me was not so much the man's speed and neatness but his light touch and gentleness. He turned and worked the dough as a potter might raise a pot from a lump of clay.

The first thing you notice about a Melton pie, apart from its design, is its sheer weight. Then, once you cut it open, you see the filling, very solid and pale in colour; this is the natural colour of the meat (think of a joint of roast pork). Encasing the meat is a layer of clear jelly made from the concentrated stock of bones and rind, and around this is the pastry case, in distinct layers. Next to the jelly it is creamy and white where it has absorbed juices from the meat, then further out it becomes drier and darker until the outside is a crisp and brown as biscuit. These features mean that hot-crust pastry is ideal for pork pies. (Incidentally do not try to freeze a Melton pie after you have bought it; the pastry will be ruined – reduced to a soft, soggy dough.)

One of the proprietors of the Dickinson and Morris shop displaying a tray of pies ready for sale. (Reproduced by kind permission of Dickinson and Morris)

A pie weighing 29 lbs was produced for a special occasion in 1868; it took seven hours to bake. More recently, a 20lb pie was sent to Arsenal Football Club for their 50th anniversary, and in October 1973 a 30-pounder was produced for the 'twinning' of Melton Mowbray with Dieppe. In return the citizens of the French town promised to try and catch a giant fish, but they did not succeed!

The Melton pie has given rise to many tales in its time, about specimens of enormous size, or consignments of several tons despatched to agricultural shows and race meetings in special trains, but my favourite story tells of a performance of *Richard III* at Drury Lane in 1876. The incident happened appropriately during the Battle of Bosworth scene, reported as follows in *The Grantham Journal*:

> *'A hungry spectator in the front row of the gallery felt inclined to enjoy his supper, and started to unwrap a Pork Pie which slipped from his grasp and dropped over the gallery and got lodged in the centre of the dress circle chandelier, which was lit by gas. As the Pork Pie began to frizzle, a most appetising odour filled the house. The contending armies of Richmond and Richard, diverted by the appetising smell, felt hunger, and their eyes were centred not on the opposing force but on the chandelier exhaling such delicious fragrance. A wag in the audience cried out, "that is a real melting Mowbray pork pie".'*

Although the best Melton pies come from Melton Mowbray, there is no copyright on the name, and any manufacturer can produce 'Melton Mowbray Pies'. Some of them are, in fact, very good indeed. (Reproduced by kind permission of Saxby's)

BREWERIES

T. HOSKINS LTD
Beaumont Road, Leicester

A small brewery which produces a bitter, a dark mild and an Old that is put into casks only for special orders.

T. HOSKINS LTD.
FINE ALES IN CASK AND BOTTLE

There is only one tied house, *The Red Lion* in Market Bosworth, but you can get draught beer from the off-licence next to the brewery. Remember to take a jug or a flagon with you.

The front view of Hoskins brewery some 50 years ago. It is more accurately a 'brew-house'. (Reproduced by kind permission of T. Hoskins)

G. RUDDLE & COMPANY LIMITED

G. RUDDLE & CO. LTD
The Brewery, Langham, Oakham

Good draught beers if kept properly: bitter, County Ale (a strong bitter that can be thick and cloudy if not looked after) and draught Rutland Barley Wine, only available in the winter and not brewed every year. It is strong and expensive.

A large number of pubs in the east and south midlands serve Ruddles beer. *The George* in Oakham market-place provides useful food; you might also try *The Falcon* in Uppingham, *The Sun* in Cottesmore, *The Bewicke Arms* in Hallaton, and *The White Lion* in Whissendine.

A scene photographed at H. H. Parry; an Oakham brewery taken over by Ruddles.

MARKETS

Cheese is the main feature of markets in the Shires, at least for people in search of regional food. Both Leicester and Melton Mowbray have superb stalls where Stilton particularly is sold at a much more aggreeable price than in most shops. Mobile pie shops, butchers and fishmongers also have regular pitches at quite a number of markets in the region.

The Cheese Fair held in the market place at Melton Mowbray in 1890. Sadly, fairs like this disappeared after the First World War. (Reproduced by kind permission of Osborne Publicity Services)

ASHBY-DE-LA-ZOUCH

General Market. *Thursday.*

LEICESTER

General Market, Corn Exchange. *Wednesday, Friday and Saturday.*
A superb market, not only for regional foods like cheese and tripe, but also fish. Considering that Leicester is so far from the coast the range is astonishing. Not strictly regional, but worth visiting nevertheless.

LOUGHBOROUGH

General market. *Thursday and Saturday.*
Seasonal WI market, Woodgate School. *Thursday morning.*

MARKET HARBOROUGH

General market. *Tuesday and Saturday.*

MELTON MOWBRAY

General market. *Tuesday and Saturday.*
Seasonal WI market, Park Road. *Tuesday morning.*

OAKHAM

General market. *Wednesday and Saturday.*
WI market, Victoria Hall. *Friday morning.*

UPPINGHAM

General market. *Friday.*
Seasonal WI market, Methodist Schoolroom. *Friday morning.*

A Stilton cheese basket, designed to contain a whole cheese. (Reproduced by kind permission of The Museum of English Rural Life, University of Reading)

The finest English cooking apple, the Bramley, was raised at Southwell in Nottinghamshire, by Matthew Bramley, butcher and innkeeper. It was introduced commercially in 1876.

A food as common and widespread as the pork pie is bound to have variations: families throughout the Shires have created their own recipes. Here are three recipes that have proved very popular in the area:

Pork and apple pie

Layers of cooking apple and pork, with chopped onion and sage, make up the filling, and the pie is either raised in the usual way or made in a dish, to be eaten hot the same day. Pork and apple pie is also known in Cheshire.

Pork pie with raisins

This pie dates back to the 14th century, but there are recipes from the 19th century for the same type of pie, and it may still be made in one or two kitchens in the region. Layers of pork and raisins are spiced with nutmeg and mace and covered with hot-crust pastry. In the Middle Ages this was known as a 'coffyn' of pastry.

Pork pie with anchovy

It may surprise you, but there is a long-standing tradition of combining meat with fish in English cookery – lamb stuffed with cockles or crab, and steak pudding with oysters are two examples – and some family recipes for pork pie included a dash of anchovy essence. The idea may have been introduced by an Italian chef working here in the 19th century. It is, today, only included in some private, household recipes. NOTE: the pies produced in Melton do not contain anchovy and, according to the makers, never have done.

MELTON HUNT CAKE

This was a favourite with the gentlemen of the Melton Hunt (now part of the Quorn), and the recipe has remained unchanged for at least 120 years. It is a very dark, rich fruit cake with dried fruit, candied peel, glacé cherries and chopped almonds, all fortified with rum. Like all cakes of this type it keeps for a long time, improving in flavour and texture as the months go by. One was apparently kept quite successfully for 11 years!

The label once used by Dickinson and Morris on their export cartons of Melton Hunt Cake. (Reproduced by kind permission of Dickinson and Morris)

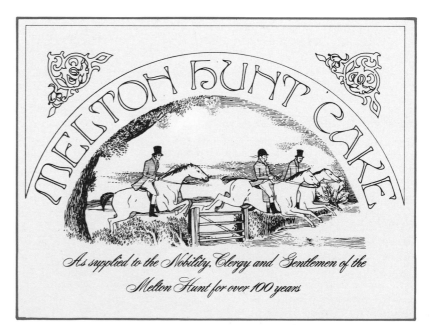

MELTON HUNT CAKE

As supplied to the Nobility, Clergy and Gentlemen of the Melton Hunt for over 100 years

Melton Mowbray pies can be made anywhere in the country, and the name is often used quite indiscriminately. Not so with Melton Hunt Cake. It has been patented, and can only be made in Melton by Dickinson and Morris. A visit to that shop is essential when you are in the area. The Hunt Cakes are large – some are oblong, others are round – but you can buy sections in the shop, which is useful if you do not want to invest in a whole cake.

If you are lazy, or have no talent for cake-making, why not buy a Melton Hunt Cake for Christmas? Dickinson and Morris will even post the cake to you if you are unable to visit the shop in person.

MELTON HUNT BEEF

Before those 19th century sportsmen went out hunting they would eat long and filling breakfasts: classic dishes like devilled kidneys and kedgeree would be lined up with more outrageous delicacies such as stuffed pig's ears and larks in aspic. There would be Melton pies too, and often a huge round of Hunt Beef. Joints weighing 15 Kg. (30 lbs) were not uncommon, the meat coming from animals that had grazed on rich Leicester pastures. The beef was rubbed with a mixture of salt, saltpetre, brown sugar and herbs, left for 10 days and then slowly baked or boiled in beer. It could be eaten hot, but was normally pressed and served cold. Sometimes, if it was not needed immediately, it would be hung in smoke for a week.

A small joint of spiced beef cured with salt, saltpetre, brown sugar, peppercorns and crushed juniper berries makes an ideal centrepiece for a Christmas supper. (Photograph by Richard Mabey)

Spiced beef, which you can make at home, is the direct descendant of Melton Hunt Beef. Much smaller joints are cured nowadays – topside or silverside are the best cuts – and they seldom weigh more than 3 Kg. (6 lbs).

POTTED MEAT

English cooks started to use potting as a method of preserving meat (and fish as well) in the 16th century. It was a way of providing supplies for travellers and sailors who needed food that would keep for months and could be stored compactly. In those days joints of meat were cooked in pots and covered with butter and a thick layer of suet. This excluded all the air, so the meat kept well and could be stored easily in its pots.

Later, cooks began to modify this technique: they chopped and pounded the meat after cooking it, packed the coarse paste into jars and covered them with a layer of butter. They made potted beef, veal, rabbit, chicken, pheasant, ham, veal and tongue mixed together, pigeon and many more. All the pounding and chopping had to be done by hand, but, once the meat had been flavoured with a secret blend from the spice-box and the children had been given the special treat of tasting and giving their verdict on the mixture, potted meat was a valuable addition to the store cupboard.

The principle behind potting was the exclusion of air, and thus all the air-borne bacteria that would attack a piece of meat or fish and cause it to decay. It was a principle that had been used by many ancient civilizations, especially the Romans. They would submerge food in jars of oil or honey to prevent them spoiling.

When did you last taste potted meat? I don't mean the products of the 'paste' manufacturers, but a tub of home-made potted beef or ham. Even though we have mincers and electric blenders to speed up the preparation, there are parts of the country where these skills seem to have vanished altogether. Not so in the Shires. People here have not forgotten the usefulness of such things. (It is no accident that potted meats still thrive in this region, with its tradition of pie-making, for potted meats also serve as fillings for raised pies and pastry cases as well as being eaten on their own.)

You have only to go to Melton Mowbray to see the butter-covered tubs in the windows of butchers' shops; I tracked down four different brands on my last visit there. They are usually made by the butcher or his wife, although sometimes the work may be farmed out to a local cook who has time and knowledge to spare.

When you buy a tub of potted meat make sure that you do not damage or break the seal made by the butter until you want to eat it. If the layer is intact the meat will keep well in a cool larder for several days. You can spread it on hot toast, or better still buy some *baps*, those flat, soft rolls so popular in the Midlands and the North of England. Baps are ideally designed; because they are large, flat and round, they can be stuffed with any kind of filling and still stay easy to eat (unlike crisp, dome-shaped rolls). You will have white fingers after eating one, though, from the light dusting of flour that each bap is given.

Baps are popular in Scotland too, where they are oval and eaten mainly at breakfast time. One Scottish folklorist, Dr Maclagan, a man with a vivid imagination, suggested an analogy between 'bap' and 'pap'. Was it their shape, size, or texture that led him to this conclusion?

BUTCHERS SHOP SPECIALITIES

When you are in a butcher's shop in the Shires, perhaps hunting for potted meat, you will see many other things worth trying.

Polony

This is a red ring of coiled sausage, made from minced pork, cereal and spices. It is already cooked, so it needs no preparation. You can eat it as soon as you have removed the skin. Polony has a delicious aromatic flavour.

Black puddings

You are free to pick out the particular pudding you want; this applies to polony as well. The black puddings are longer and thinner than those sold in Lancashire, more like Wiltshire puddings (see p. 81).

Mobile shops, like this one at Oakham market, are quite common throughout the Shires, and sell a whole range of pies, sausages and other pork products. (Photograph by David Mabey)

Brawn

It is well worth sampling the home produced variety. It is very common and highly thought of (see p. 81).

Pressed pork

This consists of pieces of lean pork cooked, pressed and set in a jelly and is usually sold in slices.

Faggots

These round meat balls are very popular, and are sold from large metal trays (see p. 81).

Pies

Pork pies are made in many different sizes, and there are also chicken pies, 'Cornish' pasties, beef and potato pies, veal, ham and egg pies, sausage rolls and large squares of minced beef flan.

Sausage meat

Often moulded into large eye-catching balls, well-made sausage meat is worth buying.

Sausages

The sage sausages here are not as roughly chopped as those of Wiltshire or Oxfordshire (see p. 83) but just as good.

Tripe

People enjoy eating tripe in the Midlands. Leicester market has stalls which sell nothing else (see p. 181).

Brawn is often sold in tubs, although it is quite common to see large blocks in the butchers' shops from which slices are cut. Either way it is a splendid food.

Opening day at one Sainsbury's shop in 1906. The range of meat and meat products is enormous, and the sight of meat and cheese together is one that is common in the Shires, where Stilton often appears in butchers' shop windows. (Reproduced by kind permission of J. Sainsbury Ltd)

QUORN BACON ROLL

Local enthusiasm for working with meat, for making your own provisions, doesn't end with brawn or potted beef. Hanging in many butchers' shops you will see home-cured bacon. It is normally 'green' (unsmoked) and divided up into large pieces.

One dish popular in the area, particularly in rough winter weather is the Quorn Bacon Roll. A mixture of chopped bacon, onions, and sage is spread on a piece of suet paste, rolled up and boiled in a cloth; the roll is eaten with winter vegetables and boiled potatoes.

A Quorn Bacon Roll: Make a suet paste with equal quantities of flour and shredded suet, a pinch of salt and a little water or stock to moisten. Make a filling of chopped bacon (either rashers or bacon scraps) with chopped onion (roughly equal amounts) and some finely chopped sage. Roll out the suet paste into an oblong about 1cm. (½ in) thick, spread the filling over it, roll it up and wrap in a pudding cloth. Tie it well and boil gently for two hours.

'I've told you before about dropping clangers.'

(Cartoon by Geoffrey Dickinson)

A similar dish to the Quorn bacon roll, eaten in some parts of the home counties until quite recently, was called 'a plugger', known by the quarrymen of Headington in Oxfordshire as 'a clanger'. But the 'Bedford clanger', made by women who worked in the Luton hat-making factory, was different. It was a complete meal enclosed in suet: meat at one end and jam filling at the other. Different names, different places; but these are all 'work foods', designed for a specific purpose. For the women who worked all day in the factory, the clanger was a way of cooking a complete dinner quickly, in one pot. The quarrymen needed bulky meals, but their food had to be improvized from a few basic ingredients – a lot of suet and a little bacon. (There is more about work foods on p. 177.)

RED LEICESTER CHEESE

Every British cheese has its own special qualities. You can recognize Red Leicester first by its colour; it is actually bright orange, despite its name.

Until quite recently the milk for Leicester cheese was delivered in churns. Nowadays it comes in bulk tankers. Once the cheese-making is under way and the curd has been formed, it needs to be cut. This is now done mechanically. (Reproduced by kind permission of Tuxford and Tebbutt)

Combine that with the fact that it is a flat cheese with very little rind and you have enough information for accurate identification. You can tell a piece of Red Leicester by handling and tasting it, too: the cheese is sold very young – within a month of being made – so it is very mild and soft, so soft that you can almost spread it; and its sharp flavour is somewhat lemony to my taste. Red Leicester is a full fat cheese and is a superb toaster. Like Double Gloucester, it melts quickly into a soft velvety mass when put under the grill.

There is nothing to stop Red Leicester cheese being made in other parts of the country, as indeed it is, but much of the cheese eaten in the Shires comes from one firm in Melton Mowbray. The factory of Tuxford and Tebbutt has a long history. In the 19th century it combined cheese-making with pies and sausages, but now confines itself to Red Leicester, butter and Stilton cheese. It is a model example of the way such foods can thrive happily on both a local and a national level.

Many of the stages in cheese-making that were traditionally performed by hand are now done with mechanical help, and many of the cheese-maker's tools, like the curd-stirrers used here are disappearing. (Reproduced by kind permission of Tuxford and Tebbutt)

After the curd has been separated from the whey, it is packed into metal moulds and pressed. Presses and moulds similar to these are still used today. A small number of Red Leicester cheeses are still bandaged with calico cloth for protection after being removed from their shallow moulds, but most are cut up and packed in film wrapping. (Reproduced by kind permission of Tuxford and Tebbutt)

It is encouraging to see rows of whole cheeses destined for local shops and market stalls, especially as much of the cheese is actually made into blocks which are cut up and prepared for the supermarkets. Farmhouse Red Leicester may be a thing of the past, but at least there is no chance of the cheese disappearing; the cheese-makers are well aware of their history and local importance.

Much of the milk for Leicester cheese came originally from local Cottesmore cattle, and others, like this prize heifer bred by Mr. R. W. Baker of Cottesmore and with a dead weight of 152 stone 3lbs, would have provided the meat for giant rounds of Melton Hunt Beef (see earlier). (Reproduced by kind permission of The Museum of English Rural Life, University of Reading)

CURD CHEESECAKES

In the Middle Ages, cooks made simple curd tarts by grinding 'new cheese' in a mortar with eggs; they sweetened the mixture with sugar, coloured it with saffron and put it into pastry cases to be baked. Later they were a feature of the annual Whitsuntide Feast in Melton Mowbray, and of Village Feasts celebrating village saint days in Cottesmore, Ridlington, Langham and other places in the region. The cheesecakes were made in their hundreds, there would be plates piled high with them in almost every kitchen. They were even put into nets slung from the ceiling.

Quite a number of bakers' shops still sell these small curd cheesecakes and they are made extensively in farmhouse kitchens.

HALLATON HARE PIE SCRAMBLING

Hallaton (Hallowed or Holy Town) was once the centre of south Leicestershire before the rise of Market Harborough, and it is the scene of two ancient, but very lively, Easter customs: Hare Pie Scrambling and Bottle Kicking, both of which take place on Easter Monday.

The Scramble was once connected with a piece of land bequeathed to the local rector of the parish, on the condition that he provided each year 'two hare pies, a quantity of ale, and two dozen penny loaves, to be scrambled for each succeeding Easter Monday at the rising ground called Hare Pie Bank.' But the real origins of the custom are probably much older, going back to the symbolic sacrifice and celebration of Easter through its sacred creature, the hare.

Hunting the Hare survived as an Easter custom in Leicester until the end of the 18th century, and it was always followed by the celebratory eating of the Hare Pie. In reality, substitutes were provided: the hunt was a drag hunt, using the corpse of a cat, and the pie was filled with beef or some other meat.

Scramble is a good description of the actual event. The pie is cut up and the pieces put into a sack which is carried to the Hare Pie Bank and emptied out. The only way to claim the pieces is to fight and struggle in a huge heap of bodies like a rugby scrum. After this the Bottle Kicking begins. The 'bottles' are actually small wooden barrels kept and decorated specially for the occasion; two contain beer, the third is a dummy. A team of men from Hallaton kicks against a team of outsiders, traditionally men from the neighbouring village of Medbourne. It is a contest to get the 'bottle' from the Bank over the boundary line. The winners of this, the first round, drink the contents of the barrel. Then the dummy is fought for. Finally the third barrel is carried to the Market Cross on Hallaton Green, and the leader of the winning team is perched on the top of the cross to take the first drink from the barrel in this highly precarious position.

Battle-scarred bottle kickers at Hallaton in about 1910. The winner is sitting in the centre with the 'barrel' between his knees. Judging by the faces of some of the characters around him, it must have been a hard-won prize. (Reproduced by kind permission of Leicester Museums)

If you want some good Easter entertainment, visit Hallaton, watch the scrambling and bottle-kicking, and then move on to The Bewicke Arms for a taste of Ruddles beer.

STILTON CHEESE

Shelves of Stilton cheese in store. (Reproduced by kind permission of Tuxford and Tebbutt)

Stilton cheese did not originate in Stilton. We have to go north into Leicestershire to find its true origins. Many villages have claimed Stilton as their own, and there are a number of different stories connected with it. The most reliable of these points to Quenby Hall, where 'Lady Beaumont's Cheese' was being made at the beginning of the 18th century. This seems to have been the true ancestor of Stilton. One of the daughters of Elizabeth Scarbrow, the Quenby housekeeper, married Cooper Thornhill, who kept *The Bell* at Stilton in Huntingdonshire, and cheeses were sent there by her sister, Mrs Paulet, from Wymondham near Melton Mowbray. (What marvellous, rich names these people had!) *The Bell* was a busy roadside inn, and soon the reputation of the cheese spread through the country when it became known as Stilton cheese.

Stilton has a unique distinction among British cheeses; it is the only one protected by a trade copyright. To be called Stilton the cheese has to be made in its traditional regions: the Vale of Belvoir in Leicestershire, the Dove Valley in Derbyshire, and parts of south Nottinghamshire.

The Bell at Stilton. A sad picture of neglect, but now in process of being restored. (Photograph by Trevor Wood)

Making the cheese has always been a tricky business. Originally it was the job of farmers' wives, working long hours in their dairies. The patience, skill and endurance of those women was prodigious. They tended their cheeses in rooms where the temperature and humidity might change at any time, where much of the cheese might not even vein up, and where it would take something like 18 months for one Stilton to ripen

This stained-glass window in Stilton's only Watneys pub is one of the few reminders that Stilton was a 'cheese village'. (Photograph by Trevor Wood)

fully. Just before the First World War many farmers in the area formed societies to try and make their cottage industry more efficient and to improve their methods. These societies and co-operatives were the forerunners of the creameries which now produce all Stilton cheese. The process is still delicate, requiring more skill and patience than any other method of cheese-making, not only in the way the cheese is formed, but also in the way it is ripened. It takes about four months to produce a fully ripe Stilton these days: 17 gallons of milk is 'invested' in every 14lb cheese. A greyish brown, wrinkled crust, a mass of blue veins and a good creamy colour are the signs of a good Stilton.

The cheese is available everywhere in the Shires, even in butchers' shops, so it is worth searching for bargains. Visit Melton Mowbray or the cheese stalls on Leicester market where they sell an enormous range of full size

and 'baby' Stiltons, which are much cheaper. This is the nearest you will get to the spirit of the old cheese fairs for which Leicester and Melton were once famous.

The quality of Stilton cheese can be tested by taking a sample with a special borer. (Reproduced by permission of Tuxford and Tebbutt)

Serving Stilton can be a problem. Scooping was the method at one time, and there were special spoons for taking out the soft centre of the cheese. According to Daniel Defoe, writing in 1724, the cheese was '*brought to the table with mites, or maggots round it, so thick that they bring a spoon with them for you to eat the mites with, as you do the cheese.*' This was a wasteful habit, since the outer part of the cheese dried out and was then not worth eating. Even worse was the fashion for pouring port or beer into the cheese, hoping to improve its flavour. A messy, pointless exercise guaranteed to ruin the cheese. The simple method of cutting is the best; you will waste none of the cheese, except the crust.

A word about White Stilton. This cheese is quite common, and as the name implies it is white, and unveined, normally sold about 20 days after it has been made. It is very pleasant in its own right, cheaper than Blue Stilton, very crumbly and quite salty, with something of the character of young Lancashire cheese.

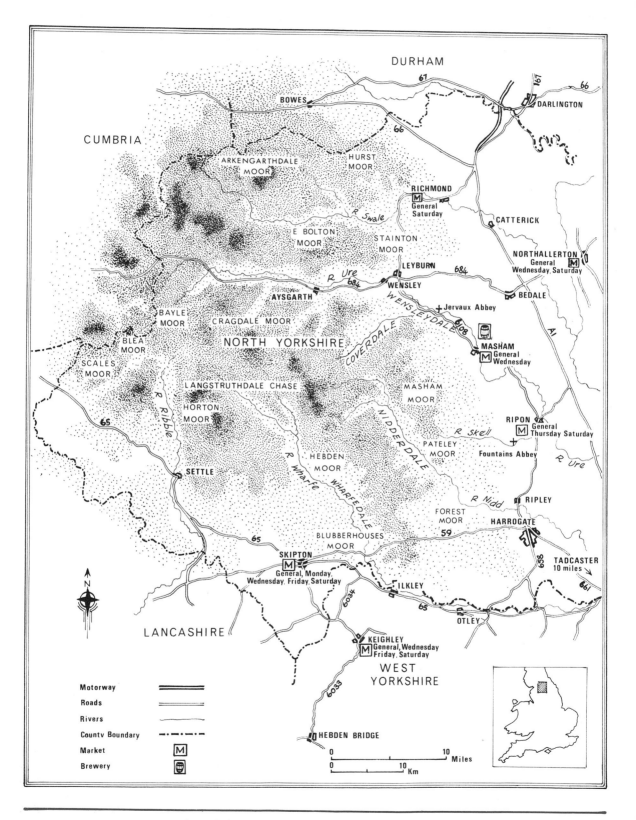

DURHAM

BOWES

CUMBRIA

ARKENGARTHDALE
MOOR

HURST
MOOR

DARLINGTON

67

66

167

66

RICHMOND
General
Saturday

CATTERICK

E BOLTON
MOOR

STAINTON
MOOR

R Swale

NORTHALLERTON
General
Wednesday, Saturday

LEYBURN

WENSLEY

684

684

BEDALE

R Ure

AYSGARTH

Jervaux Abbey

A1

BAYLE
MOOR

CRAGDALE MOOR

WENSLEYDALE

608

MASHAM
General
Wednesday

BLEA
MOOR

NORTH YORKSHIRE

COVERDALE

SCALES
MOOR

LANGSTRUTHDALE CHASE

MASHAM
MOOR

65

HORTON
MOOR

NIDDERDALE

RIPON
General
Thursday Saturday

R Skell

R Ribble

PATELEY
MOOR

Fountains Abbey

R Ure

HEBDEN
MOOR

SETTLE

R Wharfe

WHARFEDALE

R Nidd

RIPLEY

65

FOREST
MOOR

HARROGATE

BLUBBERHOUSES
MOOR

59

658

SKIPTON
General, Monday,
Wednesday, Friday, Saturday

ILKLEY

TADCASTER
10 miles

661

6034

65

OTLEY

LANCASHIRE

KEIGHLEY
General, Wednesday
Friday, Saturday

WEST
YORKSHIRE

N

6033

HEBDEN BRIDGE

Motorway

Roads

Rivers

County Boundary

Market   M

Brewery

0   10
|_____| Miles
0   10
|_____| Km

THE YORKSHIRE DALES
COTTAGE ECONOMY: SHEEP, OATCAKES AND CHEESE

Although the area of the Yorkshire Dales is now well-publicized for tourists, it is still essentially remote. And, in the days before the motor car facilitated travel, it was such an isolated region of the country that farming families had to rely almost entirely on their own provisions. They tended their animals, cured their own bacon, made their own cheese, baked their own bread and most likely brewed their own beer as well.

For much of the time the weather was, and still is, cold, rough and uncomfortable. Hardy mountain sheep could survive and perhaps a few pigs to be fattened for slaughter. But it is not an area for growing crops or of rich grazing. Consequently much of the local food was based on the uses to which the few animals could be put, and on provisions like bread and cheese which could be made in the kitchen. Those products still surviving reflect the old cottage economy of the region almost without exception.

The great symbol of food in the Yorkshire Dales was the large range and fireplace, the focal point of the kitchen. Pots and kettles were suspended above the hearth and everything from the simplest broth to the tar used for marking sheep was heated up over the fire. On one side of the fireplace was a flat metal bakestone for making oatcakes, and on the other side a brick oven, essential for baking bread, pies and cakes of all sorts. There would be racks or 'flakes' suspended from the ceiling which were draped with drying oatcakes, and outside the kitchen door there would probably stand a massive stone cheese press.

Such local food as still exists in the Dales was originally made in surroundings like this, and even though electricity has radically changed the way kitchens are now run in the area, the tradition of sheep, oatcakes and farmhouse cheese continues to thrive although it is threatened by powerful economic pressures.

SHEEP AND PIGS

Sturdy mountain sheep have grazed on the slopes of the Pennines and in the Dales for centuries. For years the large Blackfaced was the main breed, highly valued for its long, straight wool which was used for making worsted stockings. These sheep were agile creatures with long straight bones, so their chops were ideal for setting upright into a pot for cooking. The ewe's milk was originally used for making cheese. Nowadays Cheviot sheep have replaced the Blackfaced on many of the moors – like the Blackfaced they should not need to be supplied with extra food by the farmer, thriving best on what they crop from the wild.

Like much of the Lake District, the Yorkshire Dales is a National Park which openly encourages visitors, but because of its harsh climate it is best viewed in the summer, unless you are prepared to endure snow drifts and swirling fog.

Sheep dogs are very important in the Yorkshire Dales, where flocks of sheep may spread over large areas of moorland and cannot be controlled or moved without the skill of a shepherd and his dog. Sheepdog trials are a lively part of the farming calender, and arouse considerable local rivalry.

A flock of Cheviot sheep grazing in the Yorkshire Dales. (Reproduced by kind permission of The Museum of English Rural Life, University of Reading)

Mutton pot pie was also known as 'sea pie'. A similar pie, made with steak, oysters and mushrooms, used to be made at Brightlingsea in Essex, for Colne Yacht Club's 'laying-up supper' at the end of the season.

Mutton was substituted for beef in many dishes, for example in mutton sausages, and was the obvious ingredient for hot-pots and pies. There was even a recipe for a composite 'mutton pot pie'. Pieces of bacon and mutton were cooked with root vegetables, peas and beans in a strong iron pot and simmered in stock for a short while. Then a thick suet crust was cemented firmly over the top of the pot, in place of a lid, and the whole lot was simmered slowly for about an hour. The dish was eaten straight from the pot.

Barnsley chops, which are being prepared by these butchers, supposedly originated in The King's Head Hotel in Barnsley in 1849 and were supplied to farmers who required substantial lunches. The chops in this picture were eaten at a lunch celebrating the opening of Barnsley Town Hall by The Prince of Wales in 1933. There were 75 chops in all, each weighing 1lb 6ozs, two chops from a sheep. (Reproduced by kind permission of Albert Hirst of Barnsley)

The highland areas of north Lancashire, Yorkshire and the Lake District are probably the last strongholds of mutton and it is worth looking out for when you are in the area.

Yorkshire has also produced a fine breed of pig – the Large White. These Yorkshire pigs are still very highly rated. They are large sturdy animals with long, well-built legs, ideal for turning into hams.

YORK HAMS
These are the most famous of all British regional hams. It is often said that the first hams were smoked with oak sawdust and shavings left by the carpenters

A fully-grown Large White pig is a formidable beast, large enough to conceal a man, apart from his shoes! (Reproduced by kind permisssion of The Museum of English Rural Life, University of Reading)

Part of a massive display of six tons of york hams, exhibited at The Grocers' Exhibition in 1939. (Reproduced by kind permission of Fox Photos and The Museum of English Rural Life, University of Reading)

York hams have been popular throughout the country for a great many years. This picture was taken in Bournemouth in 1925, when York Hams were one shilling and threepence per pound. (Reproduced by kind permission of J. Sainsbury, Ltd)

Possibly the only surviving example of a bacon flake can be seen at the Welsh Folk Museum in Cardiff.

Portable bakestones or girdle plates came in many designs, but all were based on the idea of a circular iron plate with a handle.

during the monumental task of building York cathedral. Certainly they have a distinct smoky flavour. But, the meat itself also has a particularly fine taste, and the hams look large and long, coming as they do from Yorkshire pigs. A York ham is a substantial Christmas investment – it can weigh about 15lb. You can either buy them in London, from one of the large provision shops, order them from the curers, or buy them direct from a butcher's shop in York.

As well as hams, a great deal of bacon was cured in Dales' farmhouses. It was a regular, seasonal activity and most kitchens had a bacon *fleeak* (flake), a wooden rack on which sides of bacon and hams were laid to dry. This was suspended from the rafters, well away from the direct heat of the fireplace for about three months, then taken down when the provisions were completely dry and could be stored ready for use.

BAKING
There has always been a strong tradition of home-baking in Yorkshire, and many of the specialities are still made and sold in the region.

OATCAKES
In most kitchens in the Dales there would have been a bakestone at the side of the fireplace, which was used first of all for making oatcakes. This wasn't specific to Yorkshire – it was a feature of kitchens in all highland oat-growing areas in Britain – but the oatcakes themselves and the way they were prepared and stored was quite special.

The oatcake made in the West Riding of Yorkshire was also called 'haverbread' or 'clapbread' (see p.216), and was originally made from oatmeal and milk, mixed together and allowed to ferment. A whole day was needed for

the baking, and so a vast quantity of oatcakes would be made during one session. Some would be very thin and thrown onto the bakestone; others were rolled out to make a thicker cake. The thin cakes, floppy and about the size of a dinner plate, were draped over the wooden racks or 'flakes' which were suspended from the beams over the fireplace. This 'frame of wood laden with oatcakes', was part of the kitchen scene in *Wuthering Heights*, described by Emily Brontë, who grew up in Haworth.

Harvesting oats in the Yorkshire Dales – one of the main oat-growing areas in England. The sloping, undulating fields must have caused great problems for early mechanical harvesters. (Reproduced by kind permission of The Museum of English Rural Life, University of Reading)

A rather idyllic view of oatcake making in an 18th century farmhouse.(Reproduced by kind permission of The Museum of English Rural Life, University of Reading)

The standard piece of kitchen equipment in the Dales, and other highland regions, was the bakestone or girdle (griddle) plate on which oatcakes were cooked. (Reproduced by kind permission of The Museum of English Rural Life, University of Reading)

In the 19th century large quantities of oatcakes were transported regularly from Yorkshire bakers to London, and the cakes still appear outside Yorkshire, although mainly confined now to the north of England. They are made by many small bakers who distribute them to neighbouring counties as well as selling them locally. The recipes and baking techniques seem to vary a great deal: it's difficult to describe a typical Yorkshire oatcake these days. Most of those that I have seen, claiming the title Yorkshire oatcakes, are quite small, oval and made from coarse oatmeal. They are grey-brown in colour and quite delicious, slightly moist with a beautiful nutty flavour.

PARKIN

This heavy cake made from oatmeal, sugar, treacle and ginger is associated with Yorkshire as well as Lancashire, and there are dozens of local recipes, all slightly different (see p. 190).

Traditionally parkin was eaten throughout the north of England on Guy Fawkes' Night, November 5th. But it has ceased to have such a specific use and is now eaten throughout the year.

There are plenty of local gingerbreads – the ancient relative of parkin. I've seen recipes from Sledmere, Starnforth and Wakefield; no doubt there are many others. Families throughout Yorkshire would have devised their own variations on the basic mixture of butter, sugar, treacle, flour, eggs and ginger, and many of these recipes would have become associated with particular towns where they were made. But it is doubtful if they now survive outside the kitchens of a few local farmhouses in the region, and, indeed, the proper place for such recipes is in the home.

Before the days of cast-iron ovens and electricity, parkin and gingerbread were baked in a brick oven heated with burning brushwood and kept hot with a close-fitting door. But these ginger-based cakes were by no means the only things put into the oven. It was used for all the bread and pie baking and for cooking teacakes. These latter are common in both Yorkshire and Lancashire (see p. 189), and are made from a sweet, milk dough. They are eaten hot and toasted with butter. There were also biscuits and 'oven bottoms' – flat cakes put into the bottom of the oven, probably when the rest of the space was taken up with bread.

YORKSHIRE PUDDINGS

Yorkshire's best known dish has gained national, even international fame far beyond its local origins. The principle of this pudding was that it acted as a kind of sponge. The simple mixture of flour, egg and milk beaten together was put beneath a joint of roasting meat to absorb the juices that dripped from it. In old farmhouses the meat would be suspended from a jack in front of the range above a strong metal table. On this were put 'dripping pans' full of the pudding mixture, which would be swapped around to make sure that all of the tins got a fair share of the juicy drippings.

He's the Yorkshire pudding critic of 'The Good Food Guide'.

Tiny, bun-sized Yorkshire puddings are often served with roast beef in restaurants. They are full of air, insubstantial and are generally cooked well away from dripping meat juices. (Cartoon by Geoffrey Dickinson)

There is no denying that this is still the best way to cook Yorkshire pudding, although these days it goes with the meat inside the oven. We associate it with roast beef, but traditionally the pudding was eaten with any kind of roast meat in Yorkshire, from beef to rabbit or partridge. It was also served as a kind of first course, eaten on its own with thick gravy before the main meal arrived. This custom still survives in the north of England.

The beauty of a large tin of Yorkshire pudding, cooked under the meat, is that it has two distinct parts. I recall that my boyhood Sunday lunches would nearly always be preceded by family quarrels about rights to the 'inside' or 'outside' of the Yorkshire pudding. The inside pieces were moist and saturated with the juices from the joint, while those from the outside, in contact with the sides of the baking tin, were light, brown and crisp. The trick was to ensure that you obtained pieces from both parts of the pudding.

In Lancashire, it was often the custom to eat Yorkshire pudding at the end of the meal, covered with caster sugar. And in County Durham it was traditionally eaten not with beef, but with duck or goose.

BILBERRY PIES

In Yorkshire, the bilberry (*Vaccinium myrtillus*) is also called the blaeberry, the blueberry and even the blackberry! Certainly its berries are round and black, and the small shurbs grow in abundance on the Yorkshire moors. the time to pick bilberries is between July and September, and although the plant is common enough, picking can be a laborious task because it grows near to the ground, spreading around and beneath dense clumps of heather. Moreover the berries don't grow in convenient clusters.

The fresh fruit needs nothing more than a little cream and sugar to conteract its rather acid taste when raw. Bilberries also go into crumbles, pies, pancakes and fruit stews. Yorkshire bilberry pies are very like their famous American cousins, and were once a feature of 'funeral teas' in the region. The pies are quite simply a mixture of bilberries, sugar and lemon juice (with, occasionally, chopped apple as well) baked inside a double crust pie.

Bilberries.

(Illustrated by Carol Fowke)

MARKETS

Most of Yorkshire's best markets are outside the Dales, in the towns and cities to the south and east: the Newgate market in York is outstanding, and the markets in Barnsley, Bradford, Doncaster, Sheffield and Wakefield are worth a visit as well. There are markets in many of the towns around the Dales, but they are quite small in comparison.

Harrogate is famous for its toffee and you can still visit Farrah's Shop in the town. (Reproduced by kind permission of Farrah's Ltd)

KEIGHLEY

General market, Town Centre.   *Wednesday, Friday and Saturday.*

MASHAM

General market.   *Wednesday.*

NORTHALLERTON

General market.   *Wednesday and Saturday.*

RICHMOND

General market.   *Saturday.*

RIPON

General market, Town Square.   *Thursday and Saturday.*

SKIPTON

General market.   *Monday, Wednesday, Friday and Saturday.*

BREWERIES

T. & R. THEAKSTON
The Brewery, Masham, Ripon, Yorkshire

The bitter brewed by Theakston's is one of the palest in the country. It is not to everyone's taste, being too 'thin' for some. There is also a dark mild and the strong Old Peculier, named after a local church court called the Peculier Court; this beer is available in bottles and to a lesser extent on draught.

Theakston's only has eight tied houses in the area, but it distributes to a very large number of free trade houses. Try *The Royal Oak* at Dacre Banks, *The Oddfellows Arms* at Bedale or *The White Bear* at Masham, which is next door to the brewery.

The seal of the ancient Prebendary Court of Masham

T. & R. Theakston Ltd.
The Brewery, Masham, Ripon,
North Yorkshire HG4 4DX

Theakston's is the only brewery in the area of the Dales, but there are others nearby. Darleys beer is brewed in Doncaster and sold mainly in the east of the county; the Selby brewery, which re-started brewing in 1972, produces a bitter brewed without sugar, just hops and malt; Samuel Smith's Tadcaster brewery serves a wide area and the beer appears in many different parts of the country; Taylor's of Keighley produces among others a strong brew called Draught Landlord which appears to be available only at *The Hare and Hounds* in Hebden Bridge.

Early Brewers. (Supplied by Samuel Smith)

In the spring of 1971, bistort or Dock Pudding even made the Personal Column of The Times. 'How is your Dock Pudding?' the copy read, and invited entrants for the first World Championship Dock Pudding Contest to be held in the Calder Valley of Yorkshire.

DOCK PUDDING

Another plant which is common on the hilly pastures of the Yorkshire Dales is *Polygonum bistorta*, or bistort. Alternative names in these parts are the Passion Dock, or Easter Ledges (see also p. 219). There is still a strong traditon of eating this plant in Yorkshire, Lancashire and the Lake District, so much so that the Dock Pudding contest is an annual event in many areas. Hebden Bridge is the centre for the yearly World Championship and contests serve to raise funds in many towns and villages. (In Heptinstall in 1977 they used it to raise money for the local brass band.)

There are a great many recipes for Dock Pudding, but basically it is a mixture of green bistort leaves boiled and mixed with cooked barley or oatmeal, often bound together with beaten egg. It can either be eaten hot or allowed to go cold, then sliced and fried with bacon for breakfast or high tea.

WENSLEYDALE CHEESE

Like its Lancashire neighbour, Wensleydale cheese is still made on a small scale by one or two farmer's wives in the area around Wensleydale itself. Traditions like cheese-making die hard in these remote rural areas.

Shelves of Wensleydale cheeses being dried and matured in a Dales dairy. (Reproduced by kind permission of The Museum of English Rural Life, University of Reading)

The cheese has an even longer history than the famous Cheshire Cheese. It seems likely that the recipe was brought to the north of England by monks following in the wake of the Norman Conquest. In monasteries tucked away in the Dales and around the River Ure the monks worked to create a cheese that would brighten up their austere, meatless diet. At first Wensleydale was made from ewe's milk, understandable in an area that has sustained sheep for so long. But gradually it was transformed into a cow's milk cheese, and it is in this form that we find it today. In farms around Wensleydale, Swaledale, Cotherstone and Coverdale it was made as a regular part of cottage economy.

The great abbeys at Fountains, Kirkstall and Bolton (in Yorkshire) would have been the source of some of the first Wensleydale cheese in Britain.

This scene outside a small Wensleydale farm dairy wouldn't be tolerated by today's public health inspectors. Notice the small churn with a strap so that it could be carried on the shoulder of a man or woman. (Reproduced by kind permission of Dorothy Hartley and The Museum of English Rural Life, University of Reading)

These days it is most common to find white Wensleydale: a small, mild cheese with a soft flaky texture weighing one or two pounds. It is the cheese to eat with apple pie. As good as white Wensleydale is, I must confess that I have a preference for the rarer Blue variety, which is mild for a blue cheese, spreads easily and leaves no unpleasant acid aftertaste. A cheese for eating on its own.

Two cheese presses, very different in design but able to perform the same functions.

There is plenty of good Wensleydale to be had in towns and markets in the Dales, and I have also found the real thing in places as far apart as Carlisle and Bury.

The heavy stone press would be fixed outside the dairy, while the smaller, more ornate one would be used inside for pressing small cheeses. (Reproduced by kind permission of The Museum of English Rural Life, University of Reading)

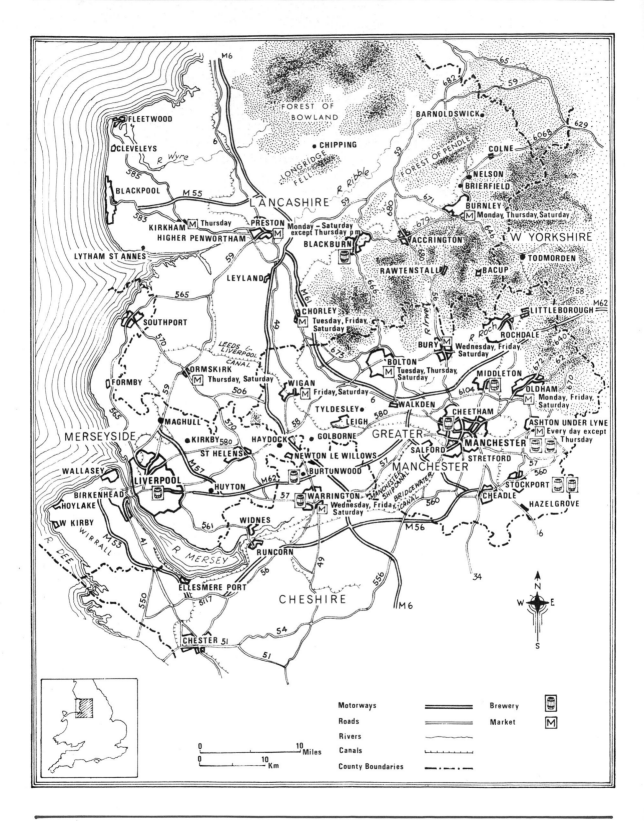

LANCASHIRE AND THE INDUSTRIAL N-W
FOODS FOR WORKING FAMILIES

Between the big industrial towns of Lancashire, the landscape is a desolate mixture of deserted mills with brick chimneys crumbling, railway tracks that lead nowhere and huge slag heaps with houses packed on and around them. It's a potent atmosphere, redolent of the history of the Industrial Revolution, and it this period which has shaped the food of the region to this day. Above all, it is functional, working food.

The pattern of the working day in this heavily industrialized region has influenced its food in many ways. Breakfast has always been important, with the long hours of work ahead; in a cold northerly climate and with time short, a man needed food that was simple, filling and quick to prepare. Those big cooked breakfasts for which the north is so famous were an ideal answer, although many families were probably too poor to afford all the ingredients we now associate with it. Bread, tea and oatmeal were the other essentials.

Dinner, at midday, was supplied at work in the earliest factory canteens, but the pie shops and fish and chip shops had a ready supply of customers too. At the end of the day it was back home for tea. Often the whole family would have been out working for the day, so the women relied heavily on cooked meats and provisions from the cooked food shops. Otherwise they tended to put everything in the pot to cook slowly during the day. The hearth and the pot have always been more important than the oven in these northern areas of the country, which is reflected in the general preference for hot-pots and rolled joints of meat for boiling. The colder climate also meant that root vegetables were grown and used much more than in the south, again finding their way into the dishes that have become associated with this part of the country. The harsh and barren landscape of the pennines supports above all sheep, so lamb and mutton are traditionally the main meat of the area.

The pressures of work weren't the only factors affecting the regional food of Lancashire, but it is still astonishing how closely the food follows these contours. Walk around the markets, hunt round the shops, call at the pie shops and chippies – the evidence is still to be found everywhere.

MEAT AND BUTCHERS

Visiting a Lancashire butcher's shop for the first time can be a bewildering and a daunting experience if you have been used to the customs and eating habits of the south of England. There's a blatant carnivorous atmosphere about the place. You can see the blood, the bones and the organs everywhere. Things that would be cut out and discarded in the south are displayed and sold quite

Bacon, black pudding and sausages are the three most important ingredients of the northern breakfast, washed down with quantities of tea.

Liver Ketchup
This manuscript recipe from Lancashire is undated but probably comes from the early 19th century. Its use of liver is very unusual, but it is purely Lancastrian.
'Take a bullock's liver, wash it extremely well, then put it with some salt in four quarts of water. Let it simmer away one-half, carefully skimming it all the time. Strain it through a hair sieve, and let it stand till next day, then pour it gently into a saucepan with spice, a clove of garlic, a few bay leaves, and a bit of horse-radish. When boiled enough to season it, let it stand till cold and bottle it for use'.
(May Byron's 'Pot luck, The British Home Cookery Book').

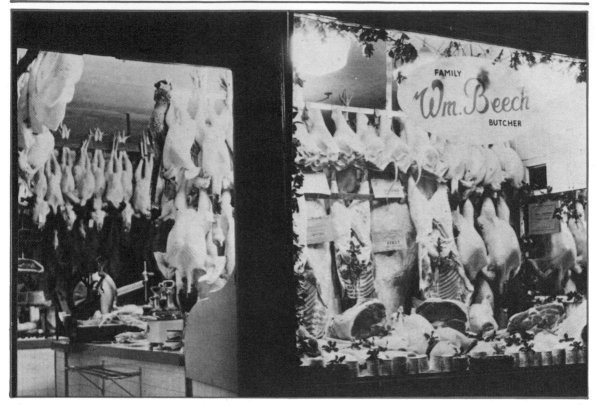

A marvellous Christmas display of meat and poultry at William Beech's shop in Barrowford near Nelson. Notice the lamb carcases dressed in a veil of caul fat. (Reproduced by kind permission of William Beech Ltd)

naturally in these parts; everything from the bare bones of a lamb carcase to the euphemistically titled 'lamb's fry' (see later). It's in the old tradition of meat eating to use up as much of an animal as possible in simple but imaginative ways – nothing is wasted. The realities of butchering aren't hidden, and this may upset the uninitiated, even if you have a stout constitution. The food may be a direct challenge to your prejudices, but persevere and you will surprised by a whole new range of tastes and textures.

LAMB AND MUTTON

There is no better reminder of the special place of lamb and mutton in the food of Lancashire than the rows of carcases hanging in butchers' shops, each dressed in a lacy loin cloth of caul fat. It's an impressive display, complemented by the range of cut meat laid out on the counters. Although mostly lamb is sold these days, you may be lucky and find mutton (it is certainly sold at Burnley market from time to time). A number of butchers still get their meat from local farmers, so the meat on the counter is likely to come from the strong hill sheep that graze on the slopes of the Pennines. There are many cheap cuts, scrag end, neck and breast as well as boned and rolled joints, and you can buy the skeletal remains after the meat has been butchered. This emphasis on lamb leads us straight to the most famous of all Lancashire dishes – the hot-pot. It is still very popular, this stew of lamb chops, kidney, and potatoes which used always to be made in tall earthenware pots that gave the dish its name. These pots, sometimes called 'pipkins', were ideally designed for the stew: the long-boned chops from the Pennine sheep could be stood vertically around the sides of the pot; in the middle would go the mixture of vegetables, kidney, mushrooms and sometimes, in the days when they were cheap, oysters as well. The dish was

Hot-pots similar to those made in Lancashire are found in many parts of Britain where mutton and lamb are important. The 'tatie pot' made in the Lake District is a good example.

covered with a layer of potatoes, cooked in the oven, and served straight from the pot. Pickled red cabbage was once the essential accompaniment to hot-pot, but, sadly, it is less common than it used to be.

Cheap lamb isn't needed only for hot-pot, however. In the area round Liverpool there is a dish call 'lobscouse', the descendant of an improvised stew eaten by seamen in the days of sail. It was a fearful mixture of salt meat, water and vinegar eaten – no doubt painfully – with hard ship's biscuits. The modern version is more palatable: mutton, vegetables (including carrots, swede, onions and potatoes), plenty of herbs and often a handful of barley – an echo of the ship's biscuit.

Miniature hot-pots are sold on some cooked meat and bakers' stalls in Lancashire markets. They don't come in the true earthenware pot, of course, but imitations made of pastry, deeper than they are wide, with little pastry lids. The mixture inside isn't equal to the full size version, but it is a nice touch, and a reminder of the function of both pastry and pots.

The are a number of small, but immensely fruitful, butchers' shops in many Lancashire towns. This one is on the corner of Pendle Street in Nelson. (Photograph by Joan Poulson)

LAMB'S FRY
A rare delicacy, actually a 'safe' name for lamb's testicles. (Not to be confused with pig's fry, which is a mixture of lights and offal.) Lamb's fry, when sliced, has the colour and texture of cod's roe.

In the 17th and 18th centuries lamb's fry were common in recipes; they were called 'lamb-stones' and were often used with sweetbreads in dishes like this one from Eliza Smith's *The Compleat Housewife* (1736):

'To make Pockets
'Cut three slices out of a leg of veal, the length of a finger, the breadth of three fingers, the thickness of a thumb, with a sharp penknife; give it a slit through the middle, leaving the bottom and each side whole, the thickness of a straw; then lard the top with small fine lards of bacon; then make forc'd-meat of (bone) marrow, sweet-breads, and lamb-stones just boiled, and make it up after 'tis seasoned and beaten together with the yolks of two eggs, and put it into your pockets as if you were filling a pincushion; then sew up the top with fine thread, flour them, and put melted butter on them, and bake them; roast three sweet-breads to put between, and serve them with gravy-sauce.'

William Verral, in 'The Complete System of Cookery' (1759), remarks that in describing a dish of 'Lambs-stones marinaded and fry'd, with parsley', the French 'are more modest, and give it a prettier name' – in this case 'Des alumelles d'agneaux'.

Sweetbreads have survived nationally, so why not 'lamb-stones'? The reason is partly prejudice, partly a decline in local slaughtering and partly a general levelling of opinion about what we do and do not eat. It is also difficult to package 'stones' to make them 'acceptable'.

MARKETS

Of all the regions covered in this book, Lancashire is best endowed with markets that are useful to people hunting for regional foods. Almost every variety of locally-produced food is sold in the covered and open-air markets of the important towns. Cooked meats, pies, bread, cakes, fish and black puddings make colourful displays and exciting eating.

(Photograph by Trevor Wood)

MORPRO LTD.
Woolton St., Woolton, L'pool L25 5NH

ASHTON-UNDER-LYNE

General market, Town Hall.   *Every day except Tuesday*

BOLTON

General market (covered), Ashburner Street.   *Tuesday, Thursday, Saturday*

BURNLEY

General Market, Market Hall.   *Monday, Thursday, Saturday*

BURY

General market (covered and open air), Shopping precinct.   *Wednesday, Friday, Saturday*
Look out for the black pudding stalls outside the covered market

CHORLEY

General market, Shopping centre.   *Tuesday, Friday, Saturday*

KIRKHAM

General market (privately owned), Shopping centre.   *Thursday*

OLDHAM

General market, Town Centre.   *Monday, Friday, Saturday*

ORMSKIRK

General street market, Shopping centre.   *Thursday, Saturday*

PRESTON

General markets (covered and open air), Town centre.   *Monday–Saturday (exc. Thursday pm)*

WIGAN

General market (covered), Market Hall.   *Friday, Saturday*

WARRINGTON

General market (covered), Market Hall.   *Wednesday, Friday, Saturday*

TRIPE

This is the stomach lining of herbivorous animals such as the ox. There are two main types: blanket tripe, which is smooth and regularly marked and comes from the first stomach, and honeycomb tripe, usually considered the better of the two, which comes from the second stomach.

There is much talk about 'tripe-dressing' in Lancashire, but this is simply the cleaning and par-boiling of the tripe which is necessary before it can be sold for human consumption. It is a technique common everywhere tripe is sold, but in Lancashire it has become something of an art, and tripe stalls and shops still maintain jealously guarded reputations. Those in Wigan have the highest reputation of all.

Tripe, cut into strips and simmered slowly for a couple of hours in milk with plenty of onions and seasoning, is a classic dish both in Lancashire and in London, which has a lot in common with the north in terms of its traditional working food (see p. 30). But tripe can also be combined with gelatinous cow-heel in a kind of stew, or fried in strips with rashers of bacon.

Some Lancashire tripe stalls sell small squares of dressed tripe pickled in vinegar, and ready for eating.

There are still plenty of good tripe stalls in Lancashire, many of which offer other regional delicacies like elder, cow-heel, pigs' feet and trotters. (Photograph by Trevor Wood)

Cow-heel, the gelatinous bovine equivalent to pigs' trotters, is common in Lancashire, where it goes into dishes such as steak and cow-heel pie. (Photograph by Trevor Wood)

Many Lancashire tripe-dressers specialize in *chitterlings*, the small intestine of the pig, which also have to be 'dressed' or cleaned and par-boiled before being sold. (See Wiltshire p. 84).

BACON

In the north of England and in Scotland bacon is rolled. The butcher or grocer may bone and tie the sides of bacon himself, or it may arrive already prepared. These long cylinders are a common sight; the bacon people most often buy is called 'middle' bacon. This is a large rasher that combines streaky and back, and would normally be sold separately in the south. Of course, you can buy different rashers, but the 'middle' bacon is by far the most commonly used. Middle bacon goes into a 'bacon barm', the northern equivalent of the bacon sandwich, made with a big rasher and a toasted barmcake (see later).

Bacon scraps are sold off cheaply as 'hot-pot' bacon.

In Southern Ireland they make a blood sausage called 'drisheen' including pig's blood (although sheep's blood was traditionally used), full cream milk, breadcrumbs or oatmeal, mace, pepper and a sprig of tansy. The drisheen is sometimes put into a membrane casing, and sometimes steamed in a bowl.

BLACK PUDDINGS

Bury is the place in Lancashire for black puddings. In most parts of the north the 'season' is about eight months, from October to May, but they say that you can sell black puddings in Bury even in high summer. Bury puddings, and indeed those from other parts of Lancashire, are small and broad; so, although they are bent and the ends tied together, they do not form the neat loop of puddings from other parts of the country. Bury puddings come in two types: fatty and dry. The dry ones are really too dry for my taste, being almost entirely composed of blood and oatmeal. The fatty ones are much better, with little cubes of pure pork fat set in the pudding mixture.

It is easy to buy black puddings, but you should make a point of finding the stalls set up just outside Bury's extensive covered market. These stalls sell only black puddings, boiled or raw. Nothing else. Your order is brief and explicit: 'Three hot, please.' The man turns and pulls three steaming puddings from one of the big coppers which are bubbling away continuously. He slits each pudding and lets the two halves open like the pages of a book. He hands them over, you pay your money and then reach for the mustard – essential with hot black puddings. A sprinkling of salt may be needed as well.

The stallholders are proud of their black puddings. They will tell you that they make and sell thousands each week on the market not only to older people, but to office girls as well; they will explain that because less beef is being slaughtered, less blood is available (they tend to use this in preference to pig's blood), but they condemn with one voice the practice of substituting dried blood. Only fresh blood provides the true taste of the black pudding, and in my experience they are right.

In the west country there is an old variation on the black pudding called 'black pot'. A mixture of pig's lights, heart and kidney is cooked, minced, mixed with groats and packed in sausage skins. These sausages are called 'gerty meat puddings'. If pig's blood is added to the mixture as well, they become 'black pots'.

Chadwick's is one of the busiest black pudding stalls on Bury market, and also claims to be the oldest. (Photograph by Trevor Wood)

There is a healthy rivalry between the Lancashire makers and those from nearby Yorkshire, where the puddings made by Albert Hirst of Barnsley are considered the finest. Mr. Hirst, seen here with a pile of puddings is not only famous in England, his efforts have also been acclaimed in the famous Black Pudding Competition held at Mortagne-Au-Perche in France. (Photograph supplied by Albert Hirst, copyright the Keystone Press Agency)

There are several ways of dealing with black puddings. You can boil them and eat them hot as part of a filling breakfast as they do in Lancashire; you can split them, fry them with bacon and eat them with fried apple rings. And a well-known pudding maker, Bill Whitfield from County Durham, maintains there is nothing to equal a black pudding baked in the oven.

COOKED MEAT SHOPS AND STALLS

The sight of the many strange foods on Lancashire cooked meat stalls is bewildering, but don't be put off. The men and women who work at them, and often make the various items, are friendly and knowledgeable, and – if they are not busy – are usually happy to talk freely about what they sell. But after such help, don't forget to purchase a selection of different items before you leave.

It is often worth buying the same food from different shops or stalls, for you will find that there are different recipes and different ways of dealing with them. It is not unusual to find that the produce of one particular stall outshines all the others. That is the beauty of these cooked meats and the places that sell them; every stall may sell corned beef or pressed chicken, for instance, but no two will taste alike.

The stalls are always worth looking at: above your head are strings of black puddings; in front of you lie trays with huge lumps of cooked liver and ox heart, various types of pressed meat in slices or moulds: beef, pork, lamb, chicken (which will be served with moist stuffing, spooned from a big bowl next to the meat), jellied veal, potted meat (usually sold loose rather than in small tubs covered with butter), and faggots. There will be other, more familiar, things as well; ham, cooked chicken, tongue and brisket, but there is less brawn than you might expect – perhaps because there is such a proliferation of other products which have similar uses.

There is a passion for all kinds of cooked meats in Lancashire. They are put into sandwiches, wedged into rolls, baps and barmcakes, or set out on plates for high tea – that distinctly northern meal which is an early supper, often completely cold but very substantial. And, incidentally, it is probably no coincidence that Lancashire supports more than its share of good European delicatessens as well, with their sausages, hams and cheeses. These establishments merely extend the range of food offered by the English cooked meat shops.

There are three items of which I'm particularly fond, and which I would like to mention in more detail:

CORNED BEEF

This is immensely popular, a classic tea food and the ideal filling for a sandwich. Some of the best sandwiches I have ever eaten were made with corned beef and onion and accompanied by a mug of tea at one of the cafe stalls on Bury market. The corned beef is very good, big blocks of it, and it is often home-made. It is much moister than the usual tinned variety, not caked with fat, and sold in thin strips which are packed into the sandwiches and barmcakes.

The term 'corning' simply means to cure or preserve meat with granulated salt. Corned beef is cured by dry-salting and then pickling in brine. The same method is applied to corned mutton, which is also sold in Lancashire. On a large, commercial scale the meat would then be pressed and packed into cans, but at home this isn't necessary.

ELDER

This is a real curiosity. I have yet to find a mention of it in any book about English regional food, but it is popular and common on market stalls particularly in south Lancashire. I found it first in Bolton market. The name is a puzzle too, for it seems to have no connection with the food itself. Elder is cooked and pressed cow's udder, eaten cold in slices, and if you have a taste for liver or tongue, the chances are that you will enjoy it. It is rather like tongue in flavour, although milder, softer and much smoother, not fibrous at all. It is pale brown in colour and is surrounded by a thin layer of beautiful golden jelly. A few slices wedged inside a barmcake, or eaten with an oatcake, are quite delicious.

SALMON PASTE

There is hardly a family in the country that does not have fond memories of tinned salmon, that weekend luxury eaten for Sunday tea. (I suspect that in recent years it has been replaced by tinned tuna.) Paste too, whether salmon, sardine, bloater or anchovy, was popular at tea-time. Sundays were the special days when work stopped and the working family could afford to devote a little more time and money to food. The contrast was important; between the food of the week – heavy filling stews for lunch, and plain flour cakes for high tea – and the delicacy and treats of Sunday tea.

In Lancashire salmon paste is still very popular and brought in large quantities. Strangely, it usually keeps company with cooked meat rather than fish on stalls and in shops, and it's home-made, served up from large tubs. Although all the pastes are made from tinned salmon, some are very coarse and dark red, while others are very smooth and pale pink in colour, more recognizable as 'paste'. The tea-time tradition, it seems, still holds.

A recipe for salmon paste on a small scale:

150 gr (6oz) butter
1 tbs hot water
1 small tin salmon
pinch of mace
salt and pepper to taste

Put the butter in a warm bowl and add the water. Beat well until soft and smooth. Remove any bits of skin or bone from the salmon and mix the flesh with the butter until you have a smooth paste. Add the spice and seasoning. Spread on bread, toast, oatcakes or crumpets.

FISH AND FISH SHOPS

When you are walking around the industrial towns of Lancashire it is easy to forget that it is a county with a coastline. But a glimpse at the quality of fish in the area will remind you that Lancashire has important fishing ports like Fleetwood, and it also has Morecambe Bay, famous for its shellfish and crustaceans. Even with today's refrigeration, ice and fast transport, the fish supply in Lancashire tends to be dominated by local resources, and, to a lesser extent, by customs and specialities from Scotland.

An inviting postcard dated 1922. (Titchfield Series Copyright)

From Sunny **Morecambe**
From one Giddy Young Shrimp to another
Hoping you are the pink of Perfection.

Titchfield Series Copyrigh **311**

The most characteristic fish in the markets, during spring and early summer, is hake – a fish often neglected in many areas. Fleetwood hake sold as whole fish, or as skinned 'silver' fillets, is very common. And very good it is too. Then there is halibut, sold in large chunks, salmon trout from the waters to the north and a wide range of shellfish, particularly cockles and whelks, also crabs, shrimps and prawns, all from the waters around Morecambe Bay.

There are echoes of Scotland in the rows of fresh filleted herrings, the Arbroath smokies tied in pairs by the tail, the Finnan haddocks and the kippers. In fact, Lancashire fish stalls reminded me strongly of the fish market at Inverness.

Arbroath smokies, which originated near that town, are small haddock, beheaded but kept whole, and hot-smoked so that the flesh is cooked and the skin outside is copper-coloured. They are one of the rarer types of smoked fish, and certainly one of the most delicious.

BAKING AND BAKERS SHOPS

The people of Lancashire have a fine reputation for home-baking, and the bakers' shops in the region, perhaps because of this, have a great deal to offer. These shops are worth investigating, and there is an essential Englishness about them, not only in their style, atmosphere and decor, but in the foods they sell; nearly everything is from Lancashire or neighbouring areas and there's hardly a Danish pastry or a Vienna slice to be seen.

PIES

Pies abound in Lancashire. They come in all shapes and sizes, with both savoury and sweet fillings. Sometimes they are made with hot-crust pastry, which tends to be much lighter coloured here than in other parts of the country, and sometimes with shortcrust, flaky, or puff pastry.

Savoury pies, from steak and kidney to cheese and onion, are one of the great convenience foods. We eat thousands of them each day, and they are perfect as a snack in the middle or at the end of the working day. They can be eaten hot or cold, straight from the shop, or neatly stuffed into a coat pocket for later.

Pie shops and 'chippies' (see p.198) are a vital part of Lancastrian daily life; they're open at lunchtime and at tea-time, after work. They may also stay open late into the night, ready for closing time in the pubs. In these shops you can buy different sorts of pies, hot peas, gravy, hot black puddings and often fish and chips as well.

It is the tradition of pie-making and eating which is important in Lancashire. Individual bakers take a pride in concocting their own recipes, fillings and pie shapes.

Among the range of savoury pies sold in Lancashire, look out for the following:

Meat and potato pies: these are a great standby in the pie shops. The pies are very heavy, with nearly-white pastry, and they really must be eaten hot from a tray with chips, peas and gravy.

Torpedoes: these are rather like large flattened Cornish pasties, and are filled with a similar mixture of meat, potato, onion and sometimes carrot as well.

Whist pies: these are tiny oval pies – no more than a couple of mouthfuls – made with minced meat (usually pork) surrounded by delicious clear jelly. The pastry again is almost white and very moist.

Cheese and onion pies: these pies are usually made with flaky pastry, and are a delicious reminder of the usefulness of Lancashire cheese in cooking (see p. 193).

Steak and kidney puddings: I include these here, although they are not strictly pies. Many individual puddings are sold ready prepared but uncooked. They are displayed next to small steamed and suet puddings on bakers' stalls in market towns.

In nearby Cumbria, the Lancashire Whist pies are called 'bridge pies'. They are round rather than oval, but their ingredients, and no doubt their function as evening tit-bits are identical.

Lancashire 'foot':

This was a special type of pasty once common in Lancashire, but rare nowadays. We can get a good idea of what they were like from Dorothy Hartley, writing at a time when they were still common.

'A foot is popular as a snappin (i.e. an odd meal that miners take down the pit). It fits into the oval tin they carry. The oval section bottles and tins are a direct result of the miner's cramped job. The name "foot" belongs to the shape, and a miner's cook usually makes a pair of feet, thus: Roll out some good short crust to a plain oval shape; then roll one end again, only, to the centre. This gives the "foot" shape, and if two are made at once, by cutting down the centre before the last roll, the likeness is more striking. It is a simple device for keeping the pies bottom crust thick, and makes the top crust thin, and larger, to flap over the filling.

The filling is not always meat, but cheese, greens, egg, and, less often, fruit and sweet stuff.' – Food in England.

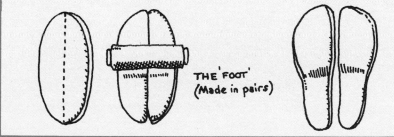

THE 'FOOT'
(Made in pairs)

You will find a large number of fruit pies and tarts in bakers' shops as well. Apple, gooseberry, damson, blackcurrant, cherry, treacle, fig, mincement all find a place as fillings for pies, or in open tarts. Sadly, the intricate pastry latticework and patterns that used to be put onto tarts and showed the baker's skill and imagination as a designer have gone out of fashion, but the tarts are still very good.

You are likely to find 'corners' in quite a number of shops. Large circular fruit pies are divided up into quarters and each of these is called a corner, although the edge of the pie is curved rather than angular. A corner is just the right size for one person, it will fit nicely on a plate, and you can see the quality of the filling before you spend your money.

In 'Food in England', Dorothy Hartley identifies six jam tart designs including Red Cross, The Star, The Well, Lattice, Gable and A Cross Tart.

BREAD, CEREALS AND YEAST PRODUCTS

Oatcakes come in all shapes and sizes, the recipes vary from area to area, and they can be found in huge piles in shops and on market stalls, or, as here, on the table of an enterprising hotel. (Photograph by Trevor Wood)

OATCAKES

In the towns of south Lancashire oatcakes are large and round, pliable and rubbery. They are slightly leavened and made with fine oatmeal; as a result, they are pitted with hundreds of tiny holes. They look as if they might serve as the lacy covering for some dressing table – very like Derbyshire oatcakes in fact. They are curious things which can be folded and rolled, stretched and curled without tearing or breaking up.

Oatcakes in the north-west of England were often known as 'havercakes' or 'haverbread', and the Lancashire Regiment were nicknamed 'the Havercake Lads'.

Move north, or north-east, towards the Yorkshire border, and oatcakes are very different. They are long and thin ('shaped like fish' one baker told me), made with coarse oatmeal, and have a grey-brown colour, not the fawn of their southern brothers. They are unleavened and definitely more substantial. These are the oatcakes for which Yorkshire is also famous (see p. 168). They have a superb, nutty flavour and, in my opinion, rival the finest wholemeal bread. They can be torn and eaten with Lancashire cheese, or warmed under the grill and spread with butter and honey or jam. All the potted and pressed meats from the butchers' shops and cooked meat stalls match the oatcake perfectly. In this context I must mention 'stew and hard', a famous pub food still eaten on Saturday nights. The name needs some explanation: the stew of the title isn't what you might think. In fact it is something between a pressed meat and a brawn, usually made from cheap cuts of beef, although other types of meat may be used. The meat is cooked and then broken down into small fibres which are pressed and set in jelly. The 'hard', or just 'ard, is oatcake warmed until it is slightly crisp. Put the two together and you have 'stew and hard', which is ideal when you are drinking; it settles the appetite, but stimulates the thirst.

BARMCAKES

These are soft rolls, usually made with brown flour, and not unlike the baps (see p.156) found in other parts of England. They are common everywhere in Lancashire: bakers' shops and market stalls sell huge piles of them; they are served in cafés where they are filled with cooked meat, or toasted with a rasher of middle bacon.

When made with white flour, they are often called 'flour cakes', and although there may be subtle variations in the recipes used for these rolls they look and taste like barmcakes. ('Barm' is an old word for yeast, or more accurately the froth of a fermenting liquor. But in the middle ages, yeast had another name: *godesgood* – a delightful word, full of astonishment and mystery, and a favourite of mine).

TEA CAKES

Although these are traditionally associated with Yorkshire they do appear frequently in Lancashire as well. They are made with a milk dough, sweetened with sugar and coloured yellow with beaten egg. These buns are eaten hot and toasted with melted butter. Sometimes the tea cake is split and each half is dipped in melted butter, then the two halves are put together and eaten hot. The toasted tea cake is treated slightly differently. The two halves are toasted on both sides, knobs of butter are laid on the bottom half, the two halves are put together and the tea cake is turned upside down and kept hot for a few minutes. The purpose of this rather elaborate procedure is to ensure that the butter is evenly distributed throughout the tea cake, and doesn't simply soak into the crust at the bottom.

MUFFINS

These are rarely seen nowadays except in Lancashire where they are still made and sold by bakers. They are simply tea cakes made from a yeast dough with a little sugar; the dough is cooked in a special metal muffin ring and the muffin itself is browned on both sides. The best way to eat muffins is to toast them in front of the fire, carefully pull top and bottom apart with your hands and stuff them with soft butter.

CRUMPETS

These are common enough throughout the country, but are usually produced by the large commercial bakers. In Lancashire, however, home-made crumpets are sold on market stalls. Crumpets are rather like muffins except that they are only cooked on one side which means that the top is white and covered with

True Lancashire oatcakes were made originally with butter-milk or with meal that had been mixed and set aside to sour. The oatmeal was mixed with a pinch of salt and enough liquid (buttermilk or water) to make a dough which was kneaded and shaped. Finally it was a flattened and cooked over a fire on a bakestone – a thick, flat, iron pan – for a few minutes. It would then be dried and stored, draped over wooden racks or beams.

All the types of oatcake made in the north-west are very similar and are often known collectively as 'haverbread'. They are found in the Lake District and the Yorkshire Dales as well as Lancashire (see p.216).

In 'A Plain Cookery Book for the Working Classes' (1852), Francatelli gives a recipe for 'Yorkshire Pie-clates for tea'. These were thick pancakes flavoured with currants. They were baked 'upon a griddle-iron fixed over a clear fire to the upper bar of the grate', for two to three minutes each side, and eaten hot with butter.

small holes. I don't think I need tell anyone how to eat crumpets, though a sprinkling of salt greatly adds to their flavour, and other toppings like cheese or bacon can be tried as well.

In Lancashire and Yorkshire, crumpets are sometimes called 'pikelets'. (This word has different meanings in different parts of the country: in the south of England it means a kind of drop scone; in Scotland and in Wales it is a *yeasted* drop scone.)

Many other items, imported from various parts of the country, are sold by Lancashire bakers. From the north come Scotch pancakes, from the west – Ireland – come potato cakes, and there are many more.

PARKIN

In Georgian times, gingerbread was prepared in moulds made from boxwood, beech, walnut and pear, and a wooden box with a close-fitting lid is still the best way to store gingerbread and parkin.

This is a kind of gingerbread common throughout the north of England and Scotland; what makes it special is the use of oatmeal instead of flour. This is mixed with brown sugar, treacle, ginger and candied peel, and these days an egg is usually included although it was never present in old recipes. In fact, there are still many recipes, all slightly different, from different areas of the country.

In Lancashire you will find plenty of parkin. It's made in huge slabs which are divided up and sold in pieces of varying size. When I first bought some I was astonished by its weight; it has an extraordinary density. Parkin must be moist and is best kept for days or even weeks before you eat it. Don't let it dry out, though, for dry parkin is not worth eating.

Guy Fawkes night, November 5th, was traditionally the night for parkin, although it was made at other times as well. Apart from being eaten on its own, it was sometimes accompanied by a slice of cheese, or eaten hot at teatime, with apple sauce.

You will also find *parkin biscuits* in many places in Lancashire and throughout the north country. These are made with similar ingredients to the slab of parkin, although in different proportions, and they are rolled and baked until crisp.

GINGERBREAD MEN

Biscuits called brown fair buttons were once a speciality of the Tombland Fair held each year in Norwich. They were similar to gingerbread biscuits, and consisted of flour, spices (including ginger), treacle, sugar, butter and lemon essence.

Gingerbread was originally a crisp biscuit, often cut into the shape of letters, numbers, or animals, and the gingerbread men, which are made by the hundred in Lancashire bakeries, must be one of the few survivors of this tradition. About six inches tall, with currants for eyes and a piece of chipped almond for a nose, these figures are a real temptation for children – they invite decapitation!

Gingerbread biscuits, made into an oval shapes, are known locally as Bobbie's feet.

GOOSNARGH CAKES

The village of Goosnargh, near Preston, was once famous for its cakes, which could more accurately be called biscuits. These 'cakes', flavoured with coriander or caraway seeds, and dredged on top with castor sugar, were made in vast numbers for the Easter and Whitsun holidays, when the village would be full of people from the area, eating Goosnargh cakes with ale. In *More Old Lancashire Recipes* Joan Poulson tells how a visitor from a nearby town might see Mrs Bramwell sitting by the window in *The Bushells Arms* preparing the sugar, grating it from a loaf using a grater one yard long.

ECCLES CAKES

These are one of the most famous cakes of the north. They are filled with a mixture of currants, candied peel, sugar and spices and the outside is a glossy,

(Reproduced by kind permission of Salford Local History Library)

golden disc of flaky pastry. In some of the very old recipes mint leaves were put into the mixture as well.

The filling is rather like a simple form of the mincemeat that goes into our Christmas mince pies, and it is possible that the original Eccles cakes may have had some religious significance. Certainly, when the Puritans forbade dancing on the village green at Eccles, they also prohibited the eating of cakes at

It was the tradition to keep watch or 'wake' in church on the eve of the anniversary of its dedication. These wakes spilled over into the churchyard, becoming rowdy drunken celebrations. (No wonder the Puritans found them offensive.) In the end these wakes became fairs, and the name continued in the north to mean the annual factory holidays. But wakes are still celebrated in some places, particularly in Ireland, where they are a curious mixture of solemnity and irreverence. They may be held in church or in private houses usually after a funeral.

Bradburn's was 'The Old Original Eccles Cake Shop'.
(Reproduced by kind permission of Salford Local History Library)

Wardle's shop sold Eccles cakes that were made at Bradburn's and it also sold herb beer, ice-cream, cigars, tobacco and chocolate. (Photograph supplied by Joan Poulson)

There are a number of similar cakes to the Eccles to be found all over England. Oval Banbury cakes from Oxfordshire are the best known, but there are also large, plate-sized Hawkshead cakes from the Lake District, and Coventry Godcakes from Warwickshire. These are triangular in shape and sold on New Year's Day and at Easter. They got their name from the time when children used to visit their godparents to receive a New Year blessing, and were given a cake as well, which no doubt tempted even the most reluctant child.

religious festivals. But the local citizens took little notice of this and continued their baking and eating in secret. The cakes remained, and continue to be associated with 'wakes' or fairs in the area. The chorus of an old local song celebrates the custom:

'With music and cakes
For to keep up the wakes
Among wenches and fine country beaux.'

Two shops were renowned for Eccles cakes in the 19th century. Bradburn's was one. It proclaimed that it was *'The only Old Original Eccles Cake Shop. Never removed. On the site of these premises Eccles Cakes were first made. Rebuilt 1835.'* The cakes were also made for another shop, Wardle's, which had no ovens for baking the cakes themselves. It was demolished in 1915 to make way for a bank which now stands opposite the Eccles Cross.

CHORLEY CAKES

These are so like Eccles cakes that it is hard to distinguish between the two if they are not labelled in a shop. Sometimes they are made rectangular rather than round and are usually larger than Eccles cakes, but that is as far as the difference goes.

SAD CAKES

These belong to the Rossendale area of north Lancashire, which is known by some as 'Sad Cake Land'. I have heard it said that the cakes were christened Desolate Cakes by local children at one time. The only ones I have seen looked like large Eccles cakes, but there are variations. In some Sad Cakes the currants are mixed with the pastry and rolled out before baking, while in others the filling is kept in the centre of the cake and the pastry is folded over it, like the corners of an envelope.

BURY SIMNEL CAKE

This used to be baked specially on Mothering Sunday, the 4th Sunday in Lent, for the simnel is a religious cake, the symbol of thousands of years of Christian and pre-Christian festivals. The decorations, traditionally 12 marzipan balls set around the top of the cake, represented the apostles, and sometimes the number was reduced to 11, a way of excluding Judas the traitor. I have seen cakes decorated with 12 blanched almonds set in the shape of a cross. The Romans baked a similar cake or bread called *siminellus*, using fine wheat flour or *simila* – from which we get the word simnel. This was made in honour of the goddess Juno on the festival of Matronalia (March 1st). Even longer ago, it is said that the Athenians honoured the Titans, the children of Uranus, with a cake not unlike our simnel.

There are many recipes for the Bury simnel cake, but they are all based on a type of Christmas cake mixture, with currants, raisins, glacé cherries, candied peel and spices. Sometimes it has a layer of almond paste filling in the middle, and sometimes the ground almonds are included in the cake mixture. After the cake has been baked, warm apricot jam is spread on the top, then it is covered with marzipan. Finally the decorations are added.

A most improbable explanation for the word simnel is that it is a contraction of 'Simon and Nellie', a couple, who were unable to agree on the ingredients for their Easter cake, so each contributed their favourite items. Future generations, it is said, married the two names into a single word, simnel. How do such tales begin?

HOME-MADE SWEETS AND TOFFEE

They are very fond of sweets and toffee in Lancashire, and if you have a taste for sweet things look out for stalls and sweet shops selling irregular chunks and pieces of home-made toffee and candy from boxes or tall, glass jars. I've seen butter toffee, herbal candy, walnut toffee, peanut brittle, treacle toffee, mint toffee and many other types throughout the region.

Lancashire is also famous for *Peggy's Leg* or Liverpool toffee, a mixture of light and dark treacle toffee rolled together, pulled, twisted and cut into lengths.

Everton toffee is rather different – it is a crisp butter toffee, cut into squares and flavoured with lemon essence. It is claimed that Everton toffee was first made by Molly Bush in Everton sometime in the 19th century.

LANCASHIRE CHEESE

The village of Chipping, tucked away in the Forest of Bowland, has a farm which produces probably the only farmhouse Lancashire cheese still made. This crumbly, loose-textured cheese is best sold and eaten young. It can be in the shops within two weeks of being fresh milk in the vats, and much of its quality and flavour comes from this. Newly-made farmhouse Lancashire, stamped with the letter N, is a superb cheese with a high fat content. It is a good spreader and toaster and in the past it was often known as 'Leigh Toaster' from the small town, not far from Manchester, that was once the centre for the cheese-making. New Lancashire cheese is graded, and you should look out for the Extra Selected, the finest quality. Also keep your eyes open for a rare version of the cheese which is speckled with chopped sage leaves.

One of the simplest and best tastes of Lancastrian food I have experienced was a frugal snack of Lancashire cheese and fresh nutty oatcakes which I consumed in a house near Colne.

BREWERIES

BODDINGTONS' BREWERY LTD
Strangeways Brewery, Manchester

A strong independent brewery that has managed to withstand a take-over bid from no less a giant than Allied Breweries. It produces a very distinctive bitter, worthy of the name 'bitter', two dark milds and a strong old ale.

Throughout Lancashire there are something like 270 tied Boddingtons' pubs, all serving traditional beer. As an introduction, try *The Shovel* at Carnforth near Morecambe Bay, *The Black Horse* in Kirkham, *The Talbot* in Chipping, or *The Victoria* in St Annes-on-sea, described by the *Good Beer Guide* as bearing 'some resemblance to a licensed rabbit warren'. In the Manchester area *The Egerton Arms* and *The Queen's Arms* in Eccles are also worth visiting.

(Reproduced by kind permission of Boddingtons' Breweries)

(Reproduced by kind permission of Burtonwood Brewery)

BURTONWOOD BREWERY CO. (FORSHAWS) LTD
Bold Lane, Burtonwood, Warrington, Cheshire

This brewery has a good reputation for its light, creamy bitter – a typical northern character, and also for its light and dark milds.

There are about 300 Burtonwood pubs scattered throughout central Lancashire, Cheshire, Staffordshire and North Wales, and interesting pubs in the Lancashire area include: *The Cavendish* in Brindle, *The Cross Gaits* in Blacko and *The Leigh Arms and Station* in Chorley.

GREENALL WHITLEY AND CO. LTD
Wilderspool Brewery, Warrington, Cheshire

This is the largest of all the independent breweries. It produces a good bitter, again creamy with a slightly sharp taste, and also a light and a dark mild. The beer is more often dispensed with electric pumps although hand pumps can still be found.

There are a considerable number of pubs to choose from – the brewery has about 1,450 tied houses in north-west England. *The Alma* in Bolton and *The Shepherd's Call* in Hyde are both friendly pubs.

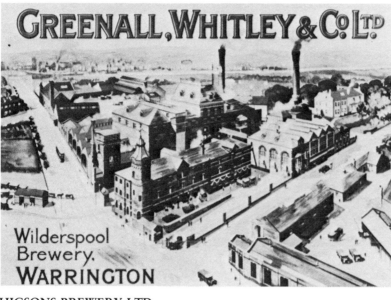

HIGSONS BREWERY LTD
127, Dale Street, Liverpool

A fairly localized brewery centred in and around Merseyside, Higsons produces a bitter and a dark mild that are well thought of in the area.

There are about 160 tied houses, mostly in the Liverpool area, with a few in North Wales as well. *The Railway* in Bootle, *The Caledonia* in Edge Hill and *The Courthouse* in Liverpool city centre are all recommended.

(Reproduced by kind permission of Greenall Whitley and Co)

(Reproduced by kind permission of Higsons Brewery)

BREWERIES

JOSEPH HOLT LTD
Derby Brewery, Empire Street, Cheetham, Manchester
Holt's is a small independent brewery producing a very drinkable bitter and a 'medium-dark' mild. Most of the 80 tied houses are within the Manchester area. For an enjoyable sampling of Holt's beer go to *The Junction* in Cheadle Hulme and *The Hare and Hounds* at Radcliffe.

HYDES' ANVIL BREWERY LTD
46, Moss Lane West, Manchester
Another small and fiercely independent brewery, Hydes produces a good bitter, two draught milds and a strong draught ale called Anvil.

There are only 50 Hydes' houses mainly in the south Manchester area with a few more scattered between Chester and Wrexham. *The Star* at Cheadle and *The Gateway* at Didsbury are worth visiting, and so is *The Pack Horse*, north of Manchester in Bury.

J. W. LEES AND CO. LTD
Greengate Brewery, Middleton, Manchester
Lees' beer has a well-earned reputation in the north-west. The brewery produces a potent bitter, a dark and a light mild. A recent addition to the range of 'John Willie' beers is Moonraker, a strong draught barley wine.

There are more than 150 pubs selling Lees' beer in Lancashire and Cheshire. *The Ring O'Bells* in Middleton is a good place to drink in provided you're not afraid of ghosts, for it is reputedly haunted. *The Wellfield* in Rochdale and *The Black Horse* in Shaw can also be recommended.

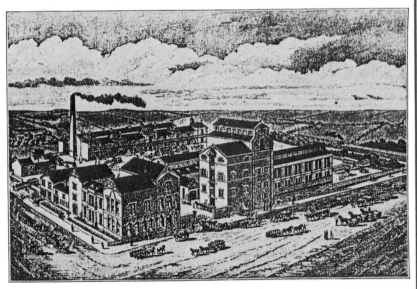

(Reproduced by kind permission of J. W. Lees and Co)

POLLARD AND CO. LTD
The Brewery, Reddish Vale Industrial Estate, Stockport, Greater Manchester
This is a new brewery, started by David Pollard in 1975, and its John Barleycorn bitter is already highly thought of.

Pollards doesn't have any tied houses, but the beer available in a few free-trade outlets in the Manchester area such as *The White Gates* in Hyde, one of the pubs owned by CAMRA Investments.

FREDERIC ROBINSON LTD

Unicorn Brewery, Stockport, Greater Manchester

Robinson's brew two bitters and two milds and also a draught barley wine called 'Old Tom', which Richard Boston nominates as 'one of the great beers'.

Out of more than 300 tied houses, there are number in south Lancashire worth visiting. A good atmosphere in which to drink Old Tom, as well as the other beers, is to be found at *The Castle* in Manchester city centre and *The Star* in Salford.

(Reproduced by kind permission of Frederic Robinson Ltd)

JOSHUA TETLEY AND SON, LTD

Dallam Brewery, Winwick Road, Warrington, Cheshire

Although Tetley's is now a subsidiary of Allied Breweries, it produces fine beer, and in the north its name is still associated with a good drink in most people's minds. It produces two bitters – Walker's and Tetley's – and a good dark mild.

Many Lancashire pubs sell Tetley's beer, although in most it is pressurized, but you can enjoy the beer in its natural state in *The Ring O'Bells* in Leigh, which is well-known for the variety of its pub games. *The Gipsy's Tent* in Bolton is a busy and friendly city pub, and *The Saddle* in Farnworth is a traditional tap room. There are plenty of good pubs in Manchester and Liverpool selling Tetley's beer.

(Reproduced by kind permission of Joshua Tetley and Son Ltd)

DANIEL THWAITES AND CO. LTD

Star Brewery, Blackburn, Lancashire

Like a few other traditional breweries, Thwaites uses shire horses to make local deliveries and is returning to cask beer in those pubs where the beer was previously pressurized. (A sign in the form of a cask is used as a display outside their tied houses.) They produce a fine bitter and two excellent milds.

Thwaites have over 300 pubs in Lancashire and Cheshire and in Staffordshire as well. *The Waterloo* is a large, pleasant pub near the centre of Bury; *The Hare and Hounds* at Bamford is modern and lively, and *The Fleece*, *The George* and *The Navigation* in Blackburn itself are all worth a visit.

FISH AND CHIPS

It may seem strange to include fish and chips in a book about regional food, when it must surely rank as one of our great *national* foods. Yet it started as a regional food and is still associated with a strong regional tradition. Not only that, but it is a food that has always had its roots and real substance in the working-class areas of the north of England and London. Although London had food and 'cook-shops' in the Middle Ages, fish and chips didn't appear until the 19th century. In a well-known passage from *Oliver Twist*, Dickens writes:

'Near to the spot on which Snow Hill and Holborn Hill meet, there opens, upon the right hand as you come out of the City, a narrow and dismal alley leading to Saffron Hill. . . . Confined as the limits of Field Lane are, it has its barber, its Coffee-shop, its beer-shop, and its fried-fish warehouse.'

The book was published between 1837 and 1839, so here in the 1830s we have talk of fried fish. But, apparently, no chips.

Fried fish shops and itinerant fish sellers proliferated in London during the middle of the 19th century. Plenty of fish was available from the fleets working in the North Sea and the best could be sold fresh, using ice to prevent it from spoiling. Fish that was less good, and often completely stale, was fried to disguise its smell and to preserve it for a day or two longer. The fish was fried in shallow pans, not deep-friers, and was usually sold cold. There are also a few references to baked potatoes being served with the fish, so evidently the idea of combining fish and potatoes in this way was beginning to take shape.

Next, we must go down to a shop called Malin's in Old Ford Road in the East End of London. This shop

The outside of Harry Ramsden's near Ilkley in Yorkshire. (Supplied by The Fish Friers Federation)

was presented with a plaque by The Fish Frier's Association, which puts the evidence quite unequivocally:

THE WORLD'S OLDEST
FISH AND CHIP BUSINESS
MALIN'S
PRESENTED 1968 BY THE
NATIONAL FEDERATION OF FISH FRIERS
TO MARK
100 YEARS OF FISH AND CHIPS

(Supplied by The Fish Friers Federation)

(Early in 1978, I went in search of Malin's original shop, but long before I got to its old site, I found myself among high-rise flats and underpasses. The shop had finally succumbed to the pressures of the developers.)

Although London makes claim to being the first fish and chip centre in the country, in the north they have different ideas. Lees' shop in Mossley, on the outskirts of Manchester, is their candidate for the distinction of being 'the original and the greatest'. In 1863 John Lees set up a wooden hut opposite *The Stamford Arms* to

sell pigs' trotters and pea soup. He added chipped potatoes to his menu after a visit to Oldham, where he probably met a tripe-dresser called Dyson, who, in turn, may well have been the first to unite fish with chips.

word of mouth as much as anything else, but it seems most likely that the border country between Lancashire and Yorkshire was the birthplace of fish and chips as we know it. And the fish and chip shops of the north are still the finest in the land – street food at its best.

Fish and chip shops fitted perfectly into the landscape of the industrial north. There was a strong tradition of potato-eating, fish supplies were increasing, there was a mass market of industrial workers who needed ready-cooked food that could be purchased and eaten quickly, especially if all the family worked and there was little time for home-cooking. In these close-knit communities the fish and chip shop was as much a meeting place for gossip as a source of food. That spirit still lives on today.

Any fish and chip shop that you visit will have its salt, vinegar and pickled onions, and nearly all nowadays supplement their wares with pies, sausages, peas and chicken, and sometimes such wayward items as Chinese spring rolls or hamburgers in batter. In the north, haddock is *the* fish (they hardly ever sell cod) and at one time hake was very popular (see p. 186). The decor of the shops themselves ranges from the austere to the flamboyant – one shop that I know in Eye in Suffolk is decked out like the interior of a sailing ship.

Outside Cadey's. (Photograph by Trevor Wood)

Fish and chips isn't just confined to family shops. At White Cross, between Leeds and Ilkley, there is *Harry Ramsden's*, a vast place employing nearly 200 people in shifts, and visited with a mixture of reverence and fanaticism by literally millions of people each year. Ramsden's thrives and maintains its reputation by producing very good food: chips that are crisp and light, not fried to a cinder or saturated with fat; fish that is the best one can buy and that is handled by chefs who have mastered the skill of making a batter that stays succulent and crisp – thin covering for the fish, which is *steamed* inside its protective coat. This is the essence of the fish frier's art.

Cadey's is decorated inside with all manner of nautical objects. (Photograph by Trevor Wood)

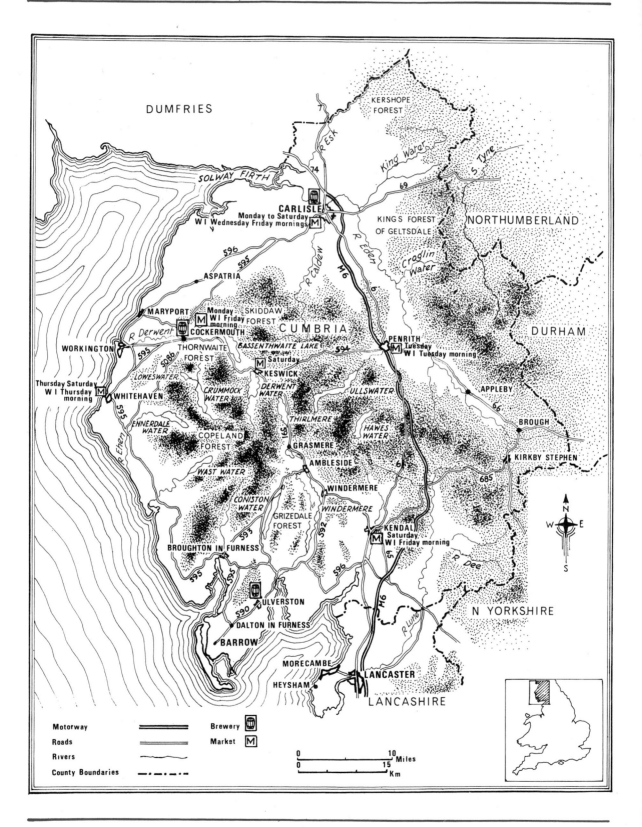

DUMFRIES

KERSHOPE FOREST

SOLWAY FIRTH

King Water

S. Tyne

R. ESK

74

69

R. Caldew

R. Eden

CARLISLE
Monday to Saturday
W I Wednesday Friday mornings

M

KINGS FOREST
OF GELTSDALE

NORTHUMBERLAND

Croglin Water

596

595

ASPATRIA

M6

6

MARYPORT
Monday
W I Friday
morning
COCKERMOUTH

SKIDDAW
FOREST

CUMBRIA

DURHAM

R. Derwent

PENRITH
Tuesday
W I Tuesday morning

M

WORKINGTON

595

THORNWAITE
FOREST

BASSENTHWAITE LAKE

594

508b

Saturday

M

KESWICK

APPLEBY

66

Thursday Saturday
W I Thursday
morning

M

WHITEHAVEN

595

LOWESWATER

CRUMMOCK
WATER

DERWENT
WATER

ULLSWATER

BROUGH

ENNERDALE
WATER

R. Eden

THIRLMERE

161

COPELAND
FOREST

GRASMERE

HAWES
WATER

6

KIRKBY STEPHEN

WAST WATER

AMBLESIDE

685

WINDERMERE

CONISTON
WATER

WINDERMERE

GRIZEDALE
FOREST

592

KENDAL
Saturday
W I Friday morning

M

N
W E
S

BROUGHTON IN FURNESS

593

596

R. Dee

595

595

ULVERSTON

590

DALTON IN FURNESS

M6

R. Lune

N YORKSHIRE

BARROW

65

MORECAMBE

LANCASTER

HEYSHAM

LANCASHIRE

Motorway
Roads
Rivers
County Boundaries

Brewery
Market M

0   10 Miles
0   15 Km

THE LAKE DISTRICT
SWEETS AND MEATS FOR THE VISITORS

It is easy to understand why the Lake District is such a popular tourist area. Ever since the 19th century, when improved transport made the Lakes accessible to people from all parts of the country, it has been a haven for walkers, climbers, anglers, naturalists and people who simply like to spend time in a beautiful landscape. Its fells and lakes, its woods and rivers, do have the kind of beauty that cannot fail to impress.

During my last visit to Carlisle I found a restaurant that served a dish called Cumbrian Kidney kebab. It was a bizarre notion. Why a mixture of kidneys, water chestnuts, bacon and tomatoes, grilled on skewers and served with rice and barbecue sauce should have any local associations, apart from the possible use of kidneys from Lakeland sheep, I failed at first to understand.

But, on reflection, I realized that it is exactly the kind of improbable advertising that is everywhere in the Lake District, where local and regional specialities can be turned into lucrative tourist attractions. Visitors are constantly reminded that the food they are buying is 'traditional', or 'original', or 'celebrated', but above all that it is 'Cumbrian'. The regional prefix is guaranteed to increase sales to newcomers to the area. (Incidentally most of the truly authentic foods like Cumberland sausage have kept their original names. No one has yet dared impose the title 'Cumbrian' on them.)

It's open to argument whether Kendal Mint Cake, or Rum Butter, or Grasmere Gingerbread, would have survived had they not been popularized, and the stream of visitors who call at the tiny shop in Wordsworth's Grasmere serves to emphasize the fascination that local foods can hold for a great many people. If advertising, packaging and an occasional celebrity can ensure that a food does not disappear, it is no bad thing, provided the food isn't altered beyond recognition in the process.

The publicity means that you will have no difficulty in finding the foods of the Lake District; they are displayed everywhere. Apart from the obvious tourist exploitation, the most striking feature of the area is the use of butter. It's the basis of rum butter; it goes into toffee, fudge, shortbread, biscuits and lemon curd; even the famous char from Lake Windermere cannot be potted without it.

Much of the central part of the Lake District is now a National Park, an area preserved for its beauty, and it attracts thousands of tourists every year. Although you need to be hardy to make a winter visit to the Lakes, almost any season will offer something of interest.

CUMBERLAND SAUSAGE

I have fond memories of a gargantuan pub breakfast that I consumed one morning in Kendal: two fried eggs, three rashers of northern 'middle' bacon (see p. 182), tomatoes and a nine-inch length of Cumberland sausage. There

Pub lunches as well as breakfasts often include Cumberland sausage in the Lake District.

Robinson's butchers shop in Penrith has been highly acclaimed for its window displays, which feature huge loops of Cumberland sausage as well as more well-known items. (Photograph by Trevor Wood)

was no choice, no cereal and no coffee. Only tea and bread and butter complemented the spread.

I say 'a nine-inch length' of sausage because that is one of its features. It is not twisted into links, but made as one piece, often several *feet* long. You are unlikely to find a more meaty pork sausage in Britain, and it is often strongly flavoured with herbs. The piece I had in Kendal was loaded with them. I could easily identify bits of rosemary, thyme and sage and there may have been more.

Although Cumberland sausage is often coiled like rope, it is not often that you will see such careful and meticulous handling of this unweildy sausage. (Photograph by Trevor Wood)

MARKETS

Most of the major towns of the Lake District boast good general markets. The meat and fish stalls are usually worth investigating, and stalls carrying home-made produce such as jams, rum butter and mint cake will also catch the eye.

Carlisle market, judging from this picture, was a bustling and very informal open-air market before the days of motorized transport. (Reproduced by kind permission of The Templeton Collection)

CARLISLE

General market, Market Place.   *Monday to Saturday.*
WI stall in the Fish Market.   *Wednesday and Friday morning.*

COCKERMOUTH

General market.   *Monday.*
WI market (seasonal), Mitchells Estate Rooms.   *Friday morning.*

KENDAL

General market.   *Saturday.*
WI market, YMCA Stricklandgate.   *Friday morning.*

KESWICK

General market, Moot Hall.   *Saturday.*

PENRITH

General market.   *Tuesday.*
WI market, Market Hall.   *Tuesday morning.*

WHITEHAVEN

General market.   *Thursday and Saturday.*
WI market, YMCA Lowther Street.   *Thursday morning.*

Although it is called Cumberland sausage it is common in butchers' shops throughout the Lake District and you can buy it in north Lancashire as well (see p.177). It is either draped in large loops from a meat hook, or coiled like rope on the counter. In the middle of the day there may even be a tray of pieces heaped together. The sausage is priced by weight, but it's traditional and more satisfying to order it by the length.

I have never been given a convincing reason why Cumberland sausage is made in one length. Is it simply that it was easier for the butcher to make it like that? Was there perhaps some special use in farmhouse cooking for a long piece of sausage? There is probably no single answer. But the puzzle only adds to the distinctive singularity of the sausage. These days quite a number of butchers sell their Cumberland sausage divided up like ordinary pork sausages – eight to the pound. The mixture inside the skin may be no different, but this trend makes the sausage more difficult to recognize.

Mr Bowman of Robinson's butchers shop in Penrith also makes a special kind of black pudding. The mixture is cooked in a large dish rather than squeezed into skins like a sausage. (Photograph by Trevor Wood)

Robinson's black pudding is cut into thick slabs which have a beautiful marbled appearance. (Photograph by Trevor Wood)

What to do with raw sausages presents a problem for the food hunter, especially when travelling, but if you are camping or using a caravan in the Lake District, you should not hesitate to buy some Cumberland sausage to cook yourself, instead of a pound of bangers for breakfast, lunch or supper. One tip: the skin of Cumberland sausage can be a nuisance. It is quite loose and isn't worth eating unless it is crisp and brown. But fry the sausage slowly, so that the filling is well cooked, before crisping it up.

In the Lake District Cumberland sausage is traditionally eaten with red cabbage that has been boiled with apple; it is also sometimes served with Yorkshire pudding and goes very well with boiled potatoes and apple rings fried in butter.

The Bell Inn at Ramsbury in Wiltshire (see p 93) specializes in English food, and serves Cumberland sausage with pickled red cabbage.

TOMATO SAUSAGES

These sound like a joke. The first time I saw them in Carlisle, next to beef and pork sausages, I thought they must surely be the peculiar invention of one eccentric butcher. But no, they turned up in several other shops in the city. They look like large chipolatas but their colour is the orange of tomato soup. They are made simply by adding tinned tomatoes to the usual pork sausage mixture before filling the skins.

I have never seen these sausages anywhere but Carlisle, and I suspect that they *were* invented by one butcher, but that others in the city subsequently began to make their own versions.

CUMBERLAND HAM

In the 18th century, Westmorland was the place for hams in the Lake District, but these days Cumberland ham has no competitors in the region. There is only one firm producing them, Cavaghan and Gray (Cavray) Ltd of Carlisle, so supplies are limited and the hams are expensive. But I've seen quite a number hanging in butchers and provision shops in Penrith and Carlisle itself.

Cumberland hams are large and long-cut, like those from nearby Yorkshire (that is the ham is cut from the pig carcase at the oyster bone and rounded off). They are dry-salted and rubbed with brown sugar, then hung up to mature for about four weeks. Sometimes they are smoked as well, although it is more usual to see them 'green' or unsmoked with light coloured skin.

Daniel Defoe described Penrith as 'a handsome market town, populous, well built, and for an inland town, has a very good share of trade.' This description is still appropriate today. Penrith is one of the few places in the Lake District that doesn't immediately strike you as a tourist centre. It's still an agricultural trading town, with Victorian red-brick corn stores and large provisions shops.

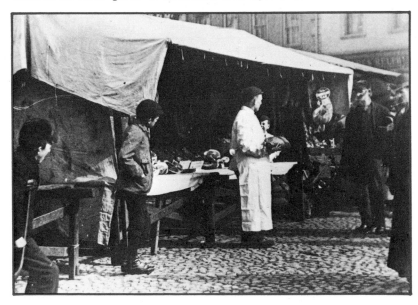

There was a time when Cumberland hams were sold on small stalls situated on Carlisle's open-air market. The boy on crutches is looking, perhaps enviously, at the meaty produce being offered by the stall holder. (Reproduced by kind permission of The Templeton Collection)

Cranberries, although much less common in the Lake District than they used to be, will make a suitable regional sauce for serving with Cumberland ham.

They are an obvious choice for hotel and restaurant menus, indeed dishes of Cumberland ham in various forms are common throughout the Lake District. Baking is the favourite method; the hams are glazed and served with garnishes like Madeira sauce. Many places also serve the ham cold. Whether genuine Cumberland ham is used in all the restaurants where it is advertised does give pause for thought.

TATIE POT

Sometimes this dish is attributed to Westmorland, sometimes to Cumberland. It is a stew of lamb chops and potatoes and is really a variation on the famous Lancashire hot-pot (see p. 178) except that black pudding is included along with the meat and vegetables. It is a dish better suited to the family kitchen than to restaurants and hotels where the long, slow cooking needed for a good result is often cut short because of the pressures of large-scale catering. Even so, restaurants in the Lake District do include it on their menus as 'a local dish', among their steaks and scampi.

I have eaten it in a restaurant in Keswick, and it was filling and tasty. Soft slices of potato at the bottom of the dish (it is served in its cooking pot), then the pieces of lamb and sliced black pudding and onions, and another layer of potatoes, slightly crisp, on top.

A lone Herdwick sheep surviving in bad weather. (Reproduced by kind permission of The Museum of English Rural Life, University of Reading)

The meat for dishes such as tatie pot and Lancashire hot-pot comes from the sheep of the Lake District, the Herdwick. The name originates from the pasture where the animals are kept, but, over the years, it has become established as the name of the breed. Herdwick sheep have a reputation for toughness and are said to be 'the breed best standing starvation'. They have to survive temporary burial in snow drifts and an improvised diet, which in the past included carefully harvested ash leaves.

CUMBERLAND SWEET PIE

Another traditional dish, prepared in many farmhouse kitchens, is Cumberland sweet pie which is also based on the fine meat from Herdwick sheep. There are two ways of making it. If the pie is to be eaten straight away, fat mutton chops are put into a pie dish with dried fruit, lemon juice, brown sugar, mixed peel and spices and covered with rough puff pastry. The pie is then baked and eaten hot.

But if it is intended to be kept, as often happens during the winter, the mutton and other ingredients are minced together with rum and packed into raised pie cases, like those made for pork pies. The pies, once baked, can be kept for several months.

The mixture inside these pies may remind you of Christmas mincemeat, and it is exactly that. For originally mincemeat did contain meat both lean and fat, not simply suet. Sometimes, if meat was scarce, no lean would be included, just mutton fat minced with the fruit. (Compare these pies with Cumberland Rum Nickies, see p. 214)

(Compare these pies with Cumberland Rum Nickies, see p. 214)

Cumberland sweet pie, unlike tatie pot, has not yet been taken out of the farmhouse kitchen and put onto menus in public eating places. But hopefully some enterprising restauranteur with sufficient skill and knowledge will introduce it in due course.

SALMON

During the summer months there is plenty of salmon to eat in the Lake District. You have to pay a high price for it, of course, but a meal of fresh poached salmon is hard to equal. Most of the fish come from the Solway Firth and the estuaries of the River Nith in Dumfries and the River Lune in north Lancashire. But the Lune and another Lancashire river, the Wyre, have become so polluted and so many fish have died in them that the fishermen have been forced to move further north to cleaner waters.

Fishermen in these areas use a special type of net called a 'haaf' or 'heave' net, which is only seen in the Solway Firth and the rivers of the north-west. The net is fixed to a wooden frame rather like a vast three-pronged fork, with a beam often 14–18 ft. across. The fisherman stands in the water and holds the net upright against the tide; when he feels a salmon in the net he has to tip and lift it out of the water. It is a clumsy instrument needing a lot of strength and skill, and there are many variations in both design and technique in different parts of the north-west. It is graphically described in the book, *Nets and Coracles*, by J. Geraint Jenkins (David and Charles 1974).

Because this effective method could lead to greediness and overfishing, licences are issued by the local river authorities much less easily than they used to be. But there is still a lot of salmon in fish shops and on restaurant menus. Look out for signs saying 'Today's Special – Fresh Salmon', especially outside pubs; this usually means that the landlord has obtained some fish and has cooked it straight away. Restaurants and hotels on the other hand may need to rely on stocks from their freezers.

Fishermen haaf-netting for salmon on the Solway Firth. (Photograph by Alastair Alpine Macgregor. Supplied by Country Life)

BREWERIES

HARTLEYS' (ULVERSTON) LTD
Old Brewery, Ulverston, Cumbria
Although this brewery is owned by Whitbread, it is still allowed to brew its own draught beer. There are two bitters, of which the XB is by far the better; it is a strong beer with a sweet heavy taste. The ordinary bitter is weaker and much lighter. There is also a dark mild sold only in a few of the brewery's tied houses.

HARTLEYS, ULVERSTON, LIMITED.
BREWERS,
WINE & SPIRIT MERCHANTS.

The Sawyers Arms in Kendal is a friendly local pub and the landlord's wife produces an extraordinary cooked breakfast – often including Cumberland sausage – for guests who stay there. Other pubs worth trying are *The Old Friends* and *The Railway* in Ulverston, *The Queen's Head* in Hawkshead and *The Golden Rule* in Ambleside.

Hartleys' brewery in Ulverston, with its splendid brick chimney, looks less like a brewery than most of its counterparts throughout the country. (Pohotograph by P. Hatfield, reproduced by kind permission of Hartleys' Brewery)

JENNINGS BROTHERS LTD
Castle Brewery, Cockermouth, Cumbria

The present brewery is situated, as the name suggests, just below Cockermouth castle, and it supplies a large number of pubs around west Cumberland. The bitter is a thin and hoppy brew, reminiscent of many southern beers; there is a dark mild as well. The Castle Pale Ale and the Export Ale are two bottled beers worth drinking.

REG. No. 24795 ENGLAND

The tiny *Ghyll Yeat* in Blindcrake, just north of Cockermouth, is a fine Jennings pub, as are most of the pubs in Cockermouth itself, like *The Railway* and *The Rampant Bull*. In Keswick *The Oddfellows Arms* is a very busy, noisy pub, and, in Embleton, *The Blue Bell* is an attractive pub to drink in.

(Reproduced by permission of Jennings Brothers Ltd)

T. & R. THEAKSTON LTD
The Old Brewery, Caldewgate, Carlisle, Cumbria

This is the former State Management Scheme brewery and is a branch of the main Theakston's brewery in Masham in north Yorkshire. The bitter brewed in Carlisle is available in a number of free houses in Cumbria. You may also be able to find bottles of Old Peculiar – a very strong bottled beer. (It is produced as a draught beer at the Masham brewery, is sometimes known as Strong Yorkshire Ale, and is claimed to be one of the strongest on draught from the wood.)

AN INDEPENDENT FAMILY BREWERY SINCE 1827

Try Theakston's bitter in *The Drunken Duck* in Ambleside, *The Sawrey Hotel* in Beatrix Potter's home village of Sawrey, and *The Crown* at High Newton.

(Reproduced by permission of T. & R. Theakston Ltd)

Although salmon trout are caught with haaf nets, most of the fish are taken in fresh water by anglers using artificial flies and spinners. Despite its name the fish only spends part of its life in the sea.

SALMON TROUT

Sometimes called sea trout or, in Wales, sewin, *Salmo trutta* is a beautiful fish to look at and superb to eat. It has a milder though similar taste to salmon, but has the moist texture of trout with very light pinkish flesh. It is in the shops during late spring and early summer, and because a single fish rarely weighs above 2kg (4lbs) it is worth buying a whole one for a special occasion.

Much of the catch comes from the river estuaries around the Solway Firth, and it is often caught, like salmon, in haaf nets.

TROUT

Anglers who come to the Lake District to catch fish come in search of trout more than anything else. Although permits and licences may be expensive and difficult to obtain, dedicated fishermen do not see this as a problem. The native brown trout lives in Lake Windermere and in other lakes in the region, and they are also found in the small mountain streams.

But if you are not an angler and want to taste really fresh trout, they are sold in quite a number of fish shops, especially those in lake villages like Windermere. They may be brown trout although the smaller rainbow trout, not a native fish but more common in shops than the brown trout, is worth buying too.

CHAR

On January 27th, 1738, the Duke of Montagu wrote from London to a Mr Atkinson of Dalton, a town near Ulverston:

'I received yours of the 1st this month, and also the Pott of Charr which you sent by that day's Carrier, which was the best I ever eat, and I would have you send me some of the same sort every Carryer, take care to pick the hen fish and those that are of the Red Kind, and let them be potted and seasoned just as that Pot was, for it cant be better.'

Char are the least known and least common members of the salmon family. In the British Isles they are confined to deep inland lakes, from the loughs of west Ireland to the lochs of the Shetlands, but they are most common in the Lake District, especially in Lake Windermere. *Salvelinus willughbii*, the Windermere char, is a handsome creature, looking rather like a trout, about 25–30 cm (10–12 inches) long, with a dark greenish-brown back fading into silver and finally orange or sometimes deep red on the belly. It has the delicate pinkish flesh characteristic of the salmon and sea trout.

This char pot was made in about 1880 from biscuitware, although most were originally made from 'delftware' – tin-glazed earthenware. The pots were supplied from factories in Liverpool from the second half of the 18th century onwards.(Reproduced by kind permission of Abbot Hall Art Gallery, Kendal)

Char would have been heavily encased in butter and the pots securely sealed to ensure that the fish withstood the jolting, discomfort and erratic temperature of an 18th century coach trip from the Lakes to London. Careful preparation and preservation was vital if the fish was to reach its destination in good condition. At Rothay Manor, in Ambleside, Bronwen Nixon uses a large, beautifully decorated pot for serving potted char. It is much deeper than its 19th century ancestors. (Photograph by Trevor Wood)

Char pies, and other recipes for the fish, had been listed in records dating back to the middle of the 17th century, but not until the 1770s, when the Lake District experienced its first tourist explosion, did potted char become really popular. With it developed a very distinctive design in ceramics, the char pot.

These char pots with their hand-painted fish – the work of freelance journeymen decorators – were specialized, non-returnable containers in which the fish could be prepared, transported and eaten. Once washed out, the empty pot could be turned into a fashionable *objet d'art* for the wealthy visitors to the Lakes in the 18th and early part of the 19th century.

The trade in potted char declined towards the end of the 19th century; there was overfishing, but better transport and refrigeration provided tourists with alternative attractions. Today it is very localized indeed; pots are no longer sent to London and the fish hardly ever appears in fish shops. You have to go to Lake Windermere and make contact with a fisherman, or catch the char yourself. Or you can go to Rothay Manor in Ambleside, one of the few places

Catching char:
By using a number of weighted lines set at different depths in the water, the fisherman can find out where the char are swimming. Some fish are caught 100ft down and are often stunned by the pressure change when brought to the surface.

A pair of chars. It is clear from this picture that the fish is related to the salmon and the trout. (Photograph by Trevor Wood)

A sample of Bronwen Nixon's collection of char spinners which are custom-built by local fishermen around Lake Windermere. (Photograph by Trevor Wood)

that regularly serves potted char as a first course on its menu. Supplies, though, are dependent on the luck and skill of the locals – postman, dustman, or butcher – all of whom call at the hotel kitchens with their catch.

They go out in boats between May and September to catch the fish using a rod and a series of lines, each ending in a hook and spinner. These spinners are the special trademark of each fisherman (just as the hand-painted fish were of the char pot decorators). They are hand-made of brass, copper or silver, or a mixture of any of these, and are polished for hours. Bronwen Nixon, the proprietor of Rothay Manor, has some that one of the char men gave her; on the side of the spinners you can see the tiny tooth marks of the fish.

POTTED SHRIMPS

Morecambe Bay has long been famous for its shrimps, which since the 18th century have been potted with butter. No doubt this was originally a way of using up surplus shrimps from a catch, but nowadays the dish has taken its place alongside other tourist attractions in the region. Potted shrimps are common in the seaside towns along the Lancashire coast, and are also sold throughout the southern half of the Lake District, especially around the Lakes tourist centres.

Most of the early recipes for potted shrimps produced something resembling a shrimp paste because the fish were shelled, pounded with butter and spices, then covered with a layer of melted butter. But these days the shrimps are shelled and left whole. They are stirred in melted butter with a little nutmeg, mace and cayenne pepper, then packed into small pots or dishes (small white china pots were always used at one time, but now disposable plastic is more common, at least in shops). Finally the buttered shrimps are covered with a layer of clarified butter and left to get cold.

You can buy potted shrimps from most fish shops in the Lake District, or you can treat yourself to a summer tea of potted shrimps, brown bread and butter in one of the tea shops or restaurants in the area.

OTHER FISH

The Lake District isn't well supplied with fish shops. There is no great tradition of fish eating in the area, apart from its famous salmon, trout and char, but the indigenous fish aren't alone on the slabs these days. From Scotland there are Finnan haddocks, Arbroath smokies (hot-smoked haddocks) and plates of filleted herrings (a familiar sight in Scottish fish shops); from English ports like Fleetwood come hake and halibut; and it is encouraging to see the small, sweet kippers from the Isle of Man being sent across the water to places like Windermere.

Fried fish shops are also quite scarce, but they do produce good fish and chips, and, as in the rest of the north of England, haddock is the fish they prefer to use.

Manx kippers are at their best during July and August and are cured from very small herrings caught off the north-west coast of England. (It's illegal to colour them with dye in the Isle of Man.) They are superb, and one batch I obtained from Geo. Devereau, Douglas, I.O.M., were the finest I have ever tasted.

RUM BUTTER

The Lake District's most popular souvenir food was once an essential part of every christening feast. Whenever a child was born a special celebration meal would be prepared, often by the midwife herself. There would be plenty of spiced ale, warmed by the fire, with rum added to it; there would be 'Groaning Cheese' – fingers of cheese handed round to all the unmarried women at the feast to tuck under their pillows at night; there would be oatcakes, too, and a large bowl of rum butter made from butter, soft Barbados sugar, nutmeg and another ration of rum. This was a special treat, handed round for everyone, but especially to the new mother to speed her recovery. Much more pleasant than many of today's prescribed tonics! It might even be given to the baby – 'as its first taste of earthly food', though this would not be the child's first contact with rum, for its head would have been washed with the spirit as soon as it was born.

It's an unlikely past for a food which has links with Christmas pudding and mince pies, but few uses otherwise. Yet there's no denying that it is delicious

One 17th century account of rum in Barbados describes it as 'rumbullion, alias kill devil . . . made of sugar canes distilled, a hot hellish and terrible liquor'.

(Reproduced by kind permission of Jennings Brothers Ltd)

Like the Yorkshire Dales, the Lake District once produced a large quantity of butter, but its cheese had little reputation. The only one I have seen mentioned is a cheese from the Whillimoor area of West Cumberland. In 'Jollie's Sketch of Cumberland Manners and Customs' (1811), there is a mention of it, where it is also called Wheelimer, Leather-hungry and Roslay Cheese. 'It is a poor sort of cheese made of skim milk, in general use among labouring people, and so tough and stubborn in its nature, that those that live upon it often find the hour of refreshment the hardest part of their day.'

Men would apparently amuse themselves in the evening by carving butter prints from it.

and worth buying. You will find it in sweetshops, delicatessens, grocers and even in souvenir shops. Usually it is packed in plastic tubs, but sometimes little stoneware pots are used. (Incidentally, look out for brandy butter as well.)

Rum butter will keep well, but a few precautions may be necessary in very hot weather, when no refrigerator is at hand. One blazing summer afternoon I had to put a tub I had bought into a glass of cold water in my hotel wash basin to stop it melting. By the morning it was perfect, and I ate a spoonful of the butter before going to breakfast.

RUM IN OTHER DISHES

Rum is important throughout the Lake District in many local dishes, in customs and folklore – no doubt to fortify the spirit during the bleak winter months, and to provide a little inner warmth and nourishment when it is freezing or blowing a blizzard outside. Why rum? During the 18th century, there was a continuous trade between ports like Whitehaven and the West Indies, and quantities of rum were brought over in ships, along with the Barbados sugar and dried fruit also used by cooks in the Lake District.

Two dishes from the Lake District's past which illustrate how rum was used in the kitchen are:

Cumberland Rum Nickies:
These were small 'mince' pies. Small rounds of shortcrust pastry were covered with a mixture of butter, rum, brown sugar, dates, currants and preserved ginger, with nutmeg. A pastry lid was put on each and they were baked in a hot oven. Compare this meatless mincemeat with that used in Cumberland Sweet Pie (see p. 207).

Rum Dog:
By soaking raisins in rum and mixing them with flour and shredded suet you could, with a little water, make a dough that could be steamed slowly and eaten after a hard day's work. Joan Poulson, in her book *Old Northern Recipes* (Hendon Publishing Co. 1975), mentions that this dish was popular after hound trailing (see below). The dogs too would be given a special concoction called 'cock-loaf' to prolong their active lives, made from flour, eggs, raisins, sherry and port, mixed and cooked like a pudding, and then sliced and toasted.

Grasmere Sports is a unique event because it features regional games and contests: Cumberland wrestling in which the contestants wear long leggings and embroidered velvet trunks; fell racing, a gruelling sprint to the top of Butter Crag and back. Also there is a hound trailing, in which the hounds – often of foxhound and greyhound ancestry – run the length of a 10 mile drag in not less than 25 minutes and not more than 45 minutes.

GRASMERE GINGERBREAD

The village of Grasmere is a classic tourist attraction, thriving on visitors and with enough attractions to draw thousands every year. It lies in the middle of the Lakes National Park, just north of Lake Windermere; you will find Dove Cottage here, the tiny home of William Wordsworth – that most English of poets; here too, every August, they hold the Grasmere Sports, the most famous in the north of England. And they sell Grasmere gingerbread.

S. Nelson

(Mrs. M. G. Wilson)

Sole Makers of the Celebrated Grasmere Gingerbread

Tucked away at one corner of the village churchyard is the Gingerbread Shop, or to give it its full title: Sarah Nelson's Original Celebrated Grasmere Gingerbread Shop. It's a tiny building that can accommodate perhaps three customers at any one time. Hardly any light filters through the windows, but it

Sarah Nelson photographed in her old age by one Herbert Bell. (Reproduced by kind permission of the proprietors of The Grasmere Gingerbread Shop)

The Grasmere Gingerbread Shop does not have a striking exterior. You might miss it altogether, were it not for the crowds that cluster round it every day. (Photograph by David Mabey)

is homely and warm, fragrant with the smell of spice and baking. All the gingerbread is made and packed on the premises where in 1855 Sarah Nelson started work. She had been given the job of baking gingerbread for the chef of a big house near her home. Quickly realizing its possibilities, she patented her recipe. After her death the secret was stored in the vaults of a bank until the present owners bought it. They didn't know exactly what they were paying for until they transcribed the notes written on that precious scrap of paper, which is once again back in the vaults.

It's rather misleading to call it gingerbread at all; it is much more like a ginger shortbread or a dry, ginger-flavoured flapjack. The gingerbread is sold in squares less than half an inch thick made of oatmeal, butter, sugar, chopped ginger and candied peel all mixed together and baked in large flat slabs – but in what proportions the makers do not say.

Grasmere gingerbread is enormously popular with visitors, especially children. You can watch them going into the shop time and time again for

(Reproduced by kind permission of the proprietors of The Grasmere Ginerbread Shop)

extra helpings which they eat as they are escorted round the village by supervising adults. And there's no better way of eating it than on the move.

If you buy a packet of gingerbread rather than a couple of loose pieces, look at the note printed in blue on the greaseproof wrapping: it tells you that if the gingerbread is rather hard you can soften it by warming it gently.

BREAD AND BAKING

> The traditional bread of the Lake District was a flat oatcake called 'haver bread' (from the Old Norse word *hafrar* meaning oats). It was also called 'clap bread' because of the way it was clapped or beaten by hand.
>
> Celia Fiennes saw clap bread being made near Kendal in 1698 and recorded these notes in the book about her travels around England.
>
> '. . . they mix their flour with water so soft as to rowle it in their hands into a ball, and then they have a board made round and something hollow in the middle riseing by degrees all round to the edge a little higher, but so little as one would take it to be only a board warp'd, this is to cast out the cake thinn and so they clap it round and drive it to the edge in a due proportion till drove as thinn as a paper, and still they clap it and drive it round, and then they have a plaite of iron same size with their clap board and so shove off the cake on it and so set it on coales and bake it . . . if their iron plaite is smooth and they take care their coales or embers are not too hot but just to make it look yellow it will bake and be as crisp and pleasant to eate as any thing you can imagine.'[1]

Celia Fiennes was fascinated by all kinds of local food and its preparation, and her book is peppered with anecdotes and descriptions of everything from making clap-bread to the extraction of rock salt in Cheshire.

The 'iron plaite' was a circular iron girdle plate or 'bakstone' to put on the fire; by the 19th century bakstones were built into stoves. Baking clap bread was a day's work so enough would be made to keep and use for several months. Most farmhouses had special carved oak bread-cupboards in which their supply was stored. (You can see one of these in the Museum of Lakeland Life and Industry in Kendal.)

In the Lake District carved oak cupboards were also known as 'court cupboards', and, in addition to haver bread, they may well have been used to hold items of silver or pewter.

1 *The Journeys of Celia Fiennes*, ed. C. Morris, Cresset Press, 1947

By the 1880s the price of wheat had dropped so low because of the import of cheap grain from the New World that the baking of traditional oatcakes or bread inevitably declined, and you will not find clap bread in bakers' shops in the Lake District today. You will find, however, traditional items imported from other regions: soda scones from Ireland; bannocks, drop scones and baps from Scotland; potato scones and pikelets from Lancashire. And, if freshly baked on the premises, they are well worth sampling. Beware mass produced imitations, though.

KENDAL MINT CAKE

This isn't a cake at all, but a tooth-rotting peppermint candy, or as the local advertisements say 'a Lakeland sweetmeat'. Although it is made in several places throughout the Lake District, Kendal is the real centre, with four manufacturers – Wipers, Wilsons, Quiggins and Romneys – all competing for the money of the tourists who buy bars of mint cake as souvenirs.

As well as being a tourist attraction, mint cake is designed specifically for giving energy in a compact form to the climbers and walkers of the region. (I have seen packets tucked into the back pockets of many a pair of jeans before a climb begins.) The makers are very proud of the use made by various international expeditions of their own brands, and publicize their clients extensively. Wilsons' list is particularly impressive:

Annapurna South Face Expedition
British Headless Valley Expedition
NAAFA Christmas Island Expedition
Sandhurst Ethiopian Expedition
British Pakistani Forces Expedition, Himalayas

Royal Navy East Greenland Expedition
Cambridge University Caving Club Expedition to Arctic Norway
University of Sheffield Expedition to Kilimanjaro

Harvesting oats by hand in the Lake District. (Photograph supplied by the Museum of English Rural Life, the University of Reading)

Most of these expeditions took place in the 1950s, a boom time for mint cake on the mountains of the world. One of the advertising posters from this period shows a line-drawing of a climber; he is a clean, neat and rather dull-looking man, not at all like today's rugged mountaineers.

(Reproduced by kind permission of Wilsons, Romneys, Quiggins and Wipers, manufacturers of Kendal Mint Cake)

Romneys' Mint Cake had the distinction of travelling with John Hunt and Sherpa Tenzing as they made their way up the slopes of Mount Everest in 1953, and the makers have re-named their mint cake after the mountain.

Mint cake is a very simple sweet, merely sugar made into a candy and flavoured with peppermint oil or essence. It comes in bars of different shapes and sizes, white or brown depending on the sugar used. (I confess that I can find no real difference in taste between these two types.) Sometimes the mint cake is coated in chocolate or made into thin fingers.

Like Kendal Mint Cake, many other locally produced sweetmeats are packaged specifically for walkers and climbers and are equally as effective as energy-producers.

Boxes of Kendal Mint Cake packed and ready for despatch to the Everest Expedition. (Reproduced by kind permission of Robert Wiper Ltd)

Quite a number of different sweetmeats are manufactured in the Lake District especially for tourists; two in particular are worth mentioning. Butter fudge is often produced by the mint cake makers and sold in what they call 'satchel packs'. Another butter sweet is butter toffee. I have bought this home-made from a stall in Carlisle market; a bag of delicious fragments which looked like pieces of amber. I'm not a great lover of toffees and sweets, but these were delicious.

Bistort.

(Illustration by Carol Fowke)

EASTER LEDGES

This is the local Lake District name for bistort (*Polygonum bistorta*), an edible plant common in wet hilly pastures in the north of England. The young leaves picked in the spring are mixed with other fresh green vegetation and made into a pudding with barley or oatmeal. This pudding isn't available in shops or markets, but people go out and pick bistort, dandelion, young nettles, lady's mantle, the leaves of the great bell flower, and the tender leaves from soft fruit bushes, anything in fact that is young, green and edible, and make the pudding themselves. In the past, after a winter diet of dried mutton, oatmeal and root vegetables, this pudding must have provided much-needed vitamins and minerals – a real spring cleaning for the blood.

In the Lake District the plant is sometimes called Easter Giant (a contraction of Easter Mangiant from the French *manger*, to eat), and in Yorkshire you will hear it called Passion Dock or Gentle Dock. (Bistort is related to the true docks, and may well have been confused with Patience Dock (*Rumex patientia*) at one time.)

NOTE: several towns in Yorkshire are famous for their Dock Pudding Contests; one held in Heptinstall during 1977 was organized to raise money for the local brass band.

There are many recipes for Easter Ledge Pudding. Here is one that I obtained from a lady in Kirkby Lonsdale:

3 good handfuls of Easter ledges
3 good handfuls of young nettle leaves
1 good handful of cabbage or broccoli leaves
a few young dandelion leaves and blackcurrant leaves (or gooseberry, or raspberry)
1 onion
1 cup barley (soaked overnight in hot water and strained)
3 eggs
salt and pepper to taste

Wash all the greens and chop or mince. Put into a muslin bag with the prepared barley, place in boiling water and boil for 1 ½ hours. Empty the contents of the bag into a warm bowl, beat in the eggs and put the dish into the oven for a few minutes before serving.

DAMSONS

The southern part of the Lake District is well known for its large, sweet damsons, known as Witherslack damsons. They are grown in many places, but the finest are said to come from the Lyth Valley, south of Windermere. They are made into chutney, cheese and jam, or pickled with sugar, spices and vinegar; they find their way into pies; they are turned into wine and used to flavour brandy in the same way that sloes do gin.

Damsons. One of a series of postcards depicting English fruit.

SCOTLAND
HIGHLANDS AND LOWLANDS: KILTS AND KIPPERS

Scottish cookery also has links with France, and especially Brittany. Many of its dishes, such as haggis, have recognisable French equivalents.

Scotland, Wales and Ireland – the Celtic countries – have a great deal in common. All of them have a strong religious inheritance, languages rooted in the same base and much that is fundamentally similar in their cooking and eating habits. While they do have many foods and dishes which are also found in England, there is still a great deal that is different.

Scottish cookery, and indeed Celtic cookery in general, is based on oatmeal and fish, while the English have founded their cookery on flour and meat. The basic features of the Scottish kitchen are the pot over the fire, the hearth as the central feature of the kitchen, and the ever-present griddle or girdle, which is a thick, round piece of iron, fitted with a handle and used for baking over an open fire. It developed from the hot stones used by the early Gaelic peoples for the same purpose. In contrast, the English cook concentrates more on the oven and the frying pan.

These differences reflect the clear variation in soil, climate and geography between the two countries. The highland areas of Scotland are cold, the growing season uncertain and the soil thin and hard to cultivate. Only oats and few root vegetables will grow with any vigour. Lush pastures are few, although Scotland does boast the Aberdeen Angus, some of the best beef cattle in

Aberdeen Angus bulls in a stately Scottish setting. (Reproduced by kind permission of The Museum of English Rural Life, University of Reading)

Britain. But the moors and heather are ideal habitats for the red grouse and for deer; the inland lakes or 'lochs' and the streams and rivers teem with salmon and trout, not to mention all the open sea has to offer. Scottish food is varied, exciting and colourful. As well as the foods that can be found on sale in different parts of Scotland, there are a great many traditional dishes (unfortunately outside the scope of this book) still made in the country's kitchens.

Breakfast and tea are the two meals which the Scots handle best, and most of their classic traditional foods belong with these occasions. The list is marvellously rich, ranging from porridge and marmalade to baps, Finnan haddock and shortbread. These foods, above all others, are identified with Scottish life today.

OATS AND PORRIDGE

The common cultivated oat (*Avena sativa*) was not established in Britain until the Iron Age, although it is known to have existed in Europe in the Bronze Age. It is the most important cereal in Scotland, mainly because it is a hardy, resilient crop, able to thrive in much poorer soil and in a worse climate than other cereals such as wheat. The Midlothian area produces the best oats in Scotland.

It is actually the oatmeal – that is the substance obtained after the oats have been ground and the husks removed – which provides the basis of so many Scottish foods. Oatmeal comes in three grades – fine, medium, and coarse – all with different uses in the kitchen. Fine oatmeal goes into soups, herrings are floured in it before cooking, and it is the basis of some bannocks (see later) and scones. Medium oatmeal is once again used for bannocks, and for mixing with other flours, while coarse oatmeal is best for oatcakes and for mixing with meat dishes.

This card, dated 1899, advertises 'The most nutritious food for infants, children and invalids'.

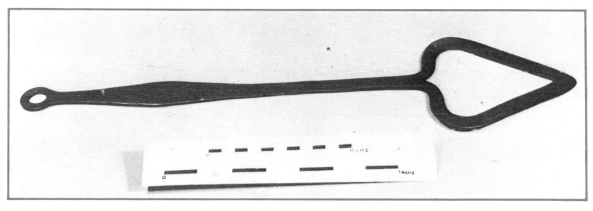

Porridge must be the most famous, and one of the simplest, of all Scottish foods. Its reputation has spread far beyond its national boundaries, but outside Scotland it is often made without care, and becomes a lumpy, cloying sludge. It should be made with medium oatmeal simmered in water with a little salt added to it. (The custom was always to stir porridge clockwise, never the other way, with a straight wooden stick rather than a spoon.) When ready, the porridge is dished into cold bowls and a small dish of cold milk is provided. Each spoonful of hot porridge is dipped into the cold milk before being eaten. The porridge is normally seasoned with extra salt, although many people prefer sugar or even treacle. One of the most fortifying winter breakfasts I have ever eaten consisted of a bowl of porridge generously laced with malt whisky.

One of the best tests of Scottish hotel cooking is the care with which the breakfast porridge is made.

A bannock spade or 'spathe', used for turning bannocks on the griddle. (Reproduced by kind permission of The Museum of English Rural Life, University of Reading)

(Reproduced by kind permission of Albany Blenders Ltd)

An impression of the Tomatin distillery, established in 1907. (Reproduced by kind permission of the Tomatin Distillers Co)

(Reproduced by kind permission of Strathdearn Scottish Distillers Ltd)

(Reproduced by kind permission of Macdonald and Muir and The Glenmorangie Distillery)

(Reproduced by kind permission of William Grant and Sons)

Part of the Glenfiddich distillery. (Reproduced by kind permission of William Grant and Sons)

SCOTCH WHISKY

So much has already been written about the virtues of Scotch whisky that it would be pointless to repeat what is common knowledge to anyone who has ever held a dram in his hand. Pure Scotch malt whisky, distilled from malted barley, is one of the finest drinks in the world, and no other country can produce anything to imitate its flavour, aroma or effect on the drinker. Everyone has their favourite, it might be Glenmorangie or Glenfiddich or Glenlivet. It might be the dark smoky Tomatin distilled in the Findhorn valley near Inverness, or the straw-coloured Jura from the Western Isles.

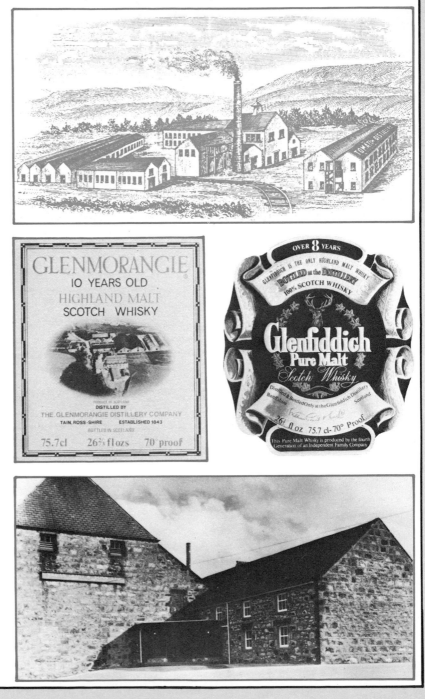

OATCAKES OR BANNOCKS

The word bannock comes from the Old Scottish *bannok*, which in turn is derived from the Latin *panicum*, suggesting that it may originally have referred to Communion bread. Through the years Scottish cooks have made bere (barley) bannocks, pease bannocks, cod liver bannocks and silverweed bannocks (which include the powdered root of the silverweed mixed with oatmeal) and many others.

Selkirk bannocks, although they bear the same name, have little in common with oatmeal bannocks. They are the Scottish equivalent of the bara brith found in Wales and the barm brack of Ireland – in other words, they are fruit loaves.

Joseph Walker started his bakery in the town of Torphins, Aberdeenshire in 1898, when he was 21 years old. The firm now has an international reputation for its oatcakes and different types of shortbread. (Reproduced by kind permission of Joseph Walker's Bakery)

Nowadays bannocks are usually made from oatmeal, buttermilk, bicarbonate of soda and a pinch of salt, in the form of a large, round cake, which is baked on both sides on a griddle. They are sometimes as big as dinner plates. Smaller oatcakes, more like thin biscuits, are sold commercially by firms such as Walkers, and you may also find 'farls' – that is quarters of much larger oatcakes which are divided up and sold separately.

HAGGIS

'The great chieftain of the pudding race', as Robert Burns called haggis, is one of the finest Scottish foods. It is also the object of a great deal of frivolous speculation. All the talk of haggis hunting and haggis eggs may be good for the tourist trade, but something as marvellous as haggis needs no promotion of this kind.

Defining the haggis (the name derives from *hag*, meaning to chop or hack) is hardly a wholesome business. It is a large round sausage whose skin is the belly or paunch of a sheep. Stuffed with a mixture of oatmeal, suet, chopped and minced liver, heart and lights, all heavily seasoned, the skin is then pricked to prevent it from bursting and boiled for 3–4 hours. If you buy a haggis from the shop, it will need to be re-heated before you eat it. It must be simmered very gently in hot water for about an hour; don't be tempted to let the water boil, or you will be in trouble because the haggis will split. Alternatively you can steam it. I have done this by putting the haggis in a colander, covering it with a cloth, and setting it over a saucepan of boiling water. The best accompaniments for haggis are 'neeps and taties' – in other words turnips and mashed potatoes. And a glass of whisky is the perfect foil to the rather heavy character of the food. The contrast between the fiery liquor and the thick mouthfuls of food suggests that there is more to this combination than simple coincidence.

The firm of Baxters claim to have made the largest haggis ever in the 1960s: it weighed 170lbs and was so vast that no sheep's stomach could contain it. In fact it was eventually secured in the ample space of two cows' stomachs.

Something similar to haggis was made by the Greeks and the Romans. There is a marvellously evocative passage in 'The Clouds' by Aristophanes in which the character Strepsiades relates a tale about a bursting haggis:

'Why, now the murder's out!
So was I served with a
    stuffed sheep's paunch I
    broiled
On Jove's day, last, just such
    a scurvy trick;
Because, forsooth, not
    dreaming of your thunder,
I never thought to give the
    rascal vent,
Bounce goes the bag, and
    covers me all over
With its rich contents of
    such varied sorts.'

A monster haggis being brought to the table accompanied by the sound of bagpipes. (Photograph supplied by Baxters of Lochaber)

In Carlisle you will find plenty of haggis sausage, but the true stuffed paunch is a rarity.

The Scots eat a lot of haggis, it isn't confined to the honoured festivals of Hogmanay, St Andrew's and Burns Night, although on these occasions it is prepared and served with great ceremony. Haggis also travels to all parts of the globe as a tonic for homesick expatriate Scots. And it crosses the border into England, finding its way into the grand provision shops of London as well as local butchers in the north country. You will sometimes see haggis sausage, which is the same mixture packed into a long synthetic casing, and tinned haggis – a very convenient package, especially when there are haggis-eating contests. But, in the end, the can is no substitute for the sheep's belly, and if you are looking for haggis, be sure to buy the real thing.

MEALY PUDDING

This is the Scottish name for the 'white puddings' sold in Wiltshire and other parts of England (see p. 81). These 'black puddings without the blood' are sold in shops throughout Scotland. The mixture of oatmeal, dripping, finely chopped onions, salt and plenty of pepper, encased in a sausage skin, keeps well if hung up in a cool place. In the past, mealy puddings were often buried in the oatmeal chest, a feature of every Scottish kitchen, until they were needed.

Mealy puddings are best cooked in the same way as haggis, that is simmered in hot water, and they can be finished off by frying quickly in bacon fat. They provide one of the most filling breakfasts you can imagine.

A similar mixture, not put into skins but fried in a pan, is called 'skirlie' in some parts of Scotland, and it is used to accompany meat and game bird dishes, and (uncooked) as a stuffing for poultry.

The ends of a mealy or 'mealie' pudding are tied together just like black puddings, and it is best to leave it looped while you simmer it. One slip of the knife could cause drastic spillage.

FRUITY PUDDING

This is something of a curiosity. It is a long mealy pudding with currants added to it, which is sold in slices and fried for breakfast. I have eaten this as part of a highland mixed grill – with slices of black pudding and beef sausage – in the area around Inverness.

AYRSHIRE ROLL

This is sometimes called Ayrshire bacon, and that is what it is. According to Victor MacClure in *Scotland's Inner Man*, (1935), the potato-growing and dairy districts of Cunningham and Kyle used to produce the best pigs for Ayrshire bacon, because the animals were reared on a diet of gleanings from the potato crop and churn milk.

Ayrshire bacon is cured with salt, saltpetre, sugar and vinegar. The treated pork is then boned, made into a long roll and left to mature. Normally it isn't smoked so the rind stays soft and cream coloured. Like other bacon, Ayrshire roll is best grilled in rashers rather than fried.

GROUSE

Of all varieties of feathered game, the red grouse (*Lagopus scoticus*) has the finest and most subtle flavour. This bird is peculiar to Scotland and a few areas in northern England, north Wales and Ireland, and all attempts to introduce it into other areas have so far failed. It thrives on the berries and tender young shoots of highland heather. (The Victorian cook, Alexis Soyer, suggested that the birds be wrapped in sprigs of heather and moistened with whisky before being roasted.)

There are three other varieties of grouse in Scotland, although they do not compare in flavour with the red grouse. They are the capercailzie, the black grouse and the white grouse or ptarmigan.

Red grouse. (Illustration from Yarrell's British Birds)

Rowanberry.

The grouse season begins on August 12th and goes on until December 15th, and young grouse (for roasting) are best taken between mid-September and mid-October. The birds should always be hung for at least three or four days, possibly as long as ten days depending on the weather. So don't be deceived into paying an exorbitant price for grouse in a restaurant at the very beginning of the season; the grouse will either be too fresh, or will have come out of the freezer.

Young grouse is roasted in a hot oven for 25–35 minutes and can be stuffed with fresh rowanberries, cranberries or even wild raspberries which can still be picked in the Yorkshire dales and the Scottish highlands. Older birds need to be casseroled, made into pies or potted.

VENISON

In Britain the term venison is applied to the meat of the red deer, roe deer and fallow deer (considered the best of the three), and Scotland is renowned for the quality of its venison. The buck is in season from late June until the end of September, the doe later in the year, between October and December. The quality of venison varies a great deal: the meat from animals culled on parks and estates may be coarse and tough, or it may be as mild and tender as young lamb. The same applies to wild deer.

All venison needs to be hung for at least a week and in most cases it needs to be marinaded as well before it is cooked. Use the haunch (the top of the hind leg), the leg and loin for roasting; the forequarter is much cheaper and can be used for stewing, jugging and for making pies, pasties and pâté. There are some excellent suggestions on the uses of venison in *Food in England* by Dorothy Hartley.

SALMON

It would be hard, and also prejudiced, to make a judgement about the quality of salmon caught, say, in the Severn, the Wye or the Tay. At their best they are all fine fish. Scotsmen naturally have a bias towards their native fish caught in rivers like the Tay and the Tweed. The prospect of salmon fishing lures droves of enthusiasts to Scotland each year, armed with elaborate gear and bulging

Cranberry.

(Illustrations by Carol Fowke)

Young salmon 'parr' being removed from ponds at the salmon hatchery at Invergarry. (Reproduced by kind permission of Marine Harvest)

wallets, since the privilege of fishing is expensive and licences are difficult to obtain.

Salmon can be used fresh in many ways, but there is also smoked salmon for which Scottish curers have a fine reputation.

A consignment of fully grown salmon ready for despatch to cities throughout Britain. Fish farming is particularly suitable for salmon and also trout. (Photograph supplied by Marine Harvest)

'Salmo salar', the Atlantic salmon. (Illustration supplied by Marine Harvest)

HERRINGS

Herrings like oats are a specific national food of the Scots, and they are used in a great many ways. Before the days of refrigeration and fast transport, fresh fish had to be preserved by salting and smoking to prevent them spoiling, and vast quantities of pickled herrings were cured in Scotland as well as in other parts of Britain where the fish were caught. The 'fisher-girls' who gutted and

Two Scotch fishwives. (A postcard dating from 1905)

Scots girls barrelling salt herrings in Great Yarmouth at the turn of the century. (Reproduced by kind permission of Great Yarmouth Maritime Museum)

salted the herrings were famous, and would follow the fish to different parts of the country. Having dealt with the summer harvest in Scotland they would converge on East Anglia for the autumn herring season.

But not all the herring catch ended up in barrels. The fish were cheap and plentiful and many were eaten fresh as well. The most common dish was 'tatties an' herrin' – potatoes cooked in a large pot with fresh herrings laid on the top.

'Occupying each a low chair, we were invited to fall to, to eat without knife, or fork, or trencher, just with our fingers out of the pot as it stood. It was a little startling, but only for a moment. After a word of grace we dipped our hand into the pot and took out a potato, hot and mealy, and with another we took a nip out of the silvery flank of the herring nearest us. It was a mouthful for a king, sir![1]

Herrings were, and still are, fried in a coating of oatmeal, and they are also potted and pickled in vinegar. Herrings are sold in fish shops everywhere, but the best and fattest come from the Loch Fyne area on the west coast of Scotland. You will see piles of herrings in places like Inverness fish market, and they are commonly filleted and sold as such. (Unlike East Anglian herring, which are almost always sold – and cooked – whole.)

But Scotland is best known for the split and smoked kipper (see p. 74) and the curers around Loch Fyne are masters of the trade. Scotch herring are ideal for kippers because they are large (much larger than East Anglian autumn herring) and they have a high fat content of about 20%. Although Loch Fyne is the kipper centre in Scotland you have only to walk around towns like Buckie and Banff on the Moray Firth to detect the smells of kipper-smoking in the air.

FINNAN HADDOCK

Inverbervie was the first centre for smoking haddock, and the fish were known as 'Bervie haddocks'.

This is a famous type of smoked haddock which originated around Aberdeen on the east coast of Scotland. The fish were at first heavily smoked with black 'stickly' peat and partly decayed Sphagnum moss from the moors. The peat smoked and flavoured the fish, while the moss flared up and partly cooked the flesh. The fish, after this treatment, looked almost black, and were hard, dry and salty. By the 1820s fisherwives in the villages between Aberdeen and Stonehaven had started to pack small quantities of smoked haddock into baskets to give to the guard of the Defiance stage coach, which ran between

1 *Nether Lochaber* by Rev. Alexander Stewart, 1883.

Finnan haddock, a speciality from the area around Aberdeen. (A postcard dated 1907)

Aberdeen and Edinburgh. At this time the curing centre was the village of Findon, about six miles south of Aberdeen, from which we get the word 'Finnan'. As the trade grew, supplies of peat were quickly exhausted and special smokehouses using wood as a fuel were built to cope with the increased demand for the fish. But smoking was a laborious, time-consuming and risky business, although it was a specialist craft. It was inevitable that a more efficient, mechanized method would be devised sooner or later. In this case it was the 'Torry kiln', ironically developed only a few miles from the old Finnan smokehouses in Aberdeen.

Finnan haddocks are easy to recognize. The fish are beheaded and split, but the backbone is left in. By the time they have been smoked they are a beautiful lemon colour. Steaming in milk and butter is the best way to cook Finnan haddock though the fish can be turned into a delicious soup as well. (The 'Cullen Skink' made around the Moray Firth is a thick soup of Finnan haddock, sieved potatoes and onions cooked in fish stock.)

Finnan haddocks are split in two distinct ways: in the Aberdeen cut, the fish is split from head to tail so the backbone lies on the right-hand side of the open fish. But these days, it is more common to find the London cut where the fish is split open so that the backbone is on the left; then an extra cut is made along the side of the backbone so that the flesh stands away from it.

ARBROATH SMOKIES

Smokies, or 'pinwiddies', are small haddock, beheaded and *hot-smoked* without being split. They did not originate in Arbroath itself, but in the hamlet of Auchmithie – between Arbroath and Montrose – on the Scottish east coast.

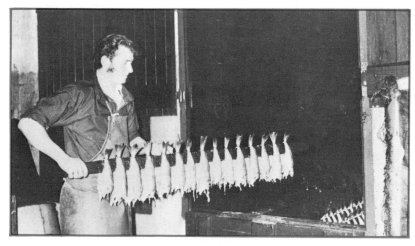

Rods of Arbroath smokies being loaded into the kiln for smoking. They are tied by the tail in pairs and simply draped over the rods. (Photograph by J. E. Manners, reproduced by kind permission of R. Spink Ltd)

Arbroath smokies being removed from the kiln by William Smith, after smoking. (Photograph supplied by R. Spink Ltd, copyright Aberdeen Journals)

'*The bight of Auchmithie is an indentation into rocky cliffs several hundred feet in perpendicular height. About the middle of the bight there is a steep ravine or gulley with a small stream, and at the bottom of this ravine there is a small piece of level ground where a fish-curing house is erected, and where also the fishermen pull up their boats, that they may be safe from easterly gales. . . . The beach is steep, and strewed with large pebbles, excellently adapted, they say, for drying fish upon.*'[1]

Although smokies are always made from haddock nowadays, in the past it was quite common to use whiting.

There was clearly plenty of fish curing in Auchmithie to judge from this description. Herrings were probably smoked in the curing house, while haddock would be dried on the rocky beach to make 'speldings'. Nearby, the writer may have seen whisky barrels with smoke billowing from them. This was the apparatus used for producing smokies; it was quite simple and made good use of local materials. The whisky barrels, cut in two, served as the kiln, a

1 *The Harvest of the Sea* by J. G. Bertram, John Murray, (1873).

kettle filled with chips from the abundant local birch trees produced the fire and smoke, and the barrel was covered with a piece of canvas. When some of the villagers from Auchmithie moved south and settled in Arbroath, they took their trade with them, so the fish became known as Arbroath smokies.

Smokies are not common outside Scotland, and they are quite unmistakable: they are copper-skinned, whole fish without heads always sold tied together in pairs. The best and simplest way of dealing with smokies is to put the fish under the grill to warm, then split it open, take out the backbone, smear it inside with butter, close it up and return it to the grill to re-heat. A perfect dish for breakfast or high tea, with toast and butter, and a mug of tea.

As the flesh of the smokie is already cooked by the smoking process, it doesn't need a great deal of extra cooking. In fact smokies are also delicious eaten cold.

BAPS

These are the traditional breakfast rolls eaten in Scotland. They are soft, oval and flat, and made from a slightly sweetened milk dough. They are similar to the baps sold in some parts of England except that they are a different shape (English baps are round), and they are always eaten warm, whereas their English relations are usually served cold, as filled rolls (see p.156).

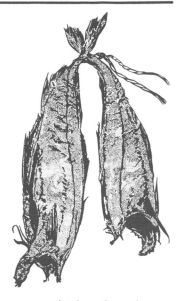

A pair of Arbroath smokies. (Crown Copyright, Her Majesty's Stationery Office)

DROP SCONES

These are also called Scotch pancakes, although the stiffer batter of the true drop scone is *dropped* onto a hot griddle, whereas pancake batter is cooked in fat in a frying pan. The small circles of drop scone batter are cooked on the griddle until they are covered with air bubbles, then turned over to brown on the other side. Drop scones can be eaten hot or cold, spread thickly with butter and honey or home-made jam.

Drop scones are very common in bakers' shops throughout Scotland, and they are also found in northern parts of England, especially in Lancashire and the Lake District.

DUNDEE CAKE

This is one of the most famous of all Scottish cakes, found not only in Scotland but in many parts of England as well. It is a rich fruit cake, reminiscent of a Christmas cake or the Melton Hunt Cake made in Leicestershire (see p.154), and it will keep for months. What distinguishes it from other similar cakes is the generous sprinkling of blanched and split almonds on the top.

BLACK BUN

This is sometimes known as Scotch currant bun, and is made for Hogmanay. It is really like an enormous mince pie. It is made in a loaf tin, which is lined with shortcrust pastry and packed with a mixture of dried fruit, sugar, spices, almonds and milk. A pastry lid is put on and the 'bun' is baked for two-and-a-half to three hours. This weighty cake keeps well, and can be made many weeks before it is needed.

SHORTBREAD

Traditionally shortbread was eaten at Christmas and Hogmanay, and in the Shetlands it was served at weddings. Nowadays it is eaten all the year round and is one of the most common souvenirs for tourists visiting Scotland. The familiar round cakes divided up into segments or sold as triangular pieces are made from a simple mixture of flour (ideally equal parts of wheat and rice flour), butter and sugar worked with the hands and rolled out to form a cake.

Dundee is also the home of Dundee marmalade. The story goes that a ship reached Tayside from Spain, early in the 18th century, loaded with a cargo of oranges. One James Keiller bought the cargo cheap, but they were bitter Seville oranges and he was unable to sell them. So his wife experimented, and eventually created a special marmalade – special because for the first time it contained thin strips of orange peel.

Mr Smart removing a rack of hand-made Highlander Shortbread from the oven at Walker's Bakery. (Reproduced by kind permission of Joseph Walker's Bakery)

Festive shortbreads were often decorated with chopped almonds, candied peel or caraway seeds.

A cake that is very similar to shortbread is called 'petticoat tails'. The name may come from the appearance of the cake which resembles that of an outspread crinoline petticoat, or it may be a corruption of the French *petites gatelles* – small cakes brought to Scotland by Mary Queen of Scots. The mixture of flour, milk, butter and sugar is rolled out into a large round. A circle is cut in the middle and the outer ring is then divided up into eight segments or 'tails'. The whole cake is then sprinkled with sugar and baked.

TRAQUAIR HOUSE ALE

Traquair Castle at Innerleithen, Peeblesshire, has the distinction of being a brewery as well as a private house. The present Laird, Peter Maxwell Stuart, discovered a collection of old brewing equipment in one of his stable blocks in 1965 dating back to about 1700 when the castle had brewed its own beer. He decided to restore the tradition. The result is a small quantity of bottled beer produced three or four times each year.

Traquair House Ale is a strong one, and it's expensive and rare. You will find it in Edinburgh and in some hotels in southern Scotland, as well as in a few well-chosen places in England. The house is open to visitors between May and September when you can see how the brew is made and sample some of it.

(Reproduced by kind permission of Traquair House)

WALES
BARA BRITH, CREMPOG, GOCOS ET AL

There is a story that in 1277 the Welsh leader Llywellyn ap Gruffydd travelled to London to pay his respects to the English king, Edward I. The courtiers were surprised to see the Welshman and his followers refusing London beer and demanding milk instead. An episode such as this suggests that beer and spirits were foreign to the Welsh, who have always made full use of their dairy products.

Welsh food still reflects Wales as it was – a pastoral country. Its rich pastures, influenced by mild weather from the Gulf Stream, produced large herds of cattle. And as the size of the herds was traditionally a mark of status, not many animals were killed off for meat but were used for their milk, of which there tended to be a permanent surplus. The Welsh consequently made great use of milk, butter and cheese in their cooking. It's no accident that Welsh rarebit – a mixture of cheese, milk and butter grilled on toast – is one of their most famous dishes.

Two of Wrexham's claims to fame are a football team successful out of proportion to the size of the place and, Border Breweries, which has invaded England successfully as far as Cheshire and the Potteries.

Welsh mountain sheep making their way along a track in the region of the 'noble Berwyn', celebrated by George Borrow in 'Wild Wales'. (Reproduced by kind permission of The Museum of English Rural Life, University of Reading)

Welshmen still identify themselves by carrying leeks, no where more emphatically than at Cardiff Arms Park, especially when J. P. R. Williams scores a try in a rugby international. Huge model leeks are raised high in the air like giant green cabers.

Welsh drinking habits were also influenced by the large quantities of milk produced in the region and buttermilk was a common drink. The tradition of beer-drinking is quite a recent phenomenon in Wales, even though transport has made the raw materials and the beer easy to come by. Wales, like other Celtic regions of north and west Britain was an oat-producing area. They didn't grow the barley essential for brewing beer.

The oats grown in Wales played an important part in the local diet and, indeed, the whole character of the kitchen. The main feature of the Welsh kitchen has always been the open-hearth fire and the bakestone or griddle, a flat piece of iron set over the fire, on which were cooked oatcakes and pancakes. Then there would be a large iron pot suspended above the fire. Boiling and stewing have always been the most important methods of cooking meat; ovens for baking or roasting, common in south and east Britain, didn't figure in Celtic kitchens. The hearth was the focal point of the kitchen, providing warmth as well as food. The family would gather round it, eating their food straight from the pot or off the bakestone. Kitchen tables were small and rarely used, and, as D. Elliston Allen suggests, this left room for the famous Welsh dresser.

LEEKS

The leek is the national vegetable of Wales. Why it has this distinction is something of a mystery, but one theory, outlined by Theodora Fitzgibbon in *A Taste Of Wales*, is that the tradition dates back to the time of Henry Tudor. The green and white colours of Valois formed part of his coat-of-arms, and while he was in exile his followers recognized each other by producing any plant which had a green stem tapering to white – an echo of the heraldic colours. The leek was an obvious choice, as it was common throughout Wales, and the same applied to that other Welsh emblem, the daffodil.

The Welsh have a great many uses for their leeks. There are leek pasties (*Pasteiod Cennin*), in which the white part of a leek is wrapped up in a pastry case with bacon sometimes added as well; leek tart (*Tarten Cennin*), an open tart rather like a French quiche; leeks are also essential to the classic Welsh 'cawl' (see p 236) and are put into many other dishes.

Bara Brith

This 'speckled bread' or 'current bread' (*bara* means bread) is very common throughout Wales, although it is no more than a variation of a fruit bread made in many parts of Britain. It is a close relative, too, of 'Barm Brack' in Ireland, Selkirk Bannock from Scotland and lardy cake from England, and originated in the days when families had regular weekly bread-baking sessions. If a little dough was left over it was brightened up with dried fruit, spices and sugar to make a special tea bread for eating at the weekend.

Bara brith is made using a milk dough recipe sweetened with sugar, coloured with egg and flavoured with currants, raisins, candid peel and mixed spice. Once the loaf has been baked it is glazed with clear honey, left to cool and eaten sliced with Welsh butter. It is one of the commonest Welsh specialities, sold in bakers' shops in most parts of the country.

Oatcakes (Bara Ceirch)

These are very similar to, though usually thinner than, Scottish oatcakes (see p. 221), and were traditionally eaten on May-day eve. They used always to be cooked on a bakestone, or *planc* as it is called in Wales, a flat piece of iron set over an open-hearth fire, but nowadays electric 'bakestones' or hot-plates are much more common. There were also special wooden outcake turners of different designs in many farmhouses, and they are still to be found around

It was traditional to eat oatcakes in Wales around the fires lit for the Beltane Quarter day.

Merioneth. If you want to taste a fine combination of Welsh food, eat oatcakes with laverbread and have a drink of buttermilk with them.

In hungry times one of these oatcakes would be crumbled up into a pot, and hot water from a tea-kettle poured over it. The mixture was then covered and cooked, flavoured with pepper, salt, butter and a bit of bacon as well. This gruel was called 'brewis' and eaten hot with a wooden or horn spoon. In even leaner times this 'tea-kettle broth' would have been made rather like Scottish 'sowans' from oat husks soaked in hot water.

Pancakes (Crempog)

Welsh pancakes are made with buttermilk and should ideally be cooked on a bakestone, although frying pans and hot-plates are used more often these days. They are a feature of local produce sold at Swansea market and no doubt elsewhere in Wales. Traditionally served hot and buttered, they are stacked in piles, not served singly as in England; they are also often covered with various meat and fish fillings to make a tall, many layered sandwich.

Look out, too, for pikelets (*Pice'r Pregethwr*), crumpets (*Crampoethau*) and sour milk pancakes (*Pancws Llaeth Sur*).

Welsh 'crempog' are close relatives of 'krampoch', the buckwheat pancakes of Lower Brittany.

MUTTON

'The leg of mutton of Wales beats the leg of mutton of any other country, and I had never tasted a Welsh leg of mutton before. Certainly I shall never forget the first Welsh leg of mutton which I tasted, rich but delicate, replete with juices derived from the aromatic herbs of the noble Berwyn, cooked to a turn and weighing just four pounds.' [1]

Welsh mountain sheep. (Reproduced by kind permission of The Museum of English Rural Life, University of Reading)

1 *Wild Wales* by George Borrow, 1862

*Once a shoulder of mutton
had been eaten, the bone had
a special function. Provided it
was from the right side of
the animal, the blade would
be picked clean and used at
Hallowe'en as a way of
divining a future husband.
The bone was pricked nine
times and then a rhyme was
chanted hopefully.*

Borrow's enthusiasm is understandable, for Welsh mutton is indeed fine meat, although it is much less common than it used to be. The Welsh sheep that graze on mountain pastures are such small animals that a hindquarter is often cut as a leg, and a whole saddle can weigh as little as eight pounds. The meat has little fat on it and has a distinctive taste, particularly if the sheep have been feeding among the patches of wild thyme growing in the Welsh hills.

A leg or saddle of Welsh mutton might well be roasted and eaten with rowanberry jelly, or laver sauce (see p. 241); chops can be cooked in a casserole with green peas and mint; and a shoulder joint tastes delicious if baked with honey – very good in parts of Wales – cider and rosemary.

MUTTON HAM

In the past, hams were not prepared only from the pig. There were beef hams, veal hams, venison hams and mutton hams. These last were especially common in Scotland and Wales, and the stocky Welsh mountain sheep were ideally suited for the purpose; the meat had a fine flavour, it wasn't tough, coarse or too fatty, and the legs, from which the hams were made, were a manageable size and could be easily cured at home. The hind leg would be cleaned and salted with a mixture of salt, brown sugar and spices, then pressed and finally smoked. Often hams would hang in the chimneys of shepherds's cottages gradually being cured by the smoke from peat and wood fires.

Mutton hams are rarely made today, and you will not find them for sale in any shop.

MUTTON PIES

*Mutton and leek pie is another
fine combination of classic
Welsh foods, although it is a
recipe which occasionally
appears in other parts of
Britain as well.*

These were once very popular at fairs in many towns and villages in Wales. Often the pies were very small, the filling consisting mainly of minced mutton with red currant jelly poured into the top of them. But sometimes a more elaborate pie could be found, like the one that used to be produced each year for the fair at Templeton in Pembrokeshire. It consisted of layers of minced mutton, currants and brown sugar, all in a pastry case, and was known as *Katt pie*. A similar product is made in the Lake District (see p. 206)

CAWL

This is the classic Welsh peasant soup or stew – their version of a dish which turns up in many forms in many different countries – a mixture of meat and vegetables all cooked together in a big cauldron over an open-hearth fire. The actual contents would depend on family preferences and what was in the larder or growing in the garden. There were no definite recipes and no two batches were the same. Cawl (pronounced 'cowl') simply means soup and it is eaten as such from bowls with a spoon. The spoons used to be made of wood – supposedly so that the soup could be eaten very hot without fear of burning the mouth.

*In 'English Food', Jane
Grigson recommends floating
a marigold flower on top of
each bowl of cawl. The bowls
themselves were traditionally
wooden or flowery patterned
Welsh earthenware.*

Although it was originally made from any meat that was available, especially bacon, cawl is now a mutton dish. It also contains considerable quantities of leeks, potatoes, onions and any other vegetables that are at hand. Sometimes the stock is eaten first, followed by the meat and vegetables (rather like the French *pot-au-feu*) or the whole lot may be eaten together.

FAGGOTS

These are found in many parts of Britain, and I have mentioned them in detail on page 81, but they are common in many parts of Wales and differ in some respects from faggots in other areas. Oatmeal often replaces breadcrumbs as the binding cereal; the herbs used once included bog myrtle, although sage is more common these days, and there's a tasty association with apples: pieces of apple are sometimes mixed in with the liver and other ingredients, and the faggots are often eaten accompanied by apple sauce, which is not unnatural if you remember that the starting meat for faggots is the pig.

SALT DUCK

The idea of salting a duck for several days before cooking is peculiar to Wales and found nowhere else in Britain as a traditional dish, although I have heard that it is a method used in the Isle of Man as well.

A large fat duck is rubbed with salt and tended for two or three days before being rinsed and packed into a large dish or pot. It is seasoned and covered with stock or a mixture of stock and cider and cooked slowly in the oven for about two hours. Once ready the duck is served hot with onion sauce – its best accompaniment.

Salt duck can also be served cold with a vinegar and mustard dressing.

SALMON

Giraldus Cambrensis (Gerald the Welshman), writing towards the end of the 12th century, noted that: '*The noble river Teivi (Teifi) flows here, and abounds with the finest salmon, more than any other river in Wales . . .*' The great feature of salmon fishing in these parts has for centuries been the use of coracles and nets. The coracle is a light, manoeuvrable craft, 'a swimmer of animal skin', as one medieval *cywydd* describes it. It was originally made of animal hide stretched over a framework of willow osiers, but now tar-coated canvas is used.

Faggots are very similar to French 'crepinettes', and an indication of ancients links between the Celtic countries of Britain and Brittany.

W. O. Jones and Trefor Jones seine-netting for sparlings (smelts or, in Welsh, 'brwyniad') at Tal-y-cafn on the River Conway in 1971. There is a tradition which states that these fish occur in no other river in the world, and do not appear until the snow on the mountain peaks has disappeared. Also it is said that when there was famine in north Wales, Saint Brigid cast a bundle of reeds ('brwyn') into the river which were transformed into 'brwyniad'. (Reproduced by kind permission of the National Museum of Wales)

Coracles were once seen on almost every Welsh river. This old man is carrying a Dee coracle used near Llangollen in 1934. (Reproduced by kind permission of the National Museum of Wales)

In E. Donovan's 'Descriptive Excursions through South Wales and Monmouthshire' (1805) there is an interesting account of Swansea market: 'Half a dozen families seated upon the panniers of their ponies . . . rode hastily down the market place with a supply of sewen . . . conveyed from Pontardulais, about ten miles to the westward . . . abounding with fish during the summer, being caught in the coracle fisheries by peasantry.'

These days coracle fishing for salmon is very limited, and only three rivers in West Wales are worked: the Teifi, Tywi and Taf, and even then coracle fishing is a rare sight. This is partly because of a decline in the skills of fishing from coracles and indeed of coracle-making as well, but also because licences and fishing regulations are more strict than they used to be.

Fishermen go out in pairs to fish for salmon from coracles. Each has his own craft, steering it with a paddle in one hand, and holding one end of a drag net in the other. Once a fish is caught, the net is lifted out of the water, the two coracles draw together and the salmon is taken out. The design of the coracles and the nets as well varies from river to river, those used on the Teifi being different from those on the Tywi for instance; this is partly because of the fishermen's own preferences but is also a calculated attempt to suit the craft to the conditions of the river – the speed of the current, depth of water and so on.

The few coracle fishermen who work on the Welsh rivers don't only go out for salmon; they are just as eager for sea-trout, called in these parts 'sewin'.

One of the favourite Welsh ways with salmon is *Eog Rhost*, or roast salmon. Either a small fish or a tail piece from a large one can be used, cooked in the oven with rosemary, cloves, and bay leaves, then served with a sauce made from butter, orange and lemon slices and vinegar. Another sauce, called Teifi Sauce, can be eaten with both salmon and sewin after it has been baked or poached. This is a mixture of salmon stock, port, anchovy, mushroom ketchup and butter all cooked together and reduced to a strong liquor.

Look out for roast salmon and Teifi sauce when you visit restaurants and eating houses in Wales. They do appear occasionally on menus.

FRESHWATER FISHING

Wales has some unusual freshwater fish for those anglers who go out with a rod and line. *Gwyniad* or whitefish (*Coregonus lavaretus*) lives in Lake Bala with *torgoch*, a red-bellied variety of char; the brown trout is caught in many of the

The grayling. (Reproduced by kind permission of The Museum of English Rural Life, University of Reading)

inland lakes and pools, and the delicate grayling can be fished from many of the rivers. This is a fish for angling connoisseurs. The 16th century angler, Izaak Walton, described it as 'very pleasant and jolly', and 'of a very fine shape', and it is still caught in the clear waters of the river Dove in his home country.

COCKLES

Cockles are very popular in South Wales, and the area around the Gower peninsula is one of the three main fisheries in Britain. The best site is at the Burry Inlet near Llanelli, but there is another area further west known as the Three Rivers Inlet, where the rivers Taf, Tawy and Gwendraeth meet.

No tractors or mechanical vehicles are allowed onto the sands around the south Wales cockle beds, so they have to be reached by horse and cart, just as they were when this photograph was taken. (Crown Copyright, Her Majesty's Stationery Office)

Welsh women cockle gatherers raking and sieving their crop from the sands. (Crown Copyright, Her Majesty's Stationery Office)

When Stone Age caves near Llandudno were excavated in the 19th century, remains of oxen, bears and pigs were found alongside cockle shells – an indication that the people lived off meat and shellfish, although not necessarily eaten together.

Cockling in South Wales is special in many ways. You cannot take mechanical vehicles like tractors onto the cockle beds, the only way of reaching the beds and of getting the crop off the sands is by horse and cart. The spectacle has changed little in 50 years except that these days it is less of a woman's trade. The pickers use a sickle-shaped iron 'scrape' to break up the sand, and then rake the cockles into piles. They have special problems because they have to compete with large flocks of overwintering oystercatchers, with sometimes up to 20,000 birds working the sands, each bird consuming around 500 cockles a day. It is a formidable task for the human gatherers. And cockling here is governed by very strict regulations – not only the usual ones relating to quantity and size of cockles to be taken and implements to be used, but also two laws unique to this region: 'No person shall fish for cockles on a Sunday, except with the written authority of the Committee' and 'No person shall fish for cockles between half-an-hour after sunset on any day and half-an-hour before sunrise on the following day'. It isn't surprising then to learn that more and more cockles sold in Swansea, Cardiff and other towns actually originate in Norfolk and are transported live to Wales.

You may still find cockles sold live in some parts of south Wales, but it is more common to see them cooked and dissected from their shells. Apart from the simple way of eating them with vinegar and brown bread, Welsh people have some good local dishes like cockle cakes (*Teisen Gocos*) which are individual cockles dipped in batter, deep-fried and consumed with buttermilk. There is cockle pie (*Pastai Gocos*), a mixture of cockles, streaky bacon or salt pork, onions and stock, all covered in short-crust pastry. The cockles can also be made into a stew or soup.

OTHER SHELLFISH

Queens, or queen scallops (Chlamys opercularis) are much smaller than the great scallop and unrelated to it, except in name. They are found in large quantities in the Irish Sea, especially off County Wicklow.

SCALLOPS: The great scallop (*Pecten maximus*) is quite common in the waters around the Welsh coast and the delicious pieces of orange coral and white muscle are served in quite a number of restaurants, although you may have to pay a high price. They are often cooked on skewers with pieces of bacon, and particularly good ones can be had at 'Y Gegin Fawr', a 14th century pilgrim's rest house at Aberdaron in Caernarvon.

In Anglesey they use scallop shells as small cake tins to make *Teisen 'Berffro* or Beffro Cakes, rather like the cakes made in East Anglia (see p. 68) in cockle shells.

OYSTERS: The ruins of Oystermouth Castle, overlooking Swansea Bay, remind you that fine oysters are sold in South Wales. The Gower oyster soup is unusual in that it uses mutton broth as its stock, with oysters, onion and mace added. It is a combination rather like cockles and pork or bacon, and a reminder of the importance of mutton in Wales (see p. 236).

RAZOR-SHELL: *Ensis siligua* is a little-known shellfish, 6–8 inches long, that looks like an old-fashioned cut-throat razor. It is only found alive in any quantity on clean, sandy shores at the edge of the lowest tides of the year. Razor-shells are treasured in Wales, where they are baked in their shells and dressed with lemon juice and butter.

Also look out for mussels and clams, especially on market stalls in South Wales.

LAVER

Porphyra umbilicalis is an edible seaweed whose thin purplish fronds cling to rocks on exposed shores, especially on the western coast of Britain. (In Ireland this seaweed is called 'sloke' and in Scotland 'slouk'.) In Wales it has become something of a speciality, especially in Swansea and south Pembrokeshire. The real centre of the laver trade is Pen-clawdd, the last village of north Gower before the peninsula joins the mainland. Although there's plenty of laver in Wales, a substantial amount is shipped from Scotland to satisfy local demand. Perhaps this is because picking is tough, uncomfortable and hardly lucrative for the few people who still gather the seaweed. In the past it was a well-organized trade; there were large drying houses built along the shore, where the weed was cured so that it would keep well.

Laver.
(Illustration by
Carol Fowke)

Laver can still be gathered by
hand, although it's an arduous
back-breaking task.
(Photograph by John L. Jones)

In 18th century Bath you would hear the cry, 'Fine potted laver'. It was fashionable at the time to be diet-conscious in that city, and its foods were carefully chosen and prepared for their health-giving properties (see p. 119).

Preparing fresh laver is an elaborate affair. It has to be washed many times and steeped for hours in water, then boiled for something like five hours. Finally the excess water is drained off and the pulp is stirred in a saucepan, traditionally with a wooden spoon or a silver fork. You end up with a brownish, gelatinous purée, not unlike discoloured spinach.

This purée is sold in Wales as 'laverbread' – a totally misleading name, because it has nothing to do with bread and it is eaten when you might least expect it, at breakfast. What they do in Wales is to roll laverbread in fine oatmeal, shape it into cakes and fry it with bacon, or in bacon fat. The other important use of laver is in laver sauce, a traditional Welsh accompaniment for mutton. Here the laver purée is mixed with the juice from a Seville orange, butter and some mutton stock. By substituting cream for the stock, this sauce is excellent with shellfish and lobster, both common in Wales.

GLAMORGAN SAUSAGES

A recipe for Glamorgan sausages

150 gr (5oz) breadcrumbs
75gr (3oz) Caerphilly cheese
1 tbs finely chopped leek or spring onion
½ tsp mixed herbs
½ tsp dry mustard powder
1 egg (separated)
pepper, salt

Mix all the dry ingredients together and bind with the egg yolk. If the mixture is a little dry you may need to add a small amount of water. Divide into portions and roll into sausage shapes on a floured board. Dip each one into the egg white, slightly whisked. Cover the sausages lightly with extra bread-crumbs and fry, preferably in bacon fat.

There isn't any meat in a Glamorgan sausage. It is made from cheese mixed with breadcrumbs, herbs and choppd leek or onion. The cheese was originally Glamorgan cheese, made from the milk of a special breed of white cattle called Gwent, but it is no longer made.

The sausage mixture is bound with the yolk of egg, and formed into small sausage shapes, rolled in flour and then dipped in egg white, which forms the 'skin'. Finally, they are covered in breadcrumbs, fried and eaten hot with potatoes.

George Borrow praised Glamorgan sausages in his book, *Wild Wales*, but he compared them with Epping sausages, which were meaty and made from pork. Were the Glamorgan sausages of his day different to the ones we eat now?

CAERPHILLY CHEESE

This is the only surviving Welsh cheese, a surprising fact, because much of lowland Wales is good dairy country, and Welsh butter is still made in quite large amounts and is justly renowned for its quality. (The same has happened in the Lake District where priority is given to butter rather than cheese.)

A selection of cheese vats. (Reproduced by kind permission of The National Museum of Wales)

It wasn't until about 1830 that farms in the area round Caerphilly began to produce this cheese – at least there are no references to it earlier than that. Across the flat pastures as far as Newport and Rhymney were dotted little farmhouse dairies where the milk of Hereford cows was turned into Caerphilly cheese. It was a seasonal activity, only performed between May and September. Each day there would be two cheese-making sessions, one with the morning milk and the other with the evening, they were never mixed, and the milk was often used while it was still warm. The cheese was creamy-white with more moisture than most British cheeses, mild in flavour, and the whole cheese would weigh between seven and fourteen pounds.

It wasn't long, however, before demand for the cheese outstripped supply. Industrialization had hit South Wales, and the mining communities were growing. Hungry Welshmen looked across the Bristol Channel to Somerset and Wiltshire where the cheese-making was an ideal proposition for dairy farmers with large areas of rich pasture. Caerphilly could be made and sold much more quickly than slow-maturing Cheddar, it didn't need the expense of bandages and greasing, and there was a ready-made market in the Welsh mining towns. It made economic sense for farmers to change over to Caerphilly cheese. The situation remains the same today. There's hardly a cheesemaker left in the Caerphilly area, but the Welsh still eat great quantities of the cheese from English and also Irish creameries.

Caerphilly is an excellent cheese. It can be eaten just as it is, used for making things like Glamorgan sausages, and, because it is a good toaster as well, is ideal for Welsh Rarebit.

Glamorgan cattle were once common in south Wales and provided milk for much of the cheese made in that area, especially in the 19th century. (Reproduced by kind permission of The Museum of English Rural Life, University of Reading)

There is a world of difference between cheese on toast and Welsh rarebit. The real thing is a mixture of grated cheese, butter, milk or beer, seasoned with salt and pepper and a little mustard, cooked until creamy and spooned over toast. After the mixture has been put under the grill to brown it is eaten with a glass of beer.

IRELAND
STOUT, SPUDS AND STILLS

Cities such as Dublin are accessible centres for Irish food, while remote areas in the south-west of the island may require much more in the way of patient exploration to yield anything of interest.

The four-and-a-half million inhabitants of Ireland are mainly dispersed in small communities through the land, apart from the conglomerations round the few big urban areas. But, although there is plenty of traditional Irish food, there isn't a great deal that can be associated with one particular area or region of the country.

Ireland is surrounded by sea and has plenty of rivers and 'loughs', and there is a noticeable difference between the eating habits of people who live on the coast and those who live inland. Fish has always been in good supply as an essential part of the Irish diet, and is commercially exploited as well. Inland, the cottagers often own small plots, probably planted with potatoes and other root crops, and they might have a pig and perhaps a few cows too. Apart from the large estates, farming is generally on a small scale and often very isolated.

The Irish landscape is full of contrast: mountainous areas that can be classed with the highland areas of Scotland and Wales, and plenty of rich lowland pasture for grazing. Irish butter has a fine reputation, and the climate and soil in some places can sustain barley in place of the more usual Celtic oats. However, it is the Celtic tradition that really dominates the character of the food here. Perhaps because of the strength of the religious tradition, there's a deep feeling about the naturalness and purity of food and there is a delightful Irish obstinacy which often preserves traditional foods for their own sake, when they do not always warrant such attention. There's a frugal simplicity about most of the dishes. The Irish do not believe in elaborate cooking.

POTATOES

The potato has not been adopted as a national emblem in Ireland as the leek has in Wales, but it is undoubtedly the most important food of that country. Potatoes arrived in Spain in the first half of the 16th century, brought back by the conquistadors from the countries of South America. Introduced into the British Isles by Spanish seamen, they were quickly taken into cultivation in Ireland, and the Irish were the first to make great use of potatoes as a basic food crop. (Potatoes were not planted in other parts of the British Isles until many decades later, and it wasn't until the end of the 18th century that they were easten in any quantity.)

The Irish became so dependent on potatoes that the failure of the crop in 1845 resulted in the terrible famine which encouraged the emigration of thousands of Irish men and women that has continued even up to the present day.

It has been claimed that Sir Walter Raleigh brought potatoes to Britain after his expedition of 1584, and planted them on his estate at Youghal in County Cork. But this is probably no more than legend.

Potatoes
'An Irish Mash.'

The Irish climate and soil suit potatoes and they are grown and used in large amounts, although there isn't the dependence on them as a single source of food today that there used to be. The potato is still used in many ways: there are potato cakes, potato soups and a number of special dishes, as well as the variety of simple methods of using it on its own – boiled, mashed, baked and fried.

COLCANNON

This dish, often called 'Kale Cannon' or 'Kailkenny', is essentially a mixture of mashed potato and chopped, cooked kale, although cabbage is usually substituted in modern versions. There is a recipe for colcannon in Eliza Acton's *Modern Cookery for Private Families*, (1845), where she also mentions that,

'Cole' is the old world name for greens, or members of the cabbage family. It survives in such dishes as 'cole slaw' – literally cabbage salad.

'In Ireland mashed parsneps and potatoes are mingled in the same way and called parsnep cannon. A good summer variety of the preparation is made there also with Windsor beans boiled tender, skinned, and bruised to a paste, then thoroughly blended with the potatoes. Turnips, too, are sometimes substituted for the parsneps; but these or any other watery vegetable should be well dried over a gentle fire before they are added to the potatoes.'

Colcannon is also made in Scotland. Sometimes the recipe is similar to that used in Ireland, but another version can be made: a mixture of potatoes, cabbage, carrots and turnips is well mashed together with butter and served from a bowl with a little meat gravy poured over it.

These days colcannon is made by mixing together the mashed potato and greens with a little hot milk, flavoured with chopped leek. The fluffy green mixture is put into a bowl, a well is made in the middle and melted butter poured in just before the dish is served. Sometimes the colcannon is fried in bacon fat until it is brown on both sides, rather like 'bubble and squeak'.

BOXTY

This is a dish made from equal quantities of cooked potatoes and grated raw potatoes, which according to this Hallowe'en rhyme could be made in two ways:

'Boxty on the griddle, boxty in the pan,
The wee one in the middle, it is for Mary Ann:
If you don't eat boxty you'll never get your man.'

Boxty 'on the griddle' is also called Boxty Bread. The potato mixture is made into a dough and baked on both sides on the griddle. The bread is buttered and eaten hot. Boxty 'in the pan' is eaten with butter and brown sugar, and is more like a pancake as the potato mixture is made into a batter with flour and milk, and then fried.

Curraghs off County Galway, loaded with export potatoes. (Photograph by Thomas H. Mason)

SODA BREAD

Soda bread must follow potatoes as a staple food of Ireland and it is made all over the country, not simply in farmhouse kitchens but in the bakeries as well. So it is easy to buy. It is made with bicarbonate of soda (baking soda), which acts as the leavening agent in place of yeast. Traditional soda bread is also made with buttermilk in preference to fresh milk.

In many country districts in Ireland, soda bread is still baked in a 'bastable oven'. This is an iron pot with a lid, handles and three short legs, which is suspended by chains over an open peat fire. The soda bread dough is put in the pot, and the lid is weighted with burning sods to ensure an even heat. However, it is much more common for the bread to be baked in a conventional oven.

Soda bread is eaten with everything from the grandest lobster to the humblest pig's trotter, and goes perfectly with that most Irish of drinks – Guinness.

Soda bread quite often migrates across the Irish Sea, and is not uncommon in north-west England and parts of Scotland as well.

BARM BRACK

This is the Irish version of the fruit bread called 'bara brith' in Wales (see p234. It is traditionally eaten in Ireland on Hallowe'en, when a ring is put in the mixture. Whoever gets the piece of cake with the ring in it will be married within the year.

The nearest Scottish equivalent to barm brack is the Selkirk bannock.

FOOD FROM THE SEA AND RIVER

As I mentioned earlier, Ireland is surrounded by water – to the west is the Atlantic, to the east the Irish sea – and has many rivers and inland lakes or 'loughs'. So it is not surprising that it has a good reputation for sea and river food.

LOBSTER

The common European lobster (*Homarus gammarus*) is common in cool waters from Norway to the Mediterranean, and fishermen in Wales, the West Country and Northumberland as well as Ireland use pots to catch these crustaceans from the rocky bottoms out at sea. The southern coast of Ireland is particularly well suited to lobsters. The season for fresh lobsters is from April or May until October, and during that time the round basketwork traps are set regularly in the best lobster waters.

The first time I saw a live lobster I was, like most people I suspect, surprised that it wasn't red at all, but dark blue. In the fishing towns of southern Ireland you could be lucky and pick up a fresh blue lobster; otherwise local restaurants will be the best places to eat them cooked and red. There's a flourishing export trade in lobsters, but they are in no way as common as some people might suppose. As a result they are an expensive, luxury food. I have never been impressed by the rich sauces often prescribed for lobster; a special treat like this needs no disguise if it is fresh and has been carefully cooked. Once a lobster has been boiled and allowed to get cold, a little mayonnaise is all that is needed to complement its delicate flesh. Alternatively it can be served hot, either split and grilled in the shell, or the pieces of flesh can be extracted and turned in hot butter.

One Irish dish worth mentioning is known as *Dublin Lawyer*. The raw chunks of lobster are heated in butter, then Irish whiskey is poured over them and lit. Finally cream is stirred into the pan juices and the mixture is put back into the shell to be served hot.

DUBLIN BAY PRAWNS

These are not prawns at all and should more accurately be called Norway lobsters (*Nephrops norvegicus*). They may also be called 'scampi', although the true scampi is larger than its relative, the Norway lobster, and is found in the Adriatic.

There is a curious story about how Dublin Bay prawns got their name. Before the days of refrigeration, about 150 years ago, shellfish had to be cooked and eaten fresh as soon as they were caught and landed. Most of the boats were not used primarily for Norway lobsters, although a fair number would be found in among the catch of the other fish, and these became perks for the crew and their families. Ships from many different countries used to anchor for provisions in Lambay Deep, off the coast of north Dublin, and their crews as well as local folk were a ready market for the shellfish that the boats had caught. The womenfolk would cook and sell them on the streets of Dublin crying 'Dublin Bay Prawns'.

Most of the Dublin Bay prawns caught nowadays are shelled, frozen and exported as 'scampi'. To end up covered in bread-crumbs and served with chips 'in the basket' is an unworthy fate for such a delicate food. The prawns are in

To add to the confusion about names, I have seen scampi also called 'lobster tails' by some producers.

season all the year round and, like lobsters, they live in cool waters, especially around the Continental shelf. If you find them fresh, only the tails are eaten. The best way is to steam and shell them, and turn them in butter with lemon juice.

OTHER SHELLFISH

Oysters, cockles, and winkles are all common in waters around the Irish coast. The best oysters come from old-established beds off County Galway, and an oyster festival, rather like the one held in Colchester (see p 32   ) serves to open the season each September.

A couple of natives.
(Photograph by Trevor Wood)

Many of the 'cockles' sold in Ireland and exported to France are really members of the clam family. Their Latin name is *Venerupis decussata*, and they are known locally as 'carpetshells'. The main fishery for these shellfish is around County Kerry.

Although winkles are common on almost every stretch of rocky or weedy shore round all British coasts, they are widely distributed and enjoyed in Ireland, where they are called 'willicks' or 'willocks'. They are one of the smallest shellfish that we eat, and the extraction of the flesh from the tiny coiled shell is a leisurely way of passing the time. In Ireland, once the flesh is 'on the pin', it is dipped in oatmeal before being eaten.

SEAWEEDS

DULSE

This red seaweed, (*Rhodomenia palmata*), is also called 'dillisk' or 'dillesk' in Ireland. Although you may find it growing on stones along many parts of the British coast, especially in the west, it is only used as a food in a few places, mainly in the west of Ireland and in a few remote parts of Scotland. After it has been gathered it is dried, so that it will keep, and this is the way it is usually sold. It is a tough, resilient weed that needs up to five hours of slow simmering to make it edible. Such an unco-operative plant must have its origins as a food in the remote past, in the hardy diet of early coastal settlers.

Once dulse has been boiled to an edible state it is mixed with butter and added to mashed potato to make a dish called *Dulse Champ*.

CARRAGEEN (IRISH MOSS)

The purple fronds of *Chondrus crispus* are common on stones and rocks on the western and southern shores of Ireland (and on other Atlantic shorelines.) They are easily recognized because the fronds branch repeatedly to form a fan-shape.

Dulse.

(Illustration by Carol Fowke)

Women gathering carrageen from the rocky shores. (Reproduced by kind permission of The Irish Press)

Carrageen is a mucilaginous plant which is an important source of alginates, or vegetable gelatines, so it isn't surprising that it has many uses in soups, jellies and even breads and pastries. It is gathered in April and May and can either be used fresh, or dried and stored. If the seaweed is gathered, cleaned and simmered in milk and sugar until it has almost completely disintegrated, strained to remove any odd strands and then poured into a mould, it will set and produce a simple 'Irish moss blancmange'.

Another traditional use is in 'Irish moss ginger jelly'. For this the seaweed is simmered in water with pieces of root ginger, sugar and lemon rind. Then the liquid is strained off and set in a jelly mould.

When carrageen is dried it takes on a bleached creamy-white colour. After it has been gathered it has to be repeatedly washed with fresh water or simply left out in the rain until it changes colour; then it is dried thoroughly indoors and stored in bags. This prepared carrageen is quite often sold in health food shops; one well-known brand is called 'Ocean Swell'.

Carrageen.

(Illustration by Carol Fowke)

LAVER

In Ireland this is called 'sloke' and, although it doesn't have the reputation that it has in Wales (see p 241), it is common and can be gathered from many rocky shores.

MEAT

There isn't a strong regional or national meat-eating tradition in Ireland. The few strictly regional items that exist are mostly derived from the 'plainer' parts of the pig, and there are a few simply prepared dishes commonly made and eaten.

CRUBEENS (CRUIBINS)

In Ireland this is the name given to pig's trotters which are often sold pickled, but not cooked, in butcher's shops. The hind trotters, which are larger and more meaty, are usually used and once they have been pickled in brine they are simmered in water with a few herbs and root vegetables and eaten hot or cold surrounded by a layer of thick jelly.

There's a connection between the Irish taste for pig's trotters, and stews, hot-pots and items like potato cakes, and the food and eating habits of people in Lancashire. This is partly the result of a similar attitude to using local resources but there is a geographical closeness as well.

One way of getting pig carcases to market in Ireland. (Reproduced by kind permission of The Museum of English Rural Life, University of Reading)

Tansy.

(Illustration by Carol Fowke)

Tansy, Chrysanthemum vulgare, was once one of the most widely used of all garden herbs, not only in the kitchen but as a medicinal plant as well. It has a strong smell and a hot bitter taste, and must have been used very cautiously when added to drisheen.

On Saturday night, in many country districts, it was the tradition to eat crubeens with soda bread and stout – a drinker's food very similar to the 'stew and hard' eaten in parts of Lancashire. (see p.189).

DRISHEEN

This is the Irish version of black pudding. It tends to be larger in diameter than its English relation, and it more closely resembles a French *boudin*. The old centres for drisheen-making were Cork, Limerick and Kerry, but a commercial variation is now sold in Dublin as well. Traditionally, drisheen was made with sheep's blood, but pig's blood is much more common nowadays. This should be mixed with cream, white breadcrumbs, pepper, mace and herbs (the classic drisheen herb is tansy, but parsley and thyme are often substituted). The mixture is packed into a membrane casing and boiled for about twenty minutes. Sometimes the mixture is poured into a dish and cooked in the oven, in a *bain-marie*. I have seen this method used for black pudding in the Lake District (see p204).

Drisheen is eaten either on Saturday night, as supper, or for breakfast on Sunday morning, with bacon, sausages or tripe. It can be grilled, fried or simmered in stock or water.

In some parts of Ireland, drisheen is called 'packet'.

IRISH HAMS

Both Limerick and Belfast are famous for their hams. In the 18th century Limerick hams were smoked with oak shavings and juniper berries, which grew freely in the area. Nowadays the Belfast ham is more common, at least on a commercial scale. It has been known in its present form for about a hundred years. The ham used always to be smoked with peat, and this method is still employed to a certain extent.

In areas of Ireland where no green crops were cultivated these hams were often eaten with cooked watercress. This is an idea worth reviving, since watercress is a sadly neglected vegetable. It can be boiled like spinach or chopped and fried lightly in butter.

In 'A Taste of Ireland', Theodora Fitzgibbon mentions that lemon sauce is one of the traditional accompaniments for Limerick ham.

IRISH STEW

Perhaps the most famous of all Irish dishes, Irish stew is in the same tradition as the Lancashire hot-pot and the tatie-pot from the Lake District. But in this case it is simply a mixture of meat, potatoes and onions, flavoured with plenty of herbs. Any extra ingredients, like carrots or turnips, distract from its pure flavour and turn it into just another stew.

Originally Irish stew was made with lean, young kid, but now lamb or mutton are always associated with it. The point about the stew is to balance the quantities of meat and potatoes, and also the time needed for cooking them, so that the result is thick and creamy, not watery. The ingredients are arranged in a pot in layers, with potatoes at the bottom and the top, sandwiching the meat and onions.

The reputation of Irish stew has even spread to France. In various recent French recipe books it is mentioned and described as a classic example of a foreign peasant dish!

1. MINTRELS AT AN IRISH FEAST
Wood engraving in Derricke's *Image of Irelande*, 1581

Minstrels at an open-air Irish feast. (Reproduced by kind permission of The Museum of English Rural Life, University of Reading)

DRINKING IN IRELAND

Three alcoholic drinks above all others belong to Ireland: Irish whiskey and Guinness, which are both legal, and *poteen*, which is not. Outside the towns and cities, in remote country districts, drinking places have a particular character. There are conventional pubs, of course, but in many cases drink has to be obtained from the back rooms of farmhouses, or from premises which serve as grocer's shop, post office and pub all rolled into one.

IRISH WHISKEY

The art of distillation came to Ireland from the Middle East about 900 years ago, and alcoholic spirits were being distilled by Irish monks long before the technique reached the British mainland. The monks made a spirit called 'Uisge Bheatha' or 'Usquebaugh' – literally 'water of life' – from which we get the

The skills of distillation drifted slowly into Scotland, but the alcoholic liquor retained its Celtic name. Scotch whisky now surpasses its Irish relative at least in terms of quantities produced.

The first recorded mention of Irish whiskey was in 'The Book of Leinster' (1494). It referred to a banquet at Dundabheann, near Bushmills, at which this new intoxicant was enjoyed – so much so that the guests veered badly off course on their homeward journey. After starting out for Louth in the east they eventually finished up in Limerick in the south.

word 'whiskey'. (Notice that, in Ireland, whiskey is spelt with an 'e'.) Distilling soon became a cottage industry, unhampered by licences or official interference, until certain Acts of Parliament were passed in an attempt to curb the activities of the whiskey-makers.

The distillery at Bushmills, now called The Old Bushmills Distillery Co. Ltd., was granted its licence in 1608, and claims to be the oldest in the world. It is certainly the only whiskey producer in the whole of Northern Ireland. The Bushmills area of Antrim, only a few miles from the legendary Giant's Causeway, is, suitably, the birthplace of this whiskey. The soil is fertile, the weather agreeable, there is a rich barley harvest, and above all the distillery makes use of the pure peat-flavoured water from Colomb's Hill, which has served as a source of supply for more than 300 years.

'Old Bushmills' is a fine whiskey, although it is actually a blend of pure malt whiskey, which is prepared from malted barley at the Bushmills distillery, and grain whiskey, made from malted barley, together with unmalted barley, maize and other cereals, distilled at the company's other plant in Coleraine. But this liquor is surpassed by their 'Black Bush', a rare whiskey only available in a few places outside Ireland. It is a dark, smooth drink that has the power to warm without producing the burning sensation of some spirits.

Irish coffee isn't a traditional drink, but seems set to become something of one. It's a combination of sweet black coffee and Irish whiskey, served in a warmed whiskey glass. Before being drunk, the coffee is 'floated' with cream, which is poured over the curved back of a teaspoon into the glass. It must not be mixed or stirred into the coffee, because the point is to drink the hot, laced coffee *through* the layer of cold cream.

POTEEN

Poteen-makers had some amazingly enterprising ways of concealing their liquor. Caesar Otway, travelling in Ireland in the early years of the 19th century, reported that a local distiller had ordered from a tinker 'a tin vessel with the head and body the shape of a woman, which he dressed to resemble his wife.' He then rode to market with his liquor-filled, metal spouse behind him.

The notorious illegal liquor, *poitín* (corrupted to poteen in English, and pronounced *potcheen*) has been distilled throughout Ireland for hundreds of years. It has been drunk at feasts, marriages and funerals or simply as a way of temporarily forgetting the rigours of life, by generations of Irish men and women. And in very poor country districts it was a vital supplement to the family income. A farm labourer with a small still could make and sell his own poteen and the proceeds would help to buy food and pay the rent.

Poteen is a kind of home-made whiskey. In the past it was always prepared from malt and barley, but any number of fermentable ingredients have been used, including potatoes, sugar, treacle and beet. This is mashed and fermented with yeast and distilled through a copper 'worm'. The liquor at this stage is called 'singlings'. One or even two more distillations are necessary to get rid of the unpalatable impurities. It is a process that has remained virtually unchanged. The main difference now is that the work is done indoors, usually in a barn or shed, with the help of bottled gas as a fuel. In the past it was an outdoor job, the still being tucked away in a secluded glen and heated over an open wood fire.

The illegality of poteen has always been a question of tax. In 1770 the Exchequer decided that it was illegal for anyone to refuse to pay tax on spirits made for their own consumption. It was enough to turn the poteen-makers into a persecuted class, so they were forced to fight, often literally, for their survival, and had to become ingenious in their work, especially in concealing the evidence.

There are suggestions that poteen should be made legal as a way of tapping this lucrative source of revenue, since a barrel of poteen can now be made for about £40 and sold for about £400!

Nowadays poteen is still made in nine or ten counties in both Northern and Southern Ireland, and is still illegal. But it is also a business with a turnover of several million pounds a year. It is manufactured with varying degrees of skill in prisons, schools and hospitals, yet the tradition is so widespread and established that the police seldom bother to hunt it down.

GUINNESS

In Ireland, dark Guinness stout is much more popular than the 'ales' drunk in other parts of Britain. Stout gets its dark colour and its flavour from the roasted malt or barley used in the brewing, as well as from the water, which is much softer than that used in brewing ales. But the important fact about Guinness is that, in both draught and bottled forms, it is unpasteurized – in other words it is a naturally-conditioned, living beer.

Guinness has been brewed at The St. James Gate Brewery in Dublin since 1759, although the brewery itself was operating a century earlier than that. It is Dublin's local stout, although much of the output of the brewery is sent abroad. The Irish drink real draught Guinness, not the brew sold in England, which is actually a keg beer, delivered in casks and expelled by gas (a unique mixture of carbon dioxide and nitrogen), but a natural beer poured with reverence and care.

In England, bottled Guinness, or Extra Stout as it is called, is the connoisseur's drink, while the brewery also produces a Foreign Extra Stout, blended from selected mature brewings to suit conditions overseas.

Guinness has always had a good medicinal reputation as these testimonies by doctors from the brewery's files indicate:

(*Reproduced by kind permission of Arthur Guinness Son and Co. Ltd*)

> NEURASTHENIA: 'Also for some years I have advised patients and friends who suffer from a more or less degree of neurasthenia, usually due to modern conditions of life, to have one bottle of Guinness in the morning and one during the evening. They invariably report much benefit, as besides acting as a tonic to a jaded appetite, the alcoholic content serves to soothe the irritable nervous condition, and the use of Guinness for this purpose is much preferable to the consumption of drugs.' M.R.C.S.
>
> CONSTIPATION: 'Guinness is of almost unfailing benefit in cases of chronic constipation, and often enables the patient to dispense with the artificial bowel stimulation.' M.R.C.S., L.R.C.P.

'No, I haven't been yet doc, but I've stopped worrying about it.'

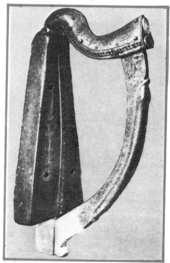

The O'Neill Harp, sometimes known as Brian Boru's Harp was introduced as the Guinness emblem in 1862. (Photograph supplied by Arthur Guinness Son and Co. Ltd)

(Cartoon by Geoffrey Dickinson)

The draught Guinness sold in Ireland was, until quite recently, called 'porter' by the brewers. In fact it is probably the nearest equivalent we have to the original dark porter of the 18th century. Guinness also brewed a weaker version of their stout, which was known commonly as 'plain'. Sadly this is no longer available.

Guinness is Dublin's native stout, but two other stouts are brewed in Cork: Beamish stout and Murphy's stout (from the Lady's Well Brewery). Both of them are pasteurized and although pleasant are much more localized in appeal than Guinness.

INDEX

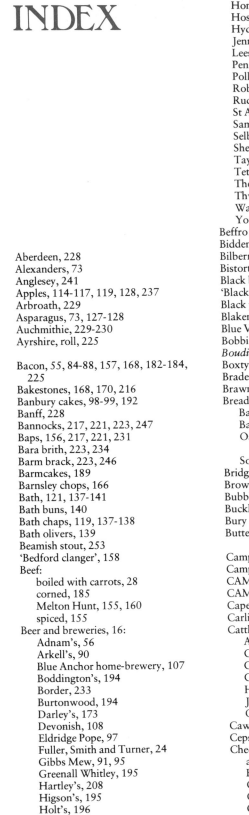

BIBLIOGRAPHY

This is a selection of books — most of which are still in print — that we have consulted during the writing of this book. It is a general list though we have excluded such specialist sources as Ministry of Agriculture leaflets and articles, many of which are mentioned by name in the text.

APPLEBY, Mrs, *Yorkshire Cookery,* Dalesman Books, 1976   ARLOTT, John, *English Cheeses of the South and West,* Harrap, 1960
AYRTON, Elisabeth, *The Cookery of England,* Andre Deutsch, 1974   BAILEY, Adrian, *The Cooking of the British Isles,* Time Life, 1969
BARTY-KING, Hugh, *A Tradition of English Wine,* Oxford Illustrated Press, 1977   BEECH, Anne, *The Gourmet's Directory,* Croom Helm,
1975   BOYD, Lizzie (ed.), *British Cookery,* Croom Helm, 1976   BOSTON, Richard, *Beer and Skittles,* Collins, 1976   *Cheeses of England,*
EP Publishing, 1974   CHEKE, Val, *The Story of Cheese-Making in Britain,* Routledge, Kegan and Paul, 1959   COX, Helen, *Traditional
English Cookery,* Angus and Robertson, 1961   'DALESMAN, The', *Lancashire Cookery and Lakeland Cookery,* Dalesman Books, 1976
DOUGLAS, Joyce, *Old Derbyshire Recipes and Customs,* and *Old Pendle Recipes,* Hendon Publishing Co., 1976   EDDEN, Helen, *County
Recipes of Old England,* Country Life Books, 1929   EHLE, John, *The Cheeses and Wines of England and France,* Harper and Row, 1972
Farmhouse Fare, 'Farmer's Weekly', 1942   FITZGIBBON, Theodora, *The Food of the Western World,* Hutchinson, 1976   *A Taste of Wales,*
Dent, 1971, *A Taste of Ireland,* Dent, 1968, *A Taste of Scotland,* Dent, 1970, *A Taste of the West Country,* Dent, 1972, *A Taste of London,*
Dent, 1973   GRAYSON, Peter, *Recipes from the Peak District,* Grayson Publications, 1976   GRIGSON, Geoffrey, *The Englishman's Flora,*
Phoenix House, 1958   GRIGSON, Jane, *English Food,* Macmillan, 1974   HARRISON, S. G., MASEFIELD, G. B., WALLIS, Michael, *The
Oxford Book of Food Plants,* Oxford University Press, 1969   HARTLEY, Dorothy, *Food in England,* Macdonald and Jane's, 1954   HEATH,
Ambrose, *English Cheeses of the North,* Harrap, 1960   HOLE, Christina, *British Folk Customs,* Hutchinson, 1976   HOSKINS, W. G., *The
Making of the English Landscape,* Hodder and Stoughton, 1955   HOWEY, Peggy, *The Geordie Cook Book,* Frank Graham, 1971
HUTCHINS, Sheila, *English Recipes,* Methuen, 1967   JACKSON, Michael, *The English Pub,* Collins, 1976   JENKINS, J. Geraint, *Nets and
Coracles,* David and Charles, 1974   LOTHIAN, Elizabeth, *Devonshire Flavour,* David and Charles, 1971   MABEY, Richard, *Food for Free,*
Collins, 1972   McGUFFIN, J., *In Praise of Poteen,* Appletree Press, 1978   McNeil, F. Marian, *The Scots Kitchen,* Blackie, 1929   MOSSOP,
M. *Lakeland Recipes,* James Pike Ltd., 1977   ODDY, Derek, J., and MILLER, Derek, S., *The Making of the Modern British Diet,* Croom
Helm, 1976   POULSON, Joan, *Old Cotswold Recipes,* Hendon Publishing, 1975, *Old Lancashire Recipes,* Hendon Publishing, 1973, *More
Lancashire Recipes,* Hendon Publishing, 1976, *Old Anglian Recipes,* Hendon Publishing, 1976, *Old Northern Recipes,* Hendon Publishing,
1975, PRIESTLAND, Gerald, *Frying Tonight,* Gentry Books, 1972   RUDDLE, Rosemary, *Rutland Recipes,* Leicestershire Library and
Information Services, 1976   SMITH, Joanna, *Village Cooking,* Sidgwick and Jackson, 1974   *Receipts and Relishes,* Whitbread and Co. Ltd.,
1950   WHITE, Florence, *Good Things in England,* Jonathan Cape, 1932   WILSON, C. Anne, *Food and Drink in Britain,* Constable, 1973.